Buffalo Soldiers in Italy

To
First Lieutenant John R. Fox, 366th Infantry,
whose willing sacrifice of his life for his country
went unrecorded and unheralded for 38 years
(Distinguished Service Cross, Posthumous, April 1, 1982).

and

Second Lieutenant Vernon J. Baker, 370th Infantry,
for gallantry above and beyond the call of duty,
and at the risk of his own life (Distinguished Service Cross).

and

Those gallant Buffalo Soldiers who died in action
in a hostile foreign land,
surrounded by enemies of their country,
loved and remembered by their comrades in arms.

Buffalo Soldiers in Italy

Black Americans in World War II

by
Hondon B. Hargrove

McFarland & Company, Inc., Publishers
Jefferson, North Carolina, and London

Author's Note

History, many times, helps to right wrongs. With the inexorable passage of time, there are those of us who dare not trust memory or judgment to validate past events. Research, documentation, and reading of books by both American and foreign authors have helped this writer put together a book about the performance of the men in the Buffalo Division and its operations in Italy during World War II. Many Americans have passed on still wondering if they should or should not believe the generally negative image of this band of black soldiers. There are those who still remember and who will acknowledge that black soldiers performed no better and no worse than others who fought in Europe in World War II. The following bit of history may serve to dispel many myths and stories and give solace to those of us who suffered and survived—and relief from a lifetime of wondering by the families of those who died fighting for their country.

The present work is a reprint of the library bound edition of Buffalo Soldiers in Italy: Black Americans in World War II, *first published in 1985.*

LIBRARY OF CONGRESS CATALOGUING-IN-PUBLICATION DATA

Hargrove, Hondon B., 1916–
    Buffalo soldiers in Italy : black Americans in World War II
      p.   cm.
    Includes bibliographical references and index.

    ISBN-13: 978-0-7864-1708-7
    softcover : 50# alkaline paper ∞

    1. World War, 1939–1945—Regimental histories—United States.
    2. United States. Army. Infantry Divisions, 92nd—History.
    3. World War, 1939–1945—Campaigns—Italy. 4. World War, 1939–1945—Afro-American troops. 5. Italy—History—German occupation, 1943–1945. I. Title.
D769.3192nd.H37   2003
940.54'12'73   84-42609

British Library cataloguing data are available

©1985 Hondon B. Hargrove. All rights reserved

No part of this book may be reproduced or transmitted in any form or by any means, electronic or mechanical, including photocopying or recording, or by any information storage and retrieval system, without permission in writing from the publisher.

Manufactured in the United States of America

McFarland & Company, Inc., Publishers
  Box 611, Jefferson, North Carolina 28640
  www.mcfarlandpub.com

Table of Contents

Dedication		ii
Introduction		vii
One	Origins and Traditions	1
	The First Buffalo Soldiers 1; Buffalo Soldiers in World War I 2; Struggle for Identity 3; Preparation for Combat 4; Festering Turbulence 7	
Two	Pre-Combat Operations	11
	The 370th Combat Team Lands 11; Allied Situation in Italy 12; The Allied Offensive Plan 14; Fifth Army Plan 14	
Three	From the Arno to the Gothic Line	15
	First Blood 15; First Score-Card 24; A New Battle Arena — New Line-Ups 26; Balance of the 92nd Division Arrives 30; The 365th Combat Team Is Committed 36; Back to the 371st 36; 370th Combat Team — Heavy Action in the Serchio Valley 39; The 366th Infantry Regiment Enters the Fray 47; An Abundance of Heroes 49	
Four	The Battles for the Serchio Valley	53
	Probing and Harassing the Enemy 53; Increased Activity in the Serchio Valley 56; Surprise Enemy Counterattack in the Serchio Valley 59; Opening Moves 62; Action on the Left Bank 68; Delays in Support Dispositions 71; Action on 27 December — East of the River 73; Operations in the Coastal Sector 77; Aftermath 78	
Five	February Attack in Coastal Sector	82
	Plan Fourth Term 82; Diversion in the Serchio Valley 84; The Main Attack Begins — 8 February 88; The 370th Infantry Attack on Strettoia Hills 89; The 371st Reaches for the Higher Ground 94; The 366th — Ordeal on the Plains 98; The Second Day of Battle — 9 February 107; The 371st	

Table of Contents

Continues the Attack 110; The 366th Fights On 112; The Third Day of Battle—10 February 116; The 371st Continues to Reach Forward 118;

Between pages 120 and 131 are 16 plates with 22 photographs

The Last Battle for the 366th 121; The 371st Clings to the Ridge Line—11 February 123; Elements of 370th and 371st Give Ground 124; Results of the Attack 126; Evaluation 127

Six   Dismemberment of the Buffalo Division   145
        High Level Discussions 145

Seven The Spring Offensive—5 April–2 May 1945   149
        The Allied Plan 149; Early Moves—Troop Dispositions 150; The 442nd Moves on the Mountains 155; Destruction and Pursuit—11 April–2 May 163; Prize for the Brazilians 169; Tedesco è Finito—(The German Is Finished) 170; Results of the Offensive 171; 365th and 371st Detached from Main Effort 174; The Partisans 176; Organization 176

Chapter Notes   181
Bibliography   187
Statistical Data, Tables   191
Index   195

Maps

Allied and Enemy Dispositions November 1944*   51
The Coastal Sector†   72
Allied and Enemy Dispositions December 1944*   76
The Serchio Valley Sector†   119
Allied and Enemy Dispositions February 1945*   138

*from 92nd Infantry Division *Book of Facts*
† from Goodman, *Fragment of Victory*

Introduction

Of the ninety American divisions deployed in World War II, many have been the object of glowing accolades. Over the years, movies, books, magazines, and radio and television "Specials" have extolled their exploits. Even divisions which fought poorly or not at all, have been praised and credited with brilliant feats of arms. One, the 106th Infantry Division, was decimated in its first contact with the enemy in December, 1944, with over 70 percent of its effectives killed, wounded, or captured. Yet, a story in the *Saturday Evening Post* of 9 September, 1946 bore the title: "The Glorious Collapse of the 106th."

Such, however, was not the case with the 92nd Infantry (Buffalo) Division, the only so-called "black" infantry division to see combat in Europe. Created in a season when complete segregation was prevalent in America, it was beset continuously by controversy because of the same rigid policy of segregation in the Army.

Except for a few chaplains and medical officers, all commanders and staff officers from division down through regiment and battalion levels, were white, as were most of the company commanders. All enlisted men were black.

In nine months of bitter combat in Italy, it was castigated by its commander, Major General Edward M. Almond, and his subordinate commanders, as a "failure," and the fighting capabilities of its black soldiers and officers were severely criticized. Stories of "melting away" and "cowardly performance " were published in news magazines and have been repeated in other media over the years. No black officer in the division was considered capable of commanding an infantry battalion and none were promoted to major.

Not surprisingly, prevailing animosities toward black people at the time—over the country and in the Army—led to negativism about black soldiers, contributing to the usually unfavorable evaluations by their commanders.

Contrary to its commanders' evaluations, however, 12,096 decorations and citations were won by the Buffalo Soldiers: Among them were 3 Distinguished Service Crosses (second highest award for valor in combat), 16 Legion of Merit Medals, 102 Silver Stars, 753 Bronze Stars, 76 Air Medals, 1910 Purple Hearts, and the Military Cross for Merit in War was awarded by the Italian government.

These were more awards for valor in combat than many American divisions received.

Casualties were heavy and were incurred in direct contact with the enemy. Five hundred eighteen (518) were killed in action and 2242 were wounded in action; 67 died of wounds, and 21 were prisoners of war. Of these casualties, only 18 were officers *above* the rank of captain; all others were junior officers (mostly black) and enlisted men.

Of all American divisions, the Buffalo Division has been least examined outside of the military establishment, yet in many ways it was one of the most fascinating and surprising of them all.

The purpose of this book is to complete the history of American arms in World War II by including the story of this unique and remarkable body of black soldiers.

Extensive research of military reports written in the field, staff orders and special reports, interviews with officers and men—all reveal much factual information and insights that negate much of the general characterizations about them. The hope is that an interested reader will be able to draw his own conclusions about this black division and the courage of its men.

I am grateful to many people for help in this venture. Mrs. Sally Aschom provided expert counsel on format and typed the manuscript with great skill and patience. Mrs. Linda Peckham, Associate Professor of English at Lansing (Michigan) Community College, provided technical guidance and continuous inspiration and encouragement. Mr. Dennette A. Harrod, president of the 366th Infantry Veterans Association and a former comrade-in-arms, provided complete access to the records of the association. Dr. Norman McRae, Director of Social Studies, Detroit Public Schools, and a historian himself, provided sound advice and shared his extensive personal history library with me. Ms. Hannah M. Ziedlick, Historical Services Division, Center of Military History, Washington, D.C., provided invaluable assistance in research of official records and other necessary services. At the beginning of the research, Congressman John Conyers, Jr. helped to guide me through the maze of Federal rules and regulations and procedures, for which I am grateful. Major Clark, Lieutenant Colonel, Retired, and a former officer in the 92nd Division, provided copies of many records and a wealth of information. Mr. Hiram Tanner, of the *Columbus Call and Post* newspaper, and also a former Buffalo Soldier, also provided copies of records and much useful information.

My wife, Lilian M. Hargrove, a former reading specialist in the Lansing School District, reviewed the manuscript and endured with great patience my demands for time and space during the long period of research and writing.

Hondon B. Hargrove
Lansing, Michigan

One

Origins and Traditions

The First Buffalo Soldiers

It was late fall on the western prairies in the year 1867. The Indian wars were raging on the rapidly expanding frontier. High on a rocky ridge, two Indian scouts lay motionless and well-nigh invisible, eyes focused intently on the tall gates of the U.S. Army Post some two miles distant.

After a week of steadily falling snow, the air was filled with a stinging sleet, and it was bitterly cold despite the occasional rays of sunshine that pierced the cloudy skies.

The gates opened slowly. The Indians stiffened and their black, piercing eyes searched the cavalry filing through the gates in a column of twos, mounts at an easy trot. They continued to scrutinize the formation after the tail end of the column cleared the post.

Gradually, the Indians began to sense something strange and different about *this* cavalry unit. The troopers seemed to be unusually animated in their movements, although they sat their mounts skillfully, almost casually. They were happy and gay, and their ribald shouts and loud laughter could be heard clearly across the brisk morning air. They resembled more a group of happy-go-lucky youths out for a lark than a detachment of heavily armed soldiers seeking mortal combat with a deadly enemy.

As the soldiers drew closer, the officer at the head of the column suddenly stopped, then raised his arm. Immediately the formation shuffled into a solid straight line, now silent, still, disciplined, and alert. Two cavalrymen dashed forward at full gallop, heading straight for the hill where lay the Indian scouts, still silent and motionless.

Finally, realizing they must withdraw, but still curious, they lingered to get a closer look at these soldiers who appeared to be so different from those they were accustomed to fighting. In the last moments before the soldiers flung themselves from their saddles at the base of the hill, the Indians suddenly realized that these men were black! Not only were they black, but they looked like buffaloes! Without further delay, they rode to the rear.

Scarcely had they reported their findings to their leaders when the charging cavalry was upon them, riding, screaming like wild men, sabres slashing and flashing in the sun, pistols and carbines spitting out death and destruction.

These black soldiers were from the Ninth and Tenth United States Cavalry Regiments. Finding the Regular Army issue overcoats inadequate for the harsh, cold, blustery winters on the plains, the men killed buffaloes and made huge robes, some of which covered them from head to toe.

To the Indians who had never seen black men, they did indeed resemble buffaloes and they also proved to be most formidable in battle.

Out of respect, the Indians dubbed them "Buffalo Soldiers." The men in the Ninth and Tenth Cavalry were proud of the comparison and it is worth noting that when the coat of arms of the Tenth Cavalry was designed, the most prominent feature in the crest was a figure of a black buffalo.

Stationed all along the rugged 2000 mile frontier were four black Regular Army Regiments, originally authorized by Congress in 1866. In addition to the cavalry regiments, two of infantry were organized, all with white officers. During the Civil War some 179,000 black men had served in the combat arms of the Union Army (33,380 were killed in action), and many of these seasoned veterans flocked to the colors of these first-class units.

These intrepid soldiers distinguished themselves in campaigns for over twenty years on the Texas and Oklahoma plains, along the Mexican border, in the mountains and deserts of Arizona, New Mexico, and Colorado, and in the barren wastes of the Dakotas. They fought and helped bring to bay the hostile Indian tribes barring the westward movement of settlers. They clung doggedly at the heels of the great war chiefs — Geronimo, Satanta, Cochise, Victorio — until, one by one, they capitulated or were killed.

They fought renegades, horse and cattle thieves, bank robbers and marauding gangs; they protected payrolls, stagecoaches, wagon trains, mail carriers, railroad working parties, and even small towns, in times of civil conflict. Many of the permanent military posts were built by these soldiers who spent long years of service in isolated, untamed frontier territory, sometimes the only force against the enemies of law and order.

They, like the good soldiers they were, endured in silence the physical hardships, the prejudice and discrimination in the communities they protected, and even the doubts and insults often expressed by many of their white contemporaries in service.

The Buffalo Soldiers continued their service in the Spanish-American War and added more honors and lustre to their colors.

To black Americans at the turn of the century, the term "Buffalo Soldiers" meant men of strength, daring and great courage; men skilled in the arts of war; men of honor and patriotism imbued with pride in self and cause; men willing to defend the nation's honor with their very lives, if necessary.

Buffalo Soldiers in World War I

It seemed natural that, when a combat division composed of black enlisted men was organized in World War I, it should be named the "Buffalo Division." And so it was. Significantly, the shoulder patch worn by every Buffalo Soldier was adorned with the figure of a black buffalo.

Although in combat in France only a few months, the Buffalo Soldiers were heavily engaged with the enemy right up to the end of hostilities in November, 1918. In that brief but bloody period, they suffered 1700 casualties, meanwhile inflicting heavy losses on the Germans and making spectacular gains. Individual officers and men received many citations, including the Distinguished Service Cross and the French Croix de Guerre. At least one of its units was cited by the grateful French.

Even so, evaluations of the 92nd Division in World War I varied widely. There were reports and rumors that some units failed to accomplish assigned missions. Some high ranking officers, including the division commander and some of his staff, tended to attach much credence to such rumored failures, in most instances casting the blame on black officers. On the other hand, many officers who have commanded the regiments, battalions and companies on the battlefields were lavish in their praise of their officers and men. Some expressed their opinions in official reports and in recommendations for unit and individual citations.

Black Americans, following the progress of the 92nd Division in reports by black newspapers, were convinced they had acquitted themselves nobly, keeping high the glorious history and traditions of the original Buffalo Soldiers.

It is likely that a true evaluation rests somewhere between the widely divergent opinions postulated.

Struggle for Identity

On December 7, 1941, a "Day of Infamy," Japan delivered a devastating air attack on Pearl Harbor (Hawaii) and, overnight, the American "Sleeping Giant" awoke and began to gear up the massive war machine that was to bring ultimate victory four long, bitter years later. England and France were already at war with Germany and Italy, and the United States was providing weapons, planes, tanks and other materials to its friends, which at that time included Russia.

Mobilization of the population for service proceeded apace with the industrial effort, and, within a short time American troops were in action in various parts of the world. As the nation's military forces rapidly expanded, black citizens hastened to join, anxious to have a part in the struggle against the enemies of Democracy; thousands joined up. Initially, as in World War I, they were assigned to noncombat duties, in accordance with policy and tradition of the War Department. A stream of protest arose from a powerful and sophisticated black press, and an emerging political black bloc made itself heard in the halls of Congress and in the White House itself.

Understandably, the leaders of the Armed Forces resisted the pressures. Beset with the mammoth problems in raising, training, equipping and transporting the largest military force in history, they viewed the utilization of black combat soldiers as a distraction from the main goals. They tended, in large part, to reflect the general attitudes and philosophies about blacks which were prevalent throughout the land. They themselves tended to doubt the combat capabilities of black soldiers. Their views developed from personal experiences and similar negative impressions which had existed historically during all prior American wars. In the American Revolution, General Washington himself, at one time, issued an order prohibiting recruitment of blacks. In the Civil War, Presidents Abraham Lincoln and Jefferson Davis had strongly resisted their use in any capacity until past the mid-point of the war. Similar reluctance flowed from the White House in the Spanish-American War; and, before and during World War I, the Congress witnessed several bills introduced (not passed) which proposed the virtual prohibition of the use of black troops in any capacity.[1]

Given the negative attitudes and prevailing racial anomosities and hostility of both the citizenry and within the Armed Forces itself, the military leadership faced the dilemma with deep concern and uncertainty. As was stated by an officer in the Adjutant General's Department in December, 1941, after Pearl Harbor:

> The Army did not create the problem.... The Army is made up of individual citizens ... who have pronounced views with respect to the Negro. Military orders will not change their views.... The Army is not a sociological laboratory.[2]

Nevertheless, every effort consistent with the times was made to reach a satisfactory resolution of the problem. Beginning in early 1942, although no change was made in the policy of separation of blacks and whites, other significant modifications were agreed to. Many branches—Marine Corps, Air Force, Navy, Coast Guard, and combat arms in Army Ground Forces, such as Infantry, Paratroopers, Combat Engineers, Tank and Tank Destroyer units—all were opened up, and several black units were formed.

Among these were two infantry divisions in which all Division Regimental and Battalion Commanders and their staff officers were white, as were most of the Company Commanders. Sprinkled throughout the divisions were some chaplains and medical officers who were captains, but most black officers were first or second lieutenants.

The 93rd Infantry Division was activated 15 May 1942, at Fort Huachuca, Arizona, and on 15 October, 1942, the 92nd Infantry (Buffalo) Division was activated at Fort McClellan, Alabama. The cadre for the nucleus of the division consisted of 128 officers and 1200 enlisted men from the 93rd Division.[3] The stated intention from the War Department was to commit both divisions to combat when training was completed. Black Americans awaited the day with bated breath—and skepticism mixed with hope.

Preparation for Combat

Major General Edward M. Almond commanded the 92nd Division throughout its training and combat operations. Born in Virginia, he graduated from Virginia Military Institute, the same school that produced General of the Army George C. Marshall. General Almond had been a professional soldier all his life. Although in combat in World War I for only a few months, he distinguished himself with the 4th Infantry Division; he was wounded in action and was awarded a Silver Star for bravery. He came to command of the Buffalo Division with excellent credentials and was highly regarded by his superiors and his peers in the Regular Army. There is no record of prior service with black troops except for his brief service as Assistant Division Commander with the 93rd Division.

As he took command, he was seen by his soldiers and by black news reporters as a typical white Southern military commander, with the traditional concepts about black people, and there was widespread suspicion and misgivings over his selection to lead the 92nd Division.

However, his words at the activation ceremonies at Fort McClellan carried a ring of hope and sincerity, which dissolved many fears and doubts:

> The 92nd Division is primarily a Combat division.... One of my principal aims is to produce a first class battlefield unit. I promise fairness to every officer and man; the best leadership of which your officers and non-commissioned officers are capable.[4]

General Almond's original staff remained with the division throughout the entire training and combat operation periods, except for his Chief of Staff, Colonel Frank E. Barber, who was killed in action in Italy, in September 1944.

As in World War I, the Buffalo Division initially trained in several widely separated locations. Fort Huachuca, where the 93rd Division was training, was the only "suitable" post which could accommodate a unit as large as a division. Most military installations were unprepared to house large numbers of black soldiers, and there were few, if any, communities which could tolerate in their midst some 15,000 black soldiers preparing for combat. Unfortunately, all the Buffalo Division's training locations, except one, were in the South, and were adjacent to communities resentful of their presence and extremely hostile to them.

Division Headquarters and Special Troops were at Fort McClellan, Alabama; the 365th Infantry Regiment and the 597th Field Artillery Battalion were at Camp Atterbury, Indiana; the 370th Infantry and the 598th Field Artillery were at Camp Breckinridge, Kentucky; and the 371st Infantry and the 599th Field Artillery were at Camp Robinson, Arkansas.

The division slogan, or motto, was "Deeds Not Words," and the shoulder patch was circular, with a black border and a black buffalo on an olive drab background symbolizing the history and traditions of Buffalo Soldiers of the past.

General Almond was given almost unlimited authority and discretion, by the War Department, to mold and shape the division. True to his promise, he immediately ordered that all efforts be directed towards creating, through realistic and imaginative training, a physically toughened, efficient battle force, thoroughly skilled and imbued with the desire to close with and destroy any enemy engaged. All the training programs prescribed for a newly activated division were followed. When tests and inspections at various stages revealed deficiencies or weaknesses, General Almond approved time extensions to permit further training and re-testing, as was the custom in most combat divisions.

By December, 1942, with the addition of officers from Officer Candidate Schools, and enlisted men from other units and Reception Centers, the division began training over-strength by 7 percent in officers and 15 percent in enlisted men.[5]

The Individual Training Program phase of the Mobilization Training Program was conducted simultaneously at all the division locations and continued until April 1943. During this period the focus was on physical conditioning, basic military training and indoctrination of each soldier. The training was physically demanding and as realistic as possible. It included knowledge and use of basic infantry weapons; and equipment, survival techniques, mines and booby-traps; basic medical and first aid practices; map reading, tank and aircraft identification; military courtesy and discipline; close combat exercises, and even the experience of crawling under machine guns firing under simulated battle conditions. Speed and endurance marches were stressed and the results were very encouraging. Ninety-two percent of the division completed the 25-mile march in an eight hour period at the 11th week of training; in physical conditioning, the ratings were high. Special schools were set up under close direction from General Almond, to deal with a serious problem of illiteracy and other educational deficiencies. It was also discovered, early in the training period, that a large number of men were inept, poorly motivated, or physically and/or emotionally unsuited for service. In an attempt to salvage these men, Casual Camps of 500-600 men were set up at each of the four unit locations for special attention and training.

During this early period another link with the traditions of the first Buffalo Soldiers was added. A real live young buffalo was acquired as the division mascot and promptly named "Buffalo Bill." Popular Staff Sergeant Valentine was assigned to care for and train Buffalo Bill. The stories that are still told about Buffalo Bill by 92nd Division veterans are legend. Although he had an impeccable pedigree, he was somewhat irascible and unpredictable. At parades or reviews, sometimes in front of scores of dignitaries and thousands of troops Buffalo Bill would stop to answer the call of nature and take all the time he needed in doing so. It has been said that when the wind was right, the aroma from Buffalo Bill was enough to fell an entire platoon. On one occasion the entire division burst into uncontrollable laughter when he broke away from Sergeant Valentine and lumbered back and forth over the parade ground until finally corralled by a small army of soldiers. Even General Almond and the other dignitaries on the reviewing stand were in stitches that day.

In May, 1943, when the entire division was assembled for the first time at Fort Huachuca, Buffalo Bill was there to greet them.

The intensity and tempo of activity was accelerated as the emphasis progressed to unit training at Fort Huachuca. Stressed was the development of each squad, platoon, company, battalion, and regiment into an effective and compact fighting force. The role each unit would play in division combat operations was constantly pressed home. The rugged Arizona mountains, with lofty peaks, deep valleys, small narrow draws, and wide stretches of arid, dusty desert land provided many opportunities for realistic training in unit proficiency. Combat firing tests were not completed to General Almond's satisfaction, and eight weeks were added to the prescribed training period.

In December, 1943, the entire division moved out of the barracks area into the desert and mountains for twenty days of field exercises (called "D" exercises). All of the things learned were put to the test under field conditions, with the added goal of improving action and control by the division, as well as regiments, battalions and companies.

Upon return to Fort Huachuca, and after endless critiques and reviews, the Buffalo Division prepared to take part in Army Maneuvers in Louisiana in February, 1944. At the conclusion of maneuvers in April, the 92nd Division was rated "satisfactory" and the consensus among reviewers was that it was adequately trained and ready for combat.

Meanwhile, the men in the Casual Camp continued to pose a serious problem. All but 300 had been taken on maneuvers, but upon return to Fort Huachuca, it was discovered that the Casual Camp had grown to over 1000 men. Hundreds of unfit soldiers had been "dumped" on the 92nd Division from other black units (from nationwide locations) which were leaving for overseas service. While continuing to salvage and train these men, the division commander also continued to divest himself of as many as possible.

The first preparations for overseas movement (POM) were finally completed and elements of the 370th Combat Team departed for Italy in June, 1944. It is worthy of note that the plan of the War Department was to commit only one combat team to action in Europe, to "represent" the 92nd Division. General Almond objected strenuously, insisting that the entire division be given an opportunity to fulfill its training mission. It was finally agreed to commit one combat team first and to have the balance of the division follow shortly thereafter.

Festering Turbulence

The 92nd Division *Book of Facts* stated:

> When the Division's first echelon left Fort Huachuca, and when the remainder followed ... they all carried with them the best in modern equipment, a full complement of trained officers and men, and the War Department's stamp of approval.[6]

On the surface this would appear to be a true statement. However, unrecognized or ignored or minimized by Headquarters, there was — in constant ferment—an intangible, elusive undercurrent of resentment, bitterness, even dispair and hopelessness among black officers and enlisted men in the division.

Most of it had to do with the effect of the Army policy of segregation and the discrimination against them that resulted. On military posts to which they were assigned, all black troops were housed in separate areas—not always the most desirable—and were subjected to discrimination in theaters, post exchanges, recreational facilities, churches, and in transportation on the posts and to and from surrounding communities. Usually, they were not welcomed by the local population; they were seldom invited into their homes, to public social events, or special veterans' functions; nor were they praised or honored as strong, courageous defenders of the nation. In most of the 92nd Division training locations, they were aware that all racial discrimination to which they were subjected was not only unnoticed by their commanders, but usually condoned and enforced by them.

There were other factors contributing to these submerged feelings. During the training period, a sense of identification with battalion and regiment and with the division as a whole, was never quite completely achieved. It is likely true that many individual soldiers never did comprehend the role of such a large fighting organization and there is no doubt that many did not even know their commanders' names, in spite of the fact that General Almond himself was very active, highly mobile and visible, and he encouraged his subordinate commanders to follow his example. As far as many black soldiers were concerned, they were distant white authority figures living apart from them, and little different from the usually hostile people surrounding them.

During the early months, officers and enlisted men never had an opportunity to see the officers and enlisted men in the other combat teams; and so, different procedures and atmospheres, influenced by the personalities and racial attitudes of the commanders and staffs, as well as the oppressive racial climate in the four widely separated training areas, led to differences in methods of resolving problems. When they assembled at Fort Huachuca, unfortunately, many of the more onerous practices were adopted on a division-wide basis. Segregation in officers' messes, officers clubs, and living quarters were uniform throughout the division. Use of racial epithets toward black officers and men increased, as did transfers of black officers to preclude command promotions. Many black officers were reclassified, thus insuring their leaving the division, or even discharge from service.[7]

There was a feeling of mutual dislike and distrust between black and white officers. Many of them—black as well as white—did not want to serve in the division because of this. Many white officers simply did not *like* black soldiers, and many submitted requests for transfers right up to the time of embarkation. General Almond's policy was to approve such requests whenever possible.

Complaints of negative racial attitudes or practices were usually investigated and acted on in a similar manner. However, he seldom took such action with his battalion or regimental commanders or members of his Headquarters Staff against whom these complaints were made. Neither did he alter the policy: "No black officers commanding companies, battalions or regiments and no black staff officers at battalion level or above."

An inspector general's report in June, 1943 is quite revealing. It was made by Brigadier General Benjamin O. Davis, the Army's only black general officer. He noted that when he had inspected units at all four locations, from January to March, 1943, he found morale to be "superior." Black and white officers got along well, with *no* complaints of racial discrimination reported to him. The Division Headquarters mess was integrated, and, at a reception at Fort McClellan, black and white officers were present, mingling freely and harmoniously. General Almond was held in high esteem by *all* officers, and he reported,

> The colored officers were especially profuse in their praise of him for his fairness and deep concern for their advancement and welfare. On all occasions, he showed a personal interest even in their comforts and entertainment.[8]

Now, however (June 1943), only a few months later, at Fort Huachuca, Davis reported that black officers and men felt that General Almond had been unduly influenced by some of his officers, and that his attitude had changed. General Davis was careful to point out that in all cases where there was deviation from his policy of fairness, General Almond was quick to discipline those found guilty. Nevertheless, he concluded that:

> General Almond had overlooked the human element in the training of the 92nd Division. Great stress has been placed upon the mechanical perfection in execution of training missions ... and not enough consideration given to ... maintenance of a racial understanding between white and colored officers and men.[9]

Many officers, black and white, and enlisted men agreed with him.

One priceless opportunity to create and develop morale and esprit de corps was never properly utilized. The history and traditions of black soldiers in the wars of the nation could have been extolled and the specific accomplishments of the Buffalo Division and its Regiments in World War I could have been utilized constructively to this end.

Officers and men in the Regular Army Divisions and in the United States Marines were continuously indoctrinated with accounts of the heroic accomplishments of their divisions, regiments and battalions. Some of them had histories extending back to the American Revolution. This was not done in the 92nd Division. Aside from the adoption of the Buffalo symbol, the free use of the "Buffalo" designation, and the highly publicized acquisition of Buffalo Bill, little else was done to make effective use of the device of unit traditions to attain esprit de corps.

Readily available was a wealth of history and military tradition established by black Americans in all previous wars. In World War I the 92nd

Buffalo Division, in spite of "rumors" of some unit failures, was referred to by General Pershing "as one of the best in the AEF."[10] The Secretary of War, Newton D. Baker, also pointed out that there was no evidence to justify the negative assumptions regarding colored troops, and that many colored officers were decorated with Distinguished Service Crosses for extraordinary heroism under fire.[11]

The sister regiments of the Buffalo Division in World War II, the 365th, 370th and 371st, all had excellent combat records in World War I. Sadly, the meaning and continuity of division and regimental tradition was not stressed or developed during the formative training period. A golden opportunity to capitalize on the legacy of bravery, gallantry, and *successes* in combat of its World War I counterpart was lost, and with it went the opportunity to lessen the gap of understanding that existed between the black officers and men and their white leaders.

Other events were occurring which contributed to low morale which could not be attributable entirely to General Almond. In each instance, he acted promptly and forcefully to correct the situation.

Large numbers of officers and men did not believe the Division would ever be committed to combat, and thus were not convinced of the seriousness and importance of their training. Said General Davis, in March, 1943:

> There is a widespread belief within the division, based on rumors, that these two divisions (92nd and 93rd) are not to be committed to combat.[12]

The intensity and realism of the training program was accelerated after this report and, at the conclusion of the Maneuver Period in 1944, General Almond assembled the troops prior to returning to Fort Huachuca and announced that the 370th Combat Team was committed to a combat theater and that the balance of the division would follow shortly thereafter. He made it quite clear that the *entire division* would see combat—and soon. His announcement ended all rumor and speculation, and contributed to an upward swing in morale in the division.

The continued presence and growth, in a highly visible and nearby separate Training Area, of hundreds of men physically and mentally unqualified for combat, was another demoralizing influence. At one time (August 1944) there were 2000 in the Casual Camp; 1700 traveled to the Port of Embarkation in September. General Almond protested vigorously, but his recommendations were ignored, and by direct order of the War Department the bulk of the 92nd Division sailed with 850 men *known* to be unfit for combat.[13]

Two

Pre-Combat Operations

The 370th Combat Team Lands

On June 6, 1944, the long-awaited invasion of Europe's mainland was launched by Allied Forces. Thousands of American soldiers stormed ashore on the Normandy beaches in France, and in the days following, thousands more landed and fought their way out of the beachhead.

On other battlefields, still other thousands of American soldiers had joined other Allied Armed Forces to drive the German and Italian forces reeling, first from North Africa and then Sicily. American General Mark Clark's Fifth Army, flushed from bloody victories at Anzio and Cassino, and the triumphant conquest of Rome, was now poised along the south bank of the Arno River.

The costs in American lives had been high, and the lists of killed, wounded, and missing in action were lengthy.

Battle honors for combat units were numerous and impressive, and the names of individual heroes became household words in America.

But there were no battle honors for black combat units or citations or awards for black individual soldiers. Alas, even though America had been at war since 1941, there were no black infantry units in action in Europe; as in most other theatres of operations, most black soldiers in Europe were service troops.

Then, on the morning of July 30, the first American black infantry combat team to fight on the European continent in World War II landed in Naples, Italy. These black soldiers, fit and ready to fight, belonged to the 370th Combat Team, which was the advance detachment of the 92nd Infantry (Buffalo) Division. This compact, self-contained fighting force consisted of the 370th Infantry Regiment, the 598th Field Artillery Battalion, and detachments from the Division Combat Engineers, Medical, Ordnance, Military Police, Quartermaster and Signal units, and the 92nd Division Headquarters Company.

Its officers and enlisted men were believed to represent the best cross-section of any Combat Team in the Division. In the months following maneuvers the 370th Combat Team was completely re-organized. Officers and men felt to be inept, poorly motivated, physically and/or mentally deficient, or who were unable to pass basic tests, were removed. They were replaced by better qualified and more capable persons, many of them volunteers. The pace and tempo of training were increased, with emphasis on physical conditioning, basic weapons proficiencies, and improvement of leadership and teamwork.

Colonel Raymond G. Sherman, commanding the 370th, believed that his unit had high morale and great expectations for success in battle; that it was secure in the knowledge that it was well-trained, in excellent physical condition, and that its personnel were "hand-picked."

Rumors of the arrival of the Buffalo Soldiers had preceded them, and hundreds of black soldiers, most of them service troops, were waiting at the docks in battered Naples Harbor. As the thousands of black fighting men, in single file, debarked from the crowded troopships, they presented an impressive and awe-inspiring spectacle. Armed with basic weapons and in full field battle dress, proudly wearing the circular shoulder patch with the black buffalo, they moved smartly and efficiently into their unit formations. As they marched away, every man in step, every weapon in place, chins up and eyes forward, a low rumbling babble of sound came from the troops on the dock, then swelled to a crescendo of thunderous cheering which continued until the last Buffalo unit had disappeared from sight. Many applications for transfer to the 92nd Division were processed after the arrival of the 370th Combat Team, and many new men participated in combat operations which followed.[1]

From July 30 until August 23, the Buffalo Soldiers were busy in orientation programs, assembling and cleaning weapons and other equipment, and in rigorous physical conditioning exercises.

Allied Situation in Italy

In the summer of 1944, the American Fifth Army was just south of the Arno River. Spread out over a 35-mile front, extending east from the Tyrrhenian Sea, the Army was resting, reorganizing, regrouping, and building up a massive supply base, preparing to penetrate the formidable Gothic Line before winter set in.

Ironically, the Fifth Army, one year earlier, after bitter and costly fighting, alongside the British Eighth Army, had driven the German-Italian Forces from Sicily and were preparing to invade the underbelly of Europe at Salerno, Italy. It was also hoped at *that* time to overwhelm and destroy the enemy before winter set in.

Aware that the Allied Forces planned to invade northern and southern France, in June 1944, Allied leaders in Italy expected to force the early surrender of Italian forces fighting with the Germans. Then, it was felt that the Germans, under aggressive pressure by American and British Armies, would soon collapse, assuring that no German troops would be available for transfer to forces contesting the Invasion in France.

The Germans, however, did not contemplate such an early collapse. On the contrary, they planned and executed a masterful delaying action to check all Allied efforts to advance into northern Italy. They had escaped from Sicily with most of their forces intact, and when Adolph Hitler ordered them to fight to hold the Italian Peninsula, more troops were assigned to them.

Fortified defensive lines at carefully selected points were constructed, usually where the natural terrain features themselves provided advantages. These defensive lines were constructed under direction of skilled German engineers and extended at various intervals the length of Italy to 125 miles north of Rome at the foot of the Northern Apennines. They were named Barbara, Bernhard, Gustav, Caesar, Trasimeno, Arezzo, Arno, and the Gothic Line (sometimes called the "Green Line").

Likely locations for allied sea landings were identified and extensively fortified; elaborate preparations were made for defensive measures intended to drive the invasion forces back into the sea, or at least to deliver another crippling blow, further delaying the advance.

In September 1943, Fifth Army Forces landed at Salerno. While the invasion fleet was still at sea, word came that the Italian government had surrendered, and the erroneous impression was created that the landing would be relatively easy. However, such notions were dispelled quickly, as the Germans reacted promptly to offset the effect of the surrender and continued to control the country and a large part of the Italian Armed Forces.

Having anticipated the invasion they were well-prepared and made a nearly successful effort to destroy the beachhead. Although a near-disaster was narrowly averted, the Allies forced the Germans to fall back, after nine days of bitter and desperate fighting. Casualties were heavy; in the Fifth Army, 500 were killed, 1800 wounded and 1200 were missing. In the Eighth Army they were heavier, with 5500 killed, wounded and missing.

Successive Allied victories followed a similar pattern in the following months as the Fifth and Eighth Armies advanced slowly against powerful and highly mobile German forces, which were now being strengthened by the arrival of more divisions.

Naples fell October 1, and the German engineers performed a massive demolitions operation on Naples Harbor and anything else in the city that might benefit the Allies. In the ensuing months many other savage battles were fought at well-defended river lines and mountain strong-points, and at the successive fortified defensive lines which extended, in most instances, across Italy from coast to coast.

At Anzio, Fifth Army troops landed unopposed, achieving almost complete surprise; however, the initial advantage was not quickly exploited and the Germans again almost succeeded in driving the Americans back into the sea. At Monte Cassino, from January 1944 to May, the Germans fought brilliantly and tenaciously, inflicting heavy losses in men and material against the combined Allied Armies, before again withdrawing.

Rome was entered June 4 and the attack was resumed against the fleeing German forces. Again, stubborn rear-guard actions effectively retarded the advance. However, by the end of July the important seaport of Leghorn and part of Pisa were captured, and the enemy was in his defensive positions at the Arno River Line.

By this time experienced combat divisions—seven British, three American, and four French—had been transferred to participate in the invasion of southern France. Despite the depletion of its forces, it was still believed that the Allied Forces could overtake and punish severely or destroy the Germans before they could reach the security of the Gothic Line before the fall rains and the winter snows came.

The plan of the German forces was clear: To halt the Allied pursuit and turn it again into a slow, grinding advance and then to stop it completely before winter, short of the Gothic Line.

The Allied Offensive Plan[2]

The 15th Army Group, comprised of the Fifth and Eighth Armies, despite the heavy casualties sustained in the drive from Sicily and the transfer of experienced units, planned an all-out offensive by both armies.

The Eighth Army was to make the main effort along the Adriatic Coast. Its mission was to strike hard at the eastern Gothic Line along a narrow front, clearing the way for a powerful lunge into the Po River Valley. It was anticipated that the enemy would be forced to withdraw troops from the other zones to meet the threat on the Adriatic Coast.

The Fifth Army was to make a secondary effort in the Central Zone north of Florence, if the Germans did in fact weaken their defenses there by transferring reserves to the east.

When Eighth Army had launched its attack, Fifth Army was to mount what would appear to the Germans to be a large-scale offensive on a front extending *west* from Pontassieve (10 miles east of Florence), to Pontedera, near Pisa.

Once the enemy committed large reserves to meet the initial threat on the Adriatic Coast as well as the possible cut-off of his troops west of Florence, Fifth Army was to deliver a sledge-hammer blow in the center, hoping to drive through to Bologna, and to link up with Eighth Army.

Fifth Army Plan

August 26 the Eighth Army attacked in force. In three days, despite stubborn resistance, the Germans gave ground and were forced to shift critically important reserves south of the Po River, to stem the British tide.

Fifth Army at this time was composed of three corps: The U.S. II and IV and the British 13th.[3] IV Corps was on the left, II Corps in the center and 13 Corps was on the right.

II Corps and 13 Corps were to make the main Fifth Army effort along a narrow eight-mile front between Florence and Pontassieve. IV Corps was to attack and contain enemy forces on a front extending from the Coast to five miles west of Florence.

The success of the Fifth Army plan hinged on achievement of surprise, and upon timing and coordination with Eighth Army.

Three

From the Arno to the Gothic Line

First Blood

The 370th Combat Team was attached to IV Corps, commanded by Major General Willis D. Crittenberger, on 17 August; on 18 August, it was attached to Major General Vernon E. Pritchard's First Armored Division. Small groups of officers and enlisted men were attached to the division's infantry battalions and artillery for orientation and indoctrination, and 20 officers and 20 enlisted men spent several days with the 85th Division.

On the night of 23-24 August, the Third Battalion moved up into the line relieving the 14th Armored Infantry Battalion near Pontedera, marking the beginning of the combat operational history of the 92nd Infantry Division.

On the next night, the Second Battalion relieved the Sixth Armored Infantry Battalion south of Pontedera; and on 26 August, the First Battalion occupied a reserve position on the extreme right flank. When the 598th Fifth Army Battalion moved its guns into firing positions just south of Pontedera, the entire 370th Combat Team was facing the enemy for the first time.

There was unusual interest in the efficiency of these unit movements into the line by IV Corps Headquarters Staff. Officer observers accompanied each battalion as it executed this most difficult of night movements. Key officers and noncommissioned officers of the relieved units remained in line with men of the 370th for the first 24 hours, a gesture that was greatly appreciated by the Buffalo Soldiers.

Distinguished visitors, including Prime Minister Winston C. Churchill, began to show up almost as soon as the 370th Combat Team maneuvered into position.

Brigadier General Benjamin O. Davis, the Army's only black general came with a motion picture team for pictures of the Division in action; many American newspaper correspondents were on hand for news, and on 28 August, Lieutenant General Mark W. Clark, Fifth Army Commander, visited the 370th Combat Team. He asked Colonel Sherman if he were having any major problems and when he referred to the slowness of promotions for some of his officers, citing First Lieutenant Charles F. Gandy as one, General Clark took the Captain's bars from his own aide and pinned them on the Lieutenant, promoting him on the spot.

On the night of 27 August, the Third Battalion Command Post was bombed by enemy aircraft, and several casualties were caused by anti-personnel bombs. Two enemy patrols attacked with machine gun support from across the Arno River, but a platoon drove them off. The Combat Team's patrols continued to move into enemy areas across the river, just as did other Fifth Army units all along the line.

On 28 August, Major Aubrey Biggs, the Combat Team Executive Officer, accompanied a small patrol which was somewhat disorganized when ambushed by a stronger German Patrol. He assumed command and re-organized the patrol, which then drove the enemy back across the Arno with heavy losses. Major Biggs was awarded a Silver Star, one of the first staff officers to receive it.

On 30 August the first German prisoners captured by black infantry-men in Europe were seized by a twenty-two man combat patrol from Company F. Led by Lieutenant Jake Chandler and joined by Captain Charles F. Gandy, the heavily armed patrol crossed the Arno and boldly entered the village of Calcinaia, where it destroyed a machine gun position, returning then safely with two prisoners. Both prisoners attempted to escape, but in the resultant gunfire one was killed and the other wounded.

Of these actions, the *New York Times* reported[1]:

> German artillery opened up heavily near — — and in the Fifth Army sector around Pontedera, thirteen miles east of Pisa. Negro troops of the 92nd Division successfully crossed the Arno River at one point and enemy patrols east of Pisa were driven across the river.

On 29 August, Battery C of the 598th Field Artillery Battalion fired the first rounds at the enemy, and First Sergeant Jerry B. Davis of Battery A was seriously wounded by the immediate counter-battery artillery fire.

On 29 August the Combat Team was ordered to move to positions in line with the south edge of the Arno River. Company G lunged forward and seized the objective, and with help from Company E and the artillery, it withstood two strong enemy counterattacks, driving the enemy in confusion from the field. By morning, the Second Battalion was firmly astride the position, and ready to cross the Arno.

On 1 September, the 370th Combat Team was ordered to join with other IV Corps units to cross the Arno at 0100.[2]

The overall objective was for IV Corps to cross the Arno in force, and occupy the two major mountains in the Arno Plain: Mount Albano and Mount Pisano. Anticipated enemy opposition was well equipped, heavily armed with automatic weapons and mortars, well situated behind extensive minefields, and certain to offer stubborn resistance.

The 370th Combat Team had as its specific mission to drive the Germans from Mount Pisano, a mountain mass running north and south, about seven miles wide and ten miles long.

The Regiment with its First Battalion on the right, its Second Battalion in the center and its Third Battalion on the left, moved across the Arno as ordered. Company C was attached to Combat Command B of the First Armored Division at that time and crossed the Arno with that unit.

At 0500, the second platoon of Company E crossed the Arno, and held the north bank to protect the crossing at Ponte Nuova, capturing one prisoner. The Second Battalion then crossed the river in force at 1000 hours, with Company E spearheading the crossing. By 1700 the battalion had reached Brientina, and began closing in the vicinity of Buti, two-three miles north of the river by 0100, on 2 September.

The Third Battalion crossed the Arno at 1000 hours as ordered, and by nightfall, its leading elements had reached the vicinity of Pieve.

The First Battalion assembled near LaRota and on 2 September, with its B Company infantrymen riding on tanks of the First Tank Battalion, moved speedily around the east side of Mount Pisano and set up positions on the northeast slopes.

On 1 September, the Regimental Command Post moved forward from Ponsaco to Pontedera, and the 589th Field Artillery Battalion displaced from positions in vicinity of Reggio Montalbona to vicinity of Sicignano, closing in and ready to fire at the exact time of the river crossing of the three battalions, 1000 hours.

On 2 September the 370th resumed the slashing offensive. By 0300, the Combat Team's 317th Engineers, working with First Armored Division Engineers, had built a bridge for armor and tanks to cross over the Arno.

By 2200, elements of the First Battalion, moving out from Cascina, had advanced to Mount Castellaccio and then to positions on the northeast slopes of Mount Pisano. Effective teamwork of tanks and black infantry soldiers led to the quick seizure and consolidation of Castelvecchio by the First Battalion.[3]

The Second Battalion left Buti at 1000, and moved directly towards the mountain and occupied it very quickly against light resistance.

At 0200, after moving around the west side of Mount Pisano, the Third Battalion pushed on and by 2200, some elements reached the Serchio River at Pappiana, five miles north of Pisa. Considerable resistance was encountered when Company K entered Ripafratta, resulting in 24 casualties from enemy machine gun, small arms fire as well as mortar and artillery fire.

On 2 September, the Regimental Command Post again moved, this time at Elvilato at 1400. The 598th Field Artillery Battalion displaced forward at 2100 to positions near Gignese. Battery A received enemy artillery fire in the gun position area with no casualties or damage.

Mount Pisano was taken by the end of 2 September. The *New York Times* had words of praise for the part played by the Buffalo Soldiers:

> The American Fifth Army lashed out in a new offensive today, burst across the Arno on a wide front, seized Pisa and stormed dominating heights on the East in concert with a new drive by the Eighth Army through a 20-mile hold in the Gothic Line. Negro troops of the Ninety-Second United States Division, making their first appearance in the battle-line, stormed up the southeast slopes of Mount Pisano, from whose

frowning heights the enemy has lobbed shells into the American lines during the long stalemate on this front. The Pisano hill mass lies East and North of Pisa, western anchor of the Gothic Line.[4]

During the next three days, the enemy continued to withdraw to the Gothic Line. Progress of fighting units was hampered and slowed by mines, demolitions, small but powerful covering forces, supported by mortars, tanks, self-propelled guns, and artillery.

Nonetheless, the 370th Combat Team pressed the attack on 4 September.

The Second Battalion moved northwest across the trails and slippery slopes of Mount Pisano, then re-organized and attacked toward the ancient city of Lucca, situated on the south bank of the Serchio River and at the very foot of the Apennines which rise steeply just beyond it. The Second Battalion arrived near Vorno, about 4 kilometers south of Lucca, at 1600 on 3 September.

At 1605, the Regimental Company Post moved to San Giuliano and Battery A and Cannon Company moved to Vorno at 1715, with the remainder of the battalion closing in positions at 2150.

At about 2200, Colonel Sherman was informed by an Italian partisan that a "Committee of Liberation" in Lucca had driven the Germans from the city and had closed the gates. Civilian factions were quarreling over control and citizens of Lucca sent him to request that American troops enter and take control of the city.

He also claimed the city was without food or water, as the retreating Germans had destroyed the viaducts supplying water. He warned that the Germans controlled the highway between Vorno and Lucca.[5]

On September 3, one of many gallant acts which occurred, resulted in the award of the Silver Star to Captain Allen L. Johnson, of the Chaplain Corps. The citation reads:

> For gallantry in action on 3 September 1944 in the vicinity of Vorno, Italy. A patrol —— ran into an enemy machine gun emplacement and was forced to withdraw. One of the members of the patrol was seriously wounded and given first aid, but had to be left behind on the field of battle when the enemy started a concentration of machine gun and artillery fire on their position, making it impracticable to evacuate the wounded man. Captain Johnson called for a medical aid man and the two of them ran approximately four hundred and fifty yards (450) over an exposed area to the aid of the wounded man. After administering first aid, although under continuous enemy artillery fire, Captain Johnson instructed the medical aid men to leave and have a vehicle ready to meet him at the nearest covered position. He then placed the wounded man on his shoulders, and although still under fire from the enemy, carried him to a place of safety from where he was evacuated. Captain Johnson's gallant act in all probability saved the wounded man's life and was in keeping with the high traditions of the Chaplain Corps of the United States Army.

On 4 September, the First Battalion was in position astride the Autostrada just southeast of Capennori, with Companies A, B, and C echeloned in depth in that order. They were just a few miles southeast of Lucca at the end of the day.

Company E (Second Battalion) sent a patrol to Pontetetto to secure and fortify a bridge two kilometers south of Lucca. At 1645, with Company E on the left and Company G on the right, the Second Battalion launched the attack from Vorno. Heavy artillery, machine gun and sniper fire slowed the attack, but by 1800, Companies E and G had advanced to the south bank of the Canale Rosio near Pontetetto, driving all enemy elements to the north bank. At 1110 a platoon from Company F, supported by tanks, patrolled to Lucca, reconnoitered the west and south gates, then seized and held them. Due to skillful use of available cover and aggressive fire and movement, the units sustained very few casualties.

By 1900 the Second Battalion lines were at the Canale Reggio.

The Third Battalion consolidated its lines around Ripafratta, only a few kilometers southwest of Lucca, after a day of running fire fights, and heavy artillery and mortar fire. Major Biggs was killed during one of the heavy artillery concentrations on this sector.

On 5 September, the First Battalion advanced about two-and-one-half miles east of Lucca to vicinity of Ponte Maggiore.

At 0600, Company E and Company G moved forward and before noon, Company E entered the city and Company F moved in at 1600. Colonel Sherman moved his Command Post into the city and posted a mobile perimeter defense around the city.

Meanwhile the Third Battalion advanced about a mile from Ripafratta to Carasoma and cleared the road from Pisa to Lucca in the face of heavy small arms, machine gun and artillery fire.

September 6 and 7 were spent consolidating positions around Lucca and resting and re-grouping units. During this brief respite the enemy harrassed all front line units continuously with mortar, artillery and long-range machine gun fire.

On their drive towards Lucca the 370th Combat Team actually reached its objective more rapidly than the Fifth Army units on its left and right flanks. On the left, Task Force 45 was held up by extensive mine fields and on the right, Combat Command B was faced with stronger German rear guard action on the afternoon of 4 September.[6]

On 8 and 9 September, the 370th Combat Team pressed forward to positions just north of Lucca and along the Serchio River, which winds westward at Lucca, and toward the Ligurian Sea.

On the ninth the 370th Combat Team was bombed in Lucca with phosphorous bombs, but little damage and no casualties resulted. The First Battalion advanced more than a kilometer to positions well north of Capannori and just east of Lucca. The Second Battalion moved along the south bank of the Serchio River, with Company F north of Lucca, and Company G due west of that city. The Third Battalion became the Combat Team Reserve and was assembled south of Lucca, and the 370th Combat Team was ready, along with other units attached to the First Armored Division, to join in the general advance toward the Gothic Line.

Now that Lucca was taken, IV Corps Headquarters took time to coordinate and firmly establish all positions along its sector front. According to plan, IV Corps had advanced aggressively from the Arno to make it appear that it was mounting a major attack to the Northwest. But IV Corps had advanced much more rapidly than anticipated, so although the temptation to continue to move forward was great, to insure the success of the II Corps effort, the orders were that the lines held September 5 were to be *held* with a *minimum* of troops. Meanwhile plans were prepared for follow-up action in event the enemy continued to withdraw north, and, in any event, to maintain pressure on him to prevent his transfer of forces to the II Corps front.

West of 370th Combat Team, Task Force 45 had driven the enemy from the coastal plain. The Third Battalion of the 370th Combat Team had reached the banks of the Serchio River at about the same as the famous 100th Battalion of the 442nd (Nisei) Regiment.[7] The British 39th Light Antiaircraft Regiment had considerably more difficulty than the 370th Combat Team or the 100th Battalion in advancing through the thick woods and heavily mined areas northwest of Pisa.

The general advance of Fifth Army toward the Gothic Line, now only a few miles away, began 10 September. The entire front surged forward.

On 10 September, the Second Battalion, again spearheaded the advance, with Company E and Company F crossing near Ponte San Quirico and Company G crossing slightly further to the North. Before daybreak, two heavily armed security patrols from each company forded the Serchio River, and immediately eliminated all enemy opposition, then established strong points around the crossing spots to assure the safety and efficiency of the crossing for the main body to follow. The battalion spread out in a three-pronged drive following the west bank of the Serchio against stubborn resistance, at times. By 1030, its companies had advanced to San Quirico di Moriana, Vignale, and Del Giglio, where Company E engaged in a vicious fire fight, clearing the area of snipers and machine guns; they also killed six of the enemy and captured several positions.

All companies of the First Battalion advanced from Capannori to the north and by dark, had advanced three kilometers to positions near Ricci, Via Piagorri and Via Boroni. The Third Battalion closed into a new position area, still in reserve, at Via Santapointe, at 0380.

The Regimental Command Post moved just outside the wall northeast of Lucca, and the 589th Field Artillery Battalion displaced its firing batteries forward near Lucca.

On 11 September, all battalions went about consolidating positions and vigorously patrolling both to the front and the flanks.

Company A, riding on tanks, moved to Ponte A Moriana, where it became embroiled in a vicious fire fight during which a tank was hit by a shell and caught fire. All battalion positions were improved — Company E moved to Mount Catina, Company F to San Quirico, and Company G to Vignale. The Third Battalion remained in reserve.

The next day all battalions moved forward again—Company A, north to Ciriana; Company B, north to the vicinity of the right flank of the 370th Combat Team, near Segromigno. The Third Battalion was pulled out of Reserve and moved through the Second Battalion up along the west bank of the Serchio River.[8]

At 0900, the 598th Field Artillery Battalion Reconnaisance party was shelled heavily, with considerable casualties, among them, the Battery Commander of Battery A.

As the Fifth Army moved forward closer to the fixed Gothic Line defenses the terrain became more difficult; minefields, demolitions, tank obstacles became more numerous, and the resistance of the Germany enemy became more stubborn and skillful as he utilized all the resources available to him—terrain, fixed defenses, machine gun emplacements, protected sometimes by steel and concrete dugouts, with automatic weapons and mortars sited for interlocking bands of fire on targets.

The task of moving up the Serchio River Valley presented many difficulties for the 370th Combat Team troops, now in action for less than a month. The Serchio flowed through deep gorges, with hills rising quick and sheer at some points, from the river bank. The troops would be fighting in hills and towns on both sides of the Serchio River and control and coordination of units would be difficult.

Up to this point, the 370th Combat Team had operated as the main infantry component of Combat Command A, First Armored Division, and successfully carried out its assignments in combined operations, such as flexible task forces for emergency missions. Such groups normally contained one company of infantry mounted on tanks, several reconnaisance half-track vehicles, and a platoon of Tank Destroyers from the 701st Tank Destroyer Battalion. The 370th Combat Team also began to take note of the extent and value of help from the Partisans, who wanted to fight with them to defeat the Germans.

The next three days marked further advances, with the Second Battalion now on the left, protecting the flank. On 16 September the front lines were quiet, but that night a patrol from Company G was ambushed in Sesta, resulting in considerable casualties.

On 17 September, the 370th Combat Team Command Post moved up to Moriano, and on that date an attack along the entire front was launched. The Second and Third Battalions fought northward through the hills, on the west side of the Serchio. Substantial gains were made, with elements of Second Battalion reaching Via Giarne and Capacci, and Third Battalion moving up to within 30 yards of Mount Castellaccio. The Germans resisted with small arms, machine gun, mortar and artillery fire; even Nebelwerfer fire fell on the Third Battalion—seventeen rockets in all.

Accentuating the aggressive, well-coordinated forward move of the 370th Combat Team was the frontal assault on Mount Dell Elto and Mount Castellaccio, two enemy strongholds on the west bank of the Serchio.

Both mountains run generally northwest, then hook around southeast for about 4000 yards. A deep draw lies between them. Castellaccio on the east is over 1800 feet high, Mount Dell Elto considerably lower with more gradual sloping and a top not so rugged.

At 1000 on 17 September the Third Battalion advanced under cover of smoke shells and by 1020 was hit with artillery, machine gun, and small arms fire from the ridges. Company L on the left moved through the vineyards on the lower slopes of Mount Castellaccio, and by 1040 was on the southwest slope 700–800 yards from the top. When, by 1120, both companies K and L were still held up by the heavy German machine gun and mortar fire they called down artillery and used anti-tank guns in an unsuccessful effort to reach the top by frontal assault. Then, a platoon worked its way around to the left and reached a point to within 400 yards of the top, but scurried for cover when fired upon by the enemy on Mount Dell Elto across the draw. Smoke again was called for, on Mount Dell Elto this time, and thus, obscured from view, one platoon was left near Villa to give the appearance of making a frontal attack, while the rest of the troops worked their way further up on the left.

They then attacked from the south and west together and began to again force their way up the long slopes. By 1320, the assault platoons were within 200 yards of the top, with one bazooka team 150 yards from a church at the ridge-top. Mines and barbed wire below the ridge prevented further advance, however, and the troops below the assault platoons again received fire from the enemy on Mount Dell Elto as well as from their own troops 200 yards ahead. Despite their situation, they doggedly hung on to the side of Mount Castellaccio all day long, and at dusk, Company K moved around the the right of the hill while Company L continued to dig in. At 1535 on September 18, Company K attacked from the southeast and Company L attacked from the west. Lieutenant Ralph G. Skinner, Company L Platoon leader, led his men through a breach in the wire and by 0900 they had surrounded the church. A vicious close-range fire fight involving the three leading platoons drove the Germans from the church, and German fixed emplacements on the ridge were attacked and destroyed one by one by two Company K platoons.[9]

During the savage battle for the mountains several officers and enlisted men distinguished themselves. The citation for the Silver Star for Private Charles J. Patterson, gives proof:

> For gallantry in action on the morning of 18 September 1944 in the vicinity of Colletta, Italy. At approximately 0930 hours the squad of which Private Patterson was a member, was fired upon by an enemy machine gun emplaced in the wall of a church. The squad continued to advance in spite of the machine gun fire until it was pinned down by another enemy machine gun which opened up from the right flank of the squad. Seeing the imminent danger that the squad was in, Private Patterson started crawling forward up a hill to attack the machine gun that was firing from the front of the squad and holding up their advance. Private Patterson worked his way to the right of the machine gun emplacement and dropped a grenade into the emplacement killing two (2) of the enemy and forcing the remainder to retire. During this time the squad leader was injured by an

enemy artillery shell. Upon observing this Private Patterson made his way back to the squad, took command of it, and led it forward up the hill. Private Patterson's gallant act enabled the platoon to reach its objective and was within keeping of the highest traditions of the United States Armed Forces. Entered military service from Fort Wayne, Indiana.

Sergeant William H. Harrison and Private John E. Toney also were cited for heroic achievement in this attack and received Bronze Stars.

Sergeant Henry Powell and Sergeant Eugene Larkins were severely wounded during the fighting for the mountains, and were evacuated.

Patrols of Task Force 92 made no contact with the enemy on September 26, so all elements of the 370th Combat Team moved forward quickly, and by the next day they had moved four to five miles up the Serchio, despite mines and small arms and machine gun fire. The Third Battalion, on the left, advanced less rapidly because of continuous fire fights and a difficult river crossing operation, but it gained some 4000 yards, reaching Borgo a Mozzano.

The First Battalion followed Highway 12 on the east side of the valley of the Serchio and reached to within a mile of the Lima Creek-Serchio River Junction. The Second Battalion fought its way over the mountains to positions overlooking Lima Creek, near Bagni Di Lucca.

On 28 September, a patrol of the Second Battalion entered Bagni Di Lucca. However, before the 370th Combat Team could consolidate their gains, Task Force 92 was reduced to 370th Combat Team alone, and assigned responsibility for a full sixteen-mile front extending from the Brazilian Expeditionary Force just west of the Serchio Valley to a line running north from Pistoia.

On the morning of the 29th, the Third Battalion began the move to the new sector. Company K arrived in the vicinity of Rosso at 1400 and received machine gun fire almost as soon as it arrived. Company I received machine gun fire upon arrival at Pitiglio. Company L closed in the new sector at 2100 and the 598th Field Artillery Battalion closed in positions near Prunetta at 2030.

On the last day of the month, the Third Battalion crossed the Lima River and entered La Lima where Highway 66 joined Highway 12. The Regimental Command Post moved up, near Prunetta.

On 1 October, facing the enemy from the Ligurian Sea to the IV Corps boundary were: Task Force 45, the Brazilian Expeditionary Force, Task Force 92, Combat Command B of the First Armored Division, and the Sixth South African Armored Division. The mission of these Fifth Army forces was to maintain pressure on the enemy while II Corps, to the east, made the main attack. Task Force 92, still consisting only of 370th Combat Team, continued to be responsible for the wide zone east of the Serchio River, straddling Highway 12.

The Third Battalion drove on through La Lima, with Company I spearheading the move and advancing about a kilometer and a half on the road to Calanche. Company K crossed the Lima River and moved parallel to

Company I along the left bank, while Company L pushed forward on the high ground west of both companies K and I. Company L then drove northward and by 1400 had reached Ponte Di Sestione, making a five-kilometer advance for the day. Company I encountered enemy small arms fire near Cutigliana, but, after a short exchange, bypassed it and continued the advance. Company K, by 1400, was nearing Vizzetta.

The Second Battalion pressed on to La Lima, somewhat ahead of its Company G which was coming up Highway 12.

Companies A and B of the First Battalion spent the day helping the Engineers repair the Highway, while Company C provided right flank security along with elements of the Second Battalion.

Battery A of 598th Field Artillery Battalion displaced forward to San Marcello at 1500.

At 1245, on 2 October, Company G reported to the Second Battalion after its long march. That afternoon, orders from IV Corps called for Task Force 92 to take over from Task Force 45 responsibility for the *entire coastal sector* from Forte dei Marmi on the coast east and southeast to the Serchio Valley, at that time the responsibility of the Brazilian Expeditionary Force.

At 1300, the Second Battalion began to move to its assembly area just south of Viareggio, passing through San Marcello, Prunetta, Marlina, Montecatina, Altopascio, Lucca, Pisa, and many other communities from where, only a few days earlier, they had fought and driven the enemy northward. The Second Battalion closed in its assembly area at 0310 on 3 October.

The First Battalion moved at 2015 on 3 October, closing in at its assembly area near Viareggio at 0200 on 4 October. Movements were by night, with black-out lights.

The Third Battalion continued to hold positions near Cutigliano. By 5 October it had closed into its new assembly area.

The 370th Regimental Command Post opened at 0030 at Pietrasanta and the 598th Field Artillery Battalion closed into positions near Pietrasanta on 5 October, at 0330.

By 5 October, 370th Combat Team was in positions under Task Force 92 (now consisting of 370th Combat Team), and Second Armored Group (which included Task Force 45's 434th and 435th Antiaircraft Artillery Battalions, fighting as infantry and supported by the 751st Tank Battalion and the 894th Tank Destroyer Battalion).[10]

First Score-Card

After 42 days of combat, the 370th Combat Team had suffered 263 casualties, including 19 killed in action, 225 wounded, and 19 missing.[11] They had driven forward nearly 30 miles against steadily increasing resistance from experienced German troops and in the face of small arms, machine gun, mortar and heavy artillery fire, as well as extensive mine fields. They had endured a night aircraft phosphorous bomb attack and at the beginning of the successful attack on Mount Castellaccio the assaulting troops were hit by ten Nebelwerfer rockets. They had skillfully and efficiently made three major river crossings and forded many canals and streams under direct observation and fire of the enemy. Their units had defeated the enemy in numerous fire fights in the villages and in the countryside, clearing out nests of snipers, and machine guns, and their aggressive patrolling was outstanding enough to win the praise of the IV Corps Commander. They had operated harmoniously with the white soldiers of the First Armored Division, and quickly adjusted to the tank-infantry team assault operations with them. Their units were able to move over wide areas maintaining good controls, proper security, and proper flank contact with other units. Their advance was more rapid than that of other more experienced units in the sector at times. The attack and reduction of the German bastions on Mount Dell Elto and Mount Castellaccio was well planned and executed, as was the successful conquest of Mount Pisano.

The performance of some non-commissioned officers in action was impressive and led to several battlefield promotions as well as decorations for valor. Outstanding leadership was discovered among junior officers as well, and the names of some both enlisted and commissioned are still mentioned almost with reverence by veterans of the 92nd Division. Among them were Captain Charles F. Gandy, Lieutenant John Birdsong, Lieutenant Ralph Skinner, Lieutenant Frank Whisonant, Lieutenant Jake Chandler, Staff Sergeant Oscar Simpson, Private Jake McInnis, all of whom won the Silver Star, some posthumously.

The coordination of its infantry units with the 317th Combat Engineer Battalion and the 598th Field Artillery Battalion was noteworthy. The Engineers cleared enemy minefields, and removed German built obstacles; built bridges for river crossings, sometimes under enemy small arms, mortar and artillery fire. They went along on Infantry-Tank missions, and not only went ahead of the tanks to check out and remove mines in their path, but, in addition, they fought as infantrymen in the many fire fights that often resulted.

The 598th Field Artillery Battalion, with its twelve 105 mm howitzers was outstanding. They displaced forward rapidly, to keep pace with the rapidly moving infantry battalions and were always prepared to deliver fire when needed, and with pin-point accuracy. The other supporting units, Signal, Quartermaster, Medical and Military Police all functioned efficiently.

The 370th Combat Team had driven through a portion of the Gothic Line, and were in control of Highway 12, which had been the enemy's main east-west route in front of IV Corps.

Although most of the advance thus far had been through the relatively flat Arno River Plain, the officers and men had developed a high esprit de corps and, according to the combat team commander, Colonel Sherman, were convinced that their combat team was far superior to the enemy.[12]

Despite all the accolades, there were voices of disparagement and reluctant praise. There was an undertone of doubt and anticipated failure, particularly in high military levels. The men of the 370th Combat Team had thought the constant stream of important military leaders of the Armed Forces which had descended on Fort Huachuca, Arizona, before their departure, including Chief of Staff George C. Marshall, Under-Secretary of War Robert Patterson, Lieutenant General Leslie McNair, and ten officers of his Ground Forces Staff, and dozens of others, would end when they entered combat. They were wrong. They had scarcely met the enemy in late August when they were "visited" by Prime Minister Winston S. Churchill, Brigadier General Benjamin O. Davis, and a coterie of newspaper correspondents. And on the night of 23-24 August when the three battalions of the combat team began to effect the night relief of white units in front line positions, staff officers from IV Corps were on hand to "observe" the "efficiency" of the combat team's movements.

Much of the attention received from top military figures was interpreted by the black soldiers as a reflection of the prevailing lack of confidence in the black soldiers' fighting capabilities by that sector of the military.

Nevertheless, the officers (white and black) at that time, faced towards the base of the Apennines, looking up at the unseen enemy with confidence, albeit with a sense of foreboding.

A New Battle Arena — New Line-Ups

By 5 October, the Fifth Army's II Corps had breached the Gothic Line in the center and had made significant advances toward Bologna. The goal now was to conquer that objective before the fall rains and heavy snowfall came. The role of the IV Corps continued to be to create a diversion and to contain enemy forces in its sector to prevent their transfer to other Fifth Army fronts.

Task Force 92 now was faced with a *six* mile front on the coastal plain on its left and steep, rugged mountains for the balance of its front, on the right.

The Northern Apennines Mountains, called the Apuan Alps in that area, became higher and wider, thus narrowing the coastal plain towards the north of Italy. Great, winding, sometimes very narrow and deep valleys were carved out among these mountains, and smaller draws fell away from ridge tops, giving the German Forces every natural defensive advantage possible. IV Corps' responsibility extended to the 35-mile-long Serchio River Valley, formed with Lima Creek. It was a winding, narrow, sometimes gorge-like valley, whose control was vital for the protection of the Fifth Army supply base at Leghorn. It was equally important to the Germans for the protection of their coastal defense troops.

Between the Serchio Valley and the Coastal Plains, rose thirteen miles of steep, rugged, virtually impassable mountains devoid of roads or passable trails, on the Allied side. This created massive supply and communications problems for the divided 92nd Division forces.

The 370th Combat Team troops were now preparing to assault the main Gothic Line defenses, against well-entrenched German Forces now committed to stand and fight to the bitter end. Mountain and plain, and the weather proved to be allies of the enemy.

In the 370th Combat Team Sector, the Gothic Line defenses were as powerful and impregnable as anywhere along its entire length. Thousands of Italian laborers and Slovak technical brigade members had worked on them since the surrender of the Italian Armies in September 1943. The operation was supervised by engineers of the German Todt Organization. The defenses were about 200 miles long and began in the valley of the River Magra, just south of La Spezia, the great Italian Naval base, and directly in front of the 370th Combat Team troops waiting for orders to move, on the Coastal Plain. It then stretched southeast through Massa, Carrara and onward through the Apuan mountains to a series of strong points located at various passes throughout the Apennines. It was especially formidable at the Vernio Pass and at the Futa Pass north of Florence. It then continued on to the Adriatic. Planned were 2,376 machine gun posts, 479 anti-tank mortar and assault gun positions, 120,000 meters of wire, and many miles of anti-tank ditches.[13]

However, there was little change in the front lines of the sector as the result of the attack. Enemy artillery, mortar, machine gun and small arms fire continued to be heavy in the Coastal sector.

The other troops attacking on the Coastal Plain, though part of Task Force 92, also did *not* reach the objective. The truth is that, just as the attack to penetrate the Gothic Line and occupy and hold Massa had failed, so had the entire Allied offensive in Italy failed. All along the Fifth Army and Eighth Army lines, the Germans' system of strong fixed fortifications, flexible mobility of their excellent quality reserve troops to meet strong threats at any point, enabled them to defend their positions successfully. Meanwhile, Allied troops drained their offensive power by continued action without rest, by difficult supply operations over rain-clogged roads, and by mounting casualties in the face of increasing enemy resistance.

So it would appear that Captain Charles F. Gandy and his fellow Buffalo soldiers, in their first crack at the German Gothic Line, had done as well as any other units in the Fifth and Eighth Armies.

After the six-day offensive ended, the 370th Infantry spent the 13th and 14th of October in reorganization and resting, making a few changes in position. On 14 October, reorganization continued, but in addition, the first of a series of "power patrols" was sent out. These "power patrols" were 35-75 man units, heavily armed, sometimes including light machine gun teams, 60 mm mortar squads, litter bearers and artillery forward observers.[14] Company E sent such a patrol to Fabbiano, but the German troops that had fired on Third Battalion troops fighting their way up MAINE on the 12th, had withdrawn from the town. A second patrol from Company E went to the *top* of MAINE and found no enemy there. The third patrol from the Company went to Mount Castellachio east of Fabbiano, and reported some enemy at La Capella; no enemy were at Mount Cavallo, northeast of Fabbiano, but they found many enemy directly north of Fabbiano.

Along with the aggressive, continuous patrolling, came the opportunity for moving units around so as to give the most hard-hit units a chance to rest, reorganize, and continue training whenever the situation permitted. Some units were quite depleted by casualties and exhaustion.

On 15 October, the Third Battalion went into reserve, and its defensive positions were taken over by the Second Battalion. There was little other activity except for relief of Company B by Company C. However, reconnaisance and security patrols continued to probe, and contact patrols reached the Brazilian Forces on the right flank.

On 17 October reconnaisance and security patrols were active. A squad of men from Company F was trapped by the enemy in a house at Giustagnana and five soldiers were killed and three were captured.[15] Company B elements probed on Mount Cutigliano.

Four men were killed and two wounded as enemy artillery shelled Battery C of the 598th Field Artillery Battalion. Reportedly, counter-battery fire on the enemy guns produced good results.[16]

On 18 October, the Third Battalion relieved the First Battalion, and the First Battalion completed its move to the reserve area, with one platoon remaining on the slopes of Mt. Cauala.

On 19 October, there was the usual patrol activity but substantially little change in the infantry battalions' positions, but the 598th Field Artillery Battalion moved to positions southeast of Pietrasanta at 0100.

On that day also, word came that the other 92nd Division units had begun to arrive at Leghorn, and Division orders were issued designating assembly and training areas for them, as well as outlining a complete and realistic training program for all units. Plans were made to arrange several days of battle indoctrination for all.

From 19 to 21 October patrolling, regrouping and re-organization continued. Company I was alerted for possible enemy on Mount Cauala and a patrol from Company F was in position on a portion of the Mountain. On the 21st, elements of Company I remained on MAINE. Plans were being developed for a night attack on Mount Strettoia by the Third Battalion. On 21 October, a patrol discovered extensive wire entanglements and mines on the approach slopes of the mountain, so a platoon of engineers was attached to the Third Battalion for the impending attack.

October 22 was a day marked by some of the heaviest fighting experienced by the 360th Combat Team. The Third Battalion, spearheaded by Company L, advanced under cover of darkness at 2100. The engineers blasted a large hole in the wire, using bangalore torpedoes, and the Company L troops moved through it and pressed on. At that point, intensive enemy machine gun and mortar fire rained down upon the company, and in the confusion and noise of battle, it became disorganized. Nevertheless, under these most trying of conditions, they were reorganized, and moved forward again. By 0300, elements of Company L had reached the objective, where they were promptly subjected to extremely intensive enemy machine gun and mortar fire, resulting in many casualties, including the Company Commander, Lieutenant Cotheren. By this time a heavy volume of enemy fire was falling all over the slopes of Mount Strettoia, particularly at the area of the gap in the wire obstacles, and Company C, by 1640, was not able to reach the beleaguerred elements of Company L fighting desperately *on the objective*. Lieutenant Reuben L. Horner, and his Company L platoon, skillfully fought off eight counterattacks hurled at them by the enemy that night, finally withdrawing when all its ammunition was used up. He was awarded the Silver Star for gallantry in action.

And on October 22, Staff Sergeant Oscar Simpson won the first of two Silver Stars he was to earn before the end of the war.

> Staff Sergeant Simpson's platoon was suddenly fired upon by an enemy gun from the rear. Under cover of counter fire by one of his officers and assisted by another member of his platoon Staff Sergeant Simpson elected to attempt to knock out the enemy weapon. Exposing himself, he moved in on the enemy, killing one, and forcing the other to surrender, thus enabling his platoon to continue in its advance.

From 20-23 October, the elements of Companies C and L, were engaged in many fire fights and after facing overwhelming small arms, machine gun, mortar and artillery fire for three days they finally withdrew. On the 23rd, the Second Battalion began to prepare to move to a new sector, and most of the day was spent in reliefs by units. Elements of Company B relieved elements of Company F on Mount Cauala on 20 October and although under heavy and continuous fire, they stood fast and continued to improve their positions and repelled every effort by the enemy to dislodge them.

On 24 October, the Second Battalion was moved and attached to Combat Command B, and on the 25th moved into an assembly area at Porretta, at 2000. Positions of Company I on Mount Cauala remained under fire most of the 24th. They attempted to advance from their positions on the south side of the top of the mountain, but met with extremely heavy resistance and made no progress.

On 26 October patrols were sent out to capture prisoners. The Fifth Army was beginning its planning to resume the offensive about 1 December, and the success of patrols became essential in determining enemy dispositions, strengths and identifications. Company I sent a patrol at 1900 on 25 October to the north peak of MAINE, but the enemy reacted violently with heavy fire, and the patrol withdrew. Company A patrol reached the enemy tactical wire at Mount Strettoia, but while trying to breach the wire, were fired on by three enemy machine guns and forced to withdraw. Company K's patrol set up an ambush on Mount Strettoia, but no enemy walked into it. "The patrol leader going into the mountain heard nothing but a cough."[17] A patrol from Company A went to vicinity of Lacapalla, killed one enemy, captured none. In the meantime, Company I remained on MAINE for the fifth day. At 1800, they threw back another enemy attack.

In the Second Battalion (under Combat Command B), the Battalion Command Post opened at Silla at 1630 and by 1930 Company G relieved Troop D of the 81st Reconnaissance Squadron and took positions near Crociale. Company F had already relieved Company A of 11th Armored Infantry Battalion near Torre Malavita.

Feverish patrolling continued on the 27th. A patrol from Company L returned from Mount Strettoia at 0800, reported tactical wire in place. At

0100 elements of Company A reported that they were on Mount Cauala and were digging in to protect Company I's right flank. A patrol from Company I moved to the north of the mountain, where they discovered the enemy dug in. A patrol from Company A found enemy on Mount Cavallo. A patrol from Company K found new enemy emplacements on Mount Strettoia. Company positions did not change.

In the vicinity of Bombiana, at 2135, Company E relieved Company C of the 11th Armored Infantry Battalion, and the Second Battalion, 370th Infantry assumed responsibility for that sector, still attached to Combat Command B.

On 28 October active patrolling continued, and Company I again beat off an enemy attack at 1120. The squad from Company A protecting the flank of Company I sustained some casualties. A combat patrol from Company A returned at 2250 from Fabbiano after a fire fight there.

On 29 October, a Company L patrol captured one prisoner and much enemy equipment. Another patrol from Company C reached Basati, found no enemy there, and a power patrol from the Third Battalion worked its way up Mount Strettoia. They overpowered two enemy prisoners and withdrew under artillery and mortar fire.

On 30 October active patrolling continued. On 31 October a patrol from Company L tried to breach the enemy wire on the third peak of Mount Cauala and ran head-on into a fire fight with the enemy, but after a hard fight and in the face of heavy machine gun and mortar fire, had to withdraw.

Balance of the 92nd Division Arrives

At 1350, the First Battalion was alerted for movement to the Serchio Valley Sector. By 1100 on 1 November, it was relieved by the First Battalion of the 371st Infantry, marking the initial entry into combat of the first of the remaining elements of the 92nd Infantry Division. It also marked the end of 69 days of fighting as the lone advance representative of the Buffalo Division of the 370th Infantry Combat Team; the move of the First Battalion was the beginning of combat action in a different portion of the front lines in which the 370th Infantry Combat Team assumed responsibility for the entire Serchio Valley, a few miles north of Lucca, near Gallicano and Barga.

An amusing notation was made in the 370th Operations report for October 1944 regarding the 371st Infantry:

> Elements of the First Battalion, "Up Front," for the first time, fought a successful engagement with an invisible and non-existent but powerful enemy horde, suspected of conducting a daring raid on Pietrasanta.

The Second Battalion, 370th Infantry, continued to be involved in Mount Belvedere action.

With the full division expected within a short time, General Almond ordered the 370th Infantry Regiment to replace the Brazilian Expeditionary

Force in the Serchio Valley Sector. On 1 November, the First Battalion, 370th Infantry moved to the Gallicano and Barga area. The Third Battalion, in the Pietrasanta sector for another day, had a difficult last day. A patrol ran into "Bouncing Betty" mines, or hand grenades, and one man was killed, two wounded and one missing. At 1220, Company I received considerable enemy mortar fire, and at least four casualties resulted from enemy mortar fire in the battalion area. Then at 1740, the Third Battalion was alerted for an attack by the enemy, and the remaining two platoons were ordered onto Mount Cauala at 1830. A Company K patrol met mortar fire at 2055. At 2400 on 3 November, another Company K patrol was ambushed by the enemy, and in withdrawing, it was chased by artillery and mortar fire; six of its men were missing. At 1310 instructions for moving to the new sector finally came to the Third Battalion. The move to the Serchio Valley sector was completed and the new 370th Regimental Command Post was opened at Fornaci di Barga.

Meanwhile, the 371st Infantry Combat Team (including 599th Field Artillery Battalion), with Colonel James Notestein commanding, prepared to begin entry into front line combat only a few weeks after its arrival in Italy. On 3 November, the Third Battalion, 371st Infantry, took over positions of the Third Battalion, 370th Infantry and the 371st Regimental Command Post moved into the building just vacated by the 370th Infantry Headquarters. By 0700 on 4 November, the 371st Infantry was functioning on its own with the First Battalion just north and east of Seravezza, and the Third Battalion just north of Pozzi.

Companies F, H, and a part of C were still in the Staging Area near Leghorn, awaiting the arrival of the balance of the Second Battalion, which had mistakenly been landed in Oran, Spanish Morocco, North Africa.

On 4 November, the 92nd Division had on the extreme left flank along the Ligurian Sea, the Second Armored Group. The 371st Combat Team was in the center, and the 370th Combat Team was in position in the Serchio Valley near Gallicano and Barga.

By 10 November, *all* Division Artillery units were in the line and the balance of the Division was arriving week by week.[18]

On 4 November the 371st Regimental Command Post was shelled for 15 minutes by German 88 mm guns. No casualties resulted. In the first few days of November, the front line troops got a demonstration of what faced them as the First Battalion received 90 to 100 rounds of mixed artillery fire daily while the Third Battalion received 80 to 85 rounds daily in addition to mortar fire and some small arms fire. It became immediately evident that Mount Cauala was strongly defended by the enemy, that the terrain was most rugged and commanded observation over most of the surrounding territory.[19]

Aggressive patrolling was begun almost immediately. Third Battalion patrols constantly encountered heavy enemy small arms fire, however, which often pinned them down. In certain places along the First Battalion front lines, patrols began to report unoccupied towns and houses. The First Battalion were convinced that some Italian civilians who had unlimited movement over the countryside were giving the enemy information as to 371st

Infantry troop dispositions, supply routes, and command posts. Blinking lights were observed. Therefore, at the request of the First Battalion Commander, all civilians were evacuated from the front lines, and guards were posted on bridges and roads leading from the front lines.[20]

On 5 November, Company F, still in the Staging Area, was attached to Company K, in position on the southern slope of Mount Cauala; it was felt added support for Company K would be required and also it provided familiarization with the mountain for a new Second Battalion unit.

On 6 November, Task Force 92 was dissolved and control of the 92nd Division passed to Fifth Army.

The 365th Combat Team arrived and was committed to action in the Coastal Sector on 9 November. In November, all 92nd Division elements were in the line, divided, however, and fighting on opposite sides of the 13-mile Appenines Mountain mass. The Buffalo Soldiers, many facing the enemy for the first time, were to experience the most savage and brutal fighting to that point, during the month of November.

Patrols reported no enemy contact on 6 November and intelligence data supported the belief the enemy was withdrawing. An advance to maintain contact *appeared* to be sound.

The plan was for First Battalion 371st Combat Team, to send a strong daylight patrol to Mount Cavallo, the next high ground to their front and then, under cover of darkness, move forward and seize the mountain. Such a maneuver would put First Battalion about 200 feet higher and in position to fire down on the east slope of Mount Cavallo. In the meantime a strong patrol from Company L was to move to occupy Hill X, to the immediate front, followed by the rest of Company L the next night. Company B was to occupy the town of Basati on the right flank.

The Third Battalion, less Company L was to exert pressure against Mount Cauala. Later the plan was amended to have troops sent to Azzano and Basati.

At 2000, the First Battalion's units moved out toward Azzano and Basati.

The Third Battalion ran into problems quickly. At 0330, a platoon from Company K moved up the slopes of Mount Cauala on 7 November. A request for artillery support from the 424th Field Artillery Group was *refused* by the field artillery because of lack of observation. In spite of this setback, the platoon continued on, but it became lost and while trying to find its way back to the company and, appearing from an unexpected direction, was subjected to hand grenade and rifle fire from Company K itself. A second patrol went out immediately, reaching the next high ground, and then a third patrol, involving the remainder of Company K, went forward.

At 0445 the patrol from L Company, proceeded toward "Hill X," led by Second Lieutenant Albert E. Seay; at the base of the hill the patrol was pinned down by enemy mortar and small arms fire from the top of the hill; because of the terraced terrain, they were unable to return the fire, but continued to advance seeking a more suitable position. Near the crest of the hill, Lieutenant Seay, stepped on a mine and though he was seriously wounded, his troops knocked out one enemy machine gun with hand grenades. The mine explosion brought down a hail of enemy machine gun and mortar fire from concealed positions. The remaining members of the platoon became disorganized and, thinking Lieutenant Seay was dead, withdrew without him. However, despite his wounds, Lieutenant Seay survived and was able to roll and crawl his way back to his own lines two days later. His citation for the Silver Star Award concludes:

> Second Lieutenant Seay's heroic performance and determined efforts to accomplish his mission ranks among the best traditions of the infantry soldier.

The First Battalion made good progress. Company A suffered some casualties in its occupation of Fabbiano, from artillery and mortar fire and minefields in the town. The wounded were evacuated with the help of litter bearers from First Battalion Headquarters personnel and Company A continued its advance towards Azzano.

A patrol from Company B drove through Basati and into the town of Levigliani. Upon returning to the Company, the patrol ran into a fire fight with a 25-man German patrol, which it scattered with hand grenades and rifle fire, and it returned with no casualties. Basati was occupied by a platoon of Company B, and by 1435 the patrol from that company was reaching out towards the town of Terrinca to the northeast.

At 1510, the First Battalion Command Post at Giustagnana was heavily shelled for 25 minutes. Later, the commanding officer, Lieutenant Colonel Weber, and three enlisted men were seriously wounded by mines. He was evacuated and replaced by Major Halterman, the battalion executive officer. Colonel Weber had led his battalion aggressively and well from forward positions until he was hit. He was awarded the Silver Star.

In the Third Battalion sector, L Company positions remained unchanged, as they were unable to penetrate the defenses on Hill X, but Company K, having advanced some 200 yards, began to dig in on the slopes of Mount Cauala.

On the morning of 8 November, Third Battalion, 371 Infantry positions were relatively unchanged, although a series of "happenings" during the post midnight hours created much movement and activity. At 0051 the L Company Commander reported a strong enemy patrol armed with small arms and machine guns was trying to envelope its right flank, forcing withdrawal of its outpost and causing him to request reinforcements. When, twenty minutes later, he reported an enemy breakthrough, Lieutenant Colonel Arthur H. Walker, the Third Battalion Commander, sent the Battalion Anti-Tank Platoon to reinforce the company, and went to the Company L area himself. He found the "enemy" had apparently withdrawn, and by 0300 the three platoons of Company L were back in position, with much confusion remaining as to just what had occurred. As a result the Company Commander was relieved, and First Lieutenant Magellan C. Mars was given command of Company L.[21]

Company K, having advanced some 200 yards, began to dig in and make preparations to advance.

At 2030 hours on 8 November, Company E (Second Battalion), commanded by Captain Winston D. Wetlaufer, moved into Seravezza. Its mission was to guard roads and approaches north and east of Seravezza, and Seravezza. It was also to assist in supply for First Battalion and to secure Seravezza to protect the supply lines.

It had become apparent by this time that Mount Cauala, and the smaller, but still formidable mountains clustered around it and extending like a spider's legs, were an important defensive strongpoint in the German coastal defense system. It was plain, too, that the Germans did not intend to give it up. Mount Cauala itself presented a very real obstacle to supply of 92nd Division troops, whose only supply access was via the Pietrasanta-Seravezza Road, plainly visible to enemy observers during daylight hours, and well covered by pre-sited, artillery and mortar fire at night.

Captain Wetlaufer and Company E on the first assignment into combat had a tough job. They experienced artillery and mortar fire throughout the night, but early on 9 November they were in position in Seravezza.

During the night of 8-9 November, the First Battalion positions remained relatively unchanged, but even the strongest patrols along the Third Battalion front met strong resistance. At 1105, Company K became involved in a wild fire fight during which the company incurred several casualties, among them Captain Curtis J. Ivey, the commanding officer. Captain Ivey was seriously wounded by mortar fire, but refused to leave his company, and succeeded in getting a platoon and a half on the objective, at the cost of ten men wounded and one killed, but the enemy, too, suffered heavy casualties. The position was consolidated, and only then did Captain Ivey consent to be evacuated and brought down from the mountain. Captain John W. Hildebrand was then assigned command of Company K.[22]

During the furious fire fight of Company K, Second Lieutenant Albert E. Seay, who had been left on "Hill X," the morning of 7 November, crawled back through the lines of Company L. In a letter to the author dated 26 June 1946, Lieutenant Seay detailed his experience, emphasizing the aggressive role played by the men in his unit in the attack during which he was wounded, and praising their efforts in trying to rescue him or recover his body.[23]

> My platoon had been on a reconnaisance patrol and returned around midnight. I was immediately called back to Battalion Headquarters to be briefed for a dawn attack; so without much of a breathing spell we were issued extra supplies and set out for the attack.
>
> During the attack James Wilson, the Automatic Rifleman, exposed himself in order to get his weapon in firing position and succeeded in silencing a machine-gun covering the hill. I sincerely believe I'd never gotten out of this if it hadn't been silenced.
>
> A Corporal of my platoon led Lieutenant Arcilious Jackson and a patrol up the same hill the next two nights in search of me or my body, but since

I had crawled away, it was useless; from my position I could observe the "Gerries" lighting the hillside up with flares and also the mortar and machine gun fire, but they *still* searched for me. I'll never forget my Buffalo comrades.

During the fighting on 8-9 November on MAINE, 92nd Division and supporting artillery fired concentrations in front of the Third Battalion, 371st Infantry. Mortars fired at a few of the located enemy machine gun emplacements. However, the enemy appeared determined to hold his position on the mountain and since many of their machine gun emplacements were cut into solid rock and supplemented by concrete bunkers, or simply dug into the rocky caves at the summit, it is doubtful that artillery and mortar concentrations were very effective.

The First Battalion was unable to give support fires to the Third Battalion front because their fire was obstructed by hill MAINE; however, on 10 November, plans were made to attach a platoon of medium tanks and two light tanks to the 371st Infantry to deliver supporting fire on call to the Third Battalion.

Meanwhile, enemy artillery became increasingly active and accurately directed into the left sector of the First Battalion zone with Companies A and C, being the forward elements on the southern outskirts of Azzano, receiving the bulk of the enemy fire. Company A was shelled intermittently all afternoon but suffered no casualties. Company C, however, had four casualties around 1200 when some enemy shells found its mortar positions. The company held its ground, but by 1545 it had sustained eighteen casualties from enemy artillery fire and Company A also had several. Although the men of the two companies were well dug in, the company positions were under direct enemy observation and thus subjected to continuous, murderous artillery and mortar fire. The company commanders of both companies thereupon requested permission to withdraw to more covered positions, but instead, after a personal reconnaisance by the battalion commander the orders were "to *advance* to more covered positions if they desired, or to move laterally, if necessary but not to move forward or to the rear."[24]

At 1945 on 10 November Companies A and C were still holding their positions. Company B, First Battalion, during the same period received intermittent mortar fire but had received no casualties thus far.

By this date, all three of the 92nd Infantry Division's Combat Teams were in action. The 370th Infantry was holding positions in the mountains and villages east and west of the Serchio River with two of its battalions in a line extending from the ridges west of Gallicano and running east of the river through Castelvecchio and Sommacolonia to Bebbio.

The 371st Infantry, newly arrived, was flexing its muscles before massive Mount Cauala and moving aggressively into positions east of the Serra River, holding its own in fire fights and standing steadfast in the face of heavy artillery and mortar fire in Azzano and other villages.

The 365th Combat Team Is Committed

On 8 November, elements of the third 92nd Division Combat Team, the 365th Infantry began to take over the Coastal sector held by the Second Armored Group. The Second Battalion began relief of the 435th Antiaircraft Battalion in the Forte dei Marmi Sector. On 13 November, the First Battalion (minus C Company which still had two platoons on board ship) and with Company I attached, completed relief of the Third Battalion, 371st Infantry. The 365th Infantry now held a sector running from the Ligurian Coast to about 1200 yards inland, with two battalions in line. Almost immediately, intensive reconnaissance patrolling became routine for these newest of Buffalo Soldiers; special attention was given to the Cinquale Canal area near the sea, which was a natural barrier between the two opposing forces. The pattern followed by the 370th and the 371st Regiments of sending large, heavily armed combat patrols into enemy territory resulted in lively fire fights in which casualties were inflicted on both sides.[25] The 365th Infantrymen fared quite well in these encounters, although the accurate heavy enemy artillery and mortar fire accounted for many casualties in this initial phase of combat. They learned quickly that any movement during daylight on the Coastal Plain was observed by enemy eyes on the many mountain peaks to their right front and would bring down a hail of shells. They learned quickly to take cover, and when to remain immobile—and to scan the front and the mountain peaks for retaliatory targets for their own artillery and mortars. On 14 November the first member of the Regiment was killed in action. He was First Lieutenant Norris E. Haines, of Company B who was hit by artillery fire. On 15 November, the 597th Field Artillery Battalion, with all-black officers from top to bottom, moved into direct-support firing positions near Forte dei Marmi. On 23 November, the Third Battalion relieved the Second Battalion in the line at 0025, and thus, within two weeks of entry into combat, the entire Regiment had been involved in front-line combat with the enemy. This included the cannon company and the Anti-Tank Company who fired direct support fire missions. To this point, casualties had been light: one officer and two enlisted men killed in action; one officer missing in action and fifteen men wounded in action.

There were many acts of heroism by officers and enlisted men of the 365th Infantry during the period, as well as encouraging examples of fine leadership.

Back to the 371st

Early in the day on 11 November, 371st reconnaissance and security patrols reached out for enemy prisoners and information. The detachment of tanks and three 57 mm anti-tank guns made available to the Third Battalion, began to seek out a single sniper in a cave in the upper reaches of Mount Cauala. He had earned the respected title of "Tootin' Tommy" and had scored "hits" on several men along the approaches to the First Battalion area. He was courageous and ingenious, and for the past three days had wreaked havoc in the area, retreating into his cave when fired upon with 30 calibre small arms and machine guns. But, by 12 November "Tootin' Tommy" tooted no more, after the tanks and 57's were finished with him.[26]

Throughout the day of 11 November, extremely accurate and heavy enemy artillery limited movement of First Battalion in its efforts to round up and evacuate townspeople from the town of Azzano, but no casualties resulted. Companies A and B continued to improve their positions, while the supporting 599th Field Artillery poured shells into located enemy gun positions throughout the day.

At 0215 on 12 November word came that the Third Battalion, 371st Infantry was to be attached to 370th Infantry in the Serchio Valley. First Battalion, 36th Infantry was to relieve Third Battalion, 371st Infantry, still clinging to positions on Mount Cauala and adjacent mountains; by 2400, Company K, close to, but not quite at the top of Mount Cauala was relieved by Company F which had been acting as Third Battalion reserve. Company G then replaced Company F at the foot of the hill. Companies A, B, and D, 365th Infantry, relieved Companies I, L, and M, 371st Infantry.

The First Battalion Command Post was moved forward from Seravezza to Minazzana, a small village high on the reverse slope of Mount Castellaccio.

With its Company E attached to First Battalion, and Company F on hill MAINE, supported by Company G, the balance of Second Battalion, 371st Infantry, commanded by Major George E. Pinard, advanced from the assembly area south of Pietrasanta, and set up its command post at Vallecchio.

Except for exchanges of artillery shelling and continuous patrol contact with the enemy the 371st Infantry front line sector was relatively quite for the next two days. However, since the "mission of the 92nd Division was to ... hold maximum enemy force in coastal area; continue to exert pressure, occupying any areas the securing of which is deemed within its capabilities, and protect the left flank of the Fifth Army,"[27] the primary mission remained defensive. Nevertheless, many "limited" local attacks were executed to instill and nourish the aggressive spirit of the troops and to maintain battle contact with the enemy.

In the Serchio Valley a full scale attack was launched 16 November to seize high ground to the front of the 370th Infantry.

Simultaneously, Second Battalion, 371st Infantry began a renewed assault on Mount Cauala on 15 November. Dawn patrols from First Battalion reported no enemy contact, but had observed recently occupied enemy emplacements. Second Battalion scouts moved up hill MAINE to the next peak without drawing enemy fire. Immediately, a reinforced platoon from Company F, followed by the entire company, occupied it and began to dig in for the night planning to continue up the hill the next morning. Company G moved up into Company F's old position. During the night Company F received some mortar fire on their new positions but the Combat Team's 599th Artillery silenced the mortars.

On the morning of 16 November, in spite of concentrated, accurate enemy mortar fire falling on Company F's position, a reinforced platoon succeeded in moving forward. At 0915 the platoon was pinned down by enemy small arms and mortar fire from the next peak to their front. Company F called for artillery fire, but it did *not* materialize, and although the men of Company F clung to the rocky sides of the mountain throughout the day, they could not advance. With no artillery support and the Germans able to observe their every movement and blast them with artillery and mortar concentrations at will, the company stood its ground for even yet one more day. Another attack was planned for 18 November, and at 1430 on that date, after several hours of harrassing fire on Mount Cauala by supporting artillery followed by a fifteen minute artillery preparation, a platoon led by Second Lieutenant Royal L. Bolling jumped off. They moved quickly up the rugged slopes, and some of the men fell behind from exhaustion. As they leap-frogged forward the enemy pounded them with mortar and artillery fire and hit them with showers of hand grenades and machine gun fire. Casualties mounted, but Lieutenant Bolling, undaunted and determined to destroy the enemy, pressed onward and upward. He finally reached the top with his platoon sergeant and two riflemen; they crawled through a stone wall and found themselves in the midst of several active enemy emplacements. In one, two Germans were frantically yelling into the phone, calling for artillery. A short but fierce hand-to-hand fight in which small arms and hand grenades were used, resulted in the death of the two Company F riflemen. Lieutenant Bolling and his platoon sergeant then withdrew, taking two prisoners, who reported that the artillery preparation had been ineffective because the enemy on Mount Cauala were dug into deep rock bunkers.

The citation for the Silver Star for Second Lieutenant Bolling concludes:

> He withdrew when all but one of his men had been killed or wounded.

The Bronze Star was awarded to Second Lieutenant Millard B. Smallwood:

> For heroic achievement in action, on 16 November, 1944, in Italy. As Second Lieutenant Smallwood proceeded down a road on his way to the regimental command post he came to a vulnerable section of the road which was enemy-observed and under threat of constant enemy artillery. At this critical point in the road, Lieutenant Smallwood noticed a soldier who had been injured by shell fragments. Seriously jeopardizing his life by not speeding through this point or taking cover in a building, he deliberately stopped his vehicle in the road and, though the area was immediately subjected to an artillery concentration, lifted the wounded man into the jeep and successfully continued on his way past the danger area.

The total casualties for Company F were 21, including the company commander, First Lieutenant Charles H. Lancaster, who was wounded. Four enlisted men were killed, fifteen were wounded and one was missing.

Mount Cauala was not taken. However, the attack resulted in many enemy killed and wounded, two prisoners taken, and indirectly led to 22 more prisoners of war surrendering to 92nd Division forces. Lieutenant Bolling's prisoners were Polish and members of a unit led by German commissioned and non-commissioned officers. On November 22, a loudspeaker system was set up in Company F's area; First Lieutenant Alfred D. Sieminski, from the Division Special Service Office, spoke to the enemy soldiers in the Polish language, promising warm food and safety. Four Poles surrendered within three hours and within 24 hours after the broadcast, twenty-two others crossed over as prisoners of war.

Second Battalion, 371st Infantry resumed its determined efforts to conquer Mount Cauala despite the stubborn resistance of the enemy. On 22 November, a heavily armed patrol from Company E, led by First Lieutenant James W. Parrish, climbed the east slope of the mountain in search of other possible routes of approach to the top. They ambushed a heavily armed group of nine Germans, killed five and returned intact 23 November, with valuable information. For his courageous leadership Lieutenant Parrish was awarded the Silver Star.

On 24 November, Company A, First Battalion, 371st Infantry, was withdrawn and attached to 370th Infantry in the Serchio Valley Sector. On 29 November, the Third Battalion was relieved from 370th Infantry and moved back to a concentration area south of Viareggio. While with the 370th Infantry the Third Battalion had suffered many casualties in one attack. The company commander, First Lieutenant Magellan C. Mars, had been killed and almost half of the company had become hospitalized with wounds. First Lieutenant Moses Allen was made company commander.[28]

Company G, 371st Infantry, commanded by First Lieutenant William E. Cooke, passed through Company F, relieving that unit of its forward position for the Third Battalion, where it had seen much bitter fighting.

During the night of November 28-29, Company E, which was providing security for the First Battalion, relieved Company C in First Battalion sector, while Company C took over positions in vicinity of Seravezza.

370th Combat Team—Heavy Action in the Serchio Valley

As the 371st Infantry Combat Team moved into the lines before MAINE and the towns and hills north and east of Seravezza during the first days of November, the 365th Infantry Combat Team was on its way to meet the enemy in the Coastal Sector.

The 370th Infantry, with only its First and Third Battalions available to cover a four-mile-wide sector in the Serchio Valley, had to spread itself out thinly, so 5 November was spent in extremely active patrolling to learn as much as possible about enemy positions. That night the last elements of Brazilian forces in the area were relieved as the Third Battalion, 370th Infantry, moved into Barga, east of the Serchio River. On 6 November, the regimental commander boldly moved his Third Battalion companies *forward* of the established positions, encountering no enemy opposition. By nightfall, both battalions and the Regimental Command Post were in position as follows:

> *Regimental Command Post* — Fornaci, east of the Serchio. *The First Battalion Command Post* was in Gallicano, a village just west of the Serchio, at the foot of a hill called "Hill 437." Gallicano was subjected to frequent shelling by enemy artillery and mortars. *Company A* was in vicinity of the village of Molazzana; *Company B*, protecting the left flank of the regiment, was in the villages of Promiana and Calomini; and *Company C* was farthest north on the west bank of the Serchio in the vicinity of Cascio.

The contact point with the 371st Infantry, to the left, was at Fornovolasco, a point reachable only by foot.

The Third Battalion Command Post was at Barga, east of the river, also frequently under shellfire. Company I was disposed on a line along the Serchio to the north of Barga; Company K was in the center holding a line running north-easterly to Sommocolonia; Company L was on the right, just north of Sommocolonia; the Anti-Tank Company was on the extreme right near Bebbio, protecting the east flank of the regiment, and the Service Company was in Borgo a Mozzano.

November 7, 8 and 9, in contrast to the previous two days, produced extremely violent reaction from the enemy as the 370th continued its aggressive patrolling all along the front. On 7 November fairly heavy and consistent fire from enemy small arms, artillery and mortars, was received. On 8 November, enemy artillery was particularly active, but patrolling was continued both by the 370th Infantry and the enemy and there were several fire fights between patrols. November 9 was a day of extremely heavy enemy artillery and mortar fire, and continued extensive patrolling by 370th Infantry. Company A, at Molazzana, was attacked by enemy forces in considerable strength, but the Buffalo Soldiers stood their ground and the enemy fled in the face of heavy rifle, mortar and artillery fire.

On 9 November, Private First Class James Robinson earned the Silver Star for gallantry in action. The citation states:

> Private First Class Robinson with a machine gun wound in his left shoulder was withdrawing from contact with the enemy with the rest of his platoon. Suddenly he saw one of the members of his Company about 150 yards from the enemy position, pinned to the ground with an unexploded mortar shell in his leg. Disregarding his own wounds, and personal safety, Private First Class Robinson went to the aid of the wounded man. In full view of the enemy, he extracted the unexploded mortar shell and carried the wounded man to his own lines.

Strong patrolling continued on 10 and 11 November, with enemy resistance increasing at every contact. A large patrol from Company I set out for the village of Colle, but a large mine field halted the advance; on the next night, however, another strong patrol from Company K worked its way into Colle, capturing considerable amount of enemy equipment. A patrol from Company C attacked enemy troops in a strongly fortified house, but did not have sufficient firepower to force them out, so it had to withdraw. There were many small engagements, largely mortar and artillery, between 370th forces and the enemy. Throughout the day all American activity or movement continued to draw fire from enemy artillery and mortars.

At 1800 on 11 November, the Second Battalion, 370th Infantry, was relieved from Combat Command "B" and attached to Brazilian Expeditionary Force, and was still unavailable to 370th Infantry. Throughout the attachment, the Second Battalion Sector had been quiet, although its units were engaged in active patrolling.

On 12 November, enemy shelling was very heavy during the night. Company C, at 1800 repulsed an enemy attack, and on 13 November Company A, at Molazzana again drove off another enemy attack. Company L. sent out a strong patrol to locate a suitable stream crossing and when they found one, they also discovered it was heavily defended by a strong enemy force whereupon, having accomplished their mission, they withdrew with no casualties.

At this time General Almond ordered the Third Battalion, 371st Infantry, then trying to claw its way up Mount Cauala, attached to the 370th Infantry, in preparation for an offensive operation in the Serchio Valley. Also attached to the 370th Infantry was the 92nd Reconnaissance Troop. On November 14, the Third Battalion, 371st Infantry entered the line near Vergemoli, attached to 370th Infantry, and the 92nd Reconnaissance Troop moved to the right flank near Bebbio, relieving Anti-Tank Company.

By this time, snow was capping the steep mountains above the 370th troops, and all the signs of winter were becoming increasingly evident.

On 14 November patrolling continued vigorously during the movements in and out of the relieving units. Enemy artillery and mortar fire were heavy and continuous and some casualties were suffered by the patrols. The determined probing by patrols continued on 15 November, however, with good results. A Company C patrol ran into heavy enemy small arms and machine gun fire after being halted before a heavily mined area. The day was spent in improving roads and bridges, analyzing still in-coming enemy information, and perfecting and reviewing plans for a full scale offensive designed to stabilize positions in the Serchio Valley Sector by taking and holding the high ground in front of the 370th Infantry.

The offensive operation called for the capture of Castelnuova di Garfagnana, the important German supply and communications Center; the high ground to be seized ran along a line Grottorotondo–Monte d'Anima–Sassi–Le Forche–Castellaccio–Lama di Sotto–Monte. The left anchor of the German defenses in the sector, Grottorotondo, was to be captured by Third Battalion, 371st Infantry. If successful, the Third Battalion was to move against Monte d'Anima, the village of Eglio, and the town of Sassi.

The First Battalion, 370th Infantry was to make a simultaneous attack on Brucciano and the hills to its north, then on to Castellaccio.

The Third Battalion, 370th Infantry was to seize control of Lama ridge system to its front, aiming for the small town of Lama.[29]

On 15 November, the 92nd Reconnaissance Troop entered combat for the first time, setting up the Troop Command Post at Coreglia, with the mission of protecting the right flank of the 92nd Division and maintaining contact with Task Force 45 on the right flank.

Its first platoon occupied Bebbio with the mission of actively patrolling to the front for indications of enemy movement.

A provisional platoon was made up of cooks, mechanics, radio operators and every man who could be spared from Reconnaissance Troop Headquarters, and sent to Scarpello with the same patrolling mission.

Supplies for these two platoons were transported by jeep and mules.

On 16 November, two Germans surrendered to the First platoon at Bebbio; one was a former German captain, who stated that he had fought on the Russian front and had deserted; when apprehended, he said he had been reduced to the grade of private and sent to the Italian front.[30]

The Third Battalion, 371st Infantry, on the left, moved forward at 0700 on 16 November and, fighting their way aggressively, were in position on several assigned objectives on Grottorotondo at the end of the day. In the First Battalion area, 370th Infantry, Company B was to seize Brucciano, then move against two hills to the north, with the attack to be supported by fire from Company A positions in Promiana and Molazzana. Once this objective was taken, Companies A and B together were to attack to the north, seizing Mount Altissimo, and then drive on to the high ground of Le Forche. The attack of these last two objectives was to be supported by the fires of Company C from the town of Cascio. This ambitious, but complex plan did not develop as envisioned. The First Battalion jumped off on schedule, but Companies B and A both came under very heavy shelling from enemy artillery, mortars and small arms fire stopping the attack almost as soon as it jumped off. On the right, the Third Battalion, 370th Infantry, had as its objective the formidable Lama ridge running from Lama di Sotto southwest of Monte San Quirico. Company L was to climb up the ridge and seize Lama di Sotto; Company K was assigned the ridge to the north near Colle, while Company I was taking Monte San Quirico. Company L scaled the slopes and reached Lama di Sotto. Company K took part of its objective and Company I had advanced to a point just north of Castelvecchio and Caproni by nightfall.

The first day's fighting again gave proof that the German command intended to defend vigorously its present positions in the 92nd Division Sector. There was further evidence of the thorough defensive planning of the designers of the Gothic Line System. Minefields abounded at all approaches to prospective objectives; scores of machine guns and mortars were sited to fire on call on roads, trails, draws and were usually so placed as to deliver mutually supporting fires. Artillery pieces of various calibers were laid and adjusted to deliver fire on call quickly and devastatingly. They seemed able to fire at will when necessary.

The German observers, high on the ridges and mountain tops, with radios and telephones at hand, must have been completely amazed to look down through the bright sunshiny day and clearly see three battalions of targets moving towards them, far below.

Their amazement did not immobilize them. At daybreak, the Third Battalion, 371st Infantry, resumed the attack, with Company I moving up to Hill 832, on schedule. However, Company L was sent north through a draw between Hill 832 and Hill 1029, where Company K was located, with the mission of seizing Monte d'Anima. Near the base of Monte d'Anima, Company L came under extremely heavy and evidently pre-arranged mortar fire, while enemy machine gun fire, from the slopes above, literally cut the company to pieces. The company commander, Lieutenant Magellan C. Mars was killed, and over half of the company was killed or wounded. At the same time Company I, on Hill 832 was hit by a strong enemy counterattack, preceded by heavy mortar fire, driving it from the hill; Company K was also counterattacked and subjected to a heavy concentration of mortar fire, and was driven from the hill, but held on to Hill 1031. Fighting by the men of the Third Battalion, 371st Infantry, was hard and desperate and there were many instances of intrepid bravery and outstanding leadership on that day. Lieutenant Mars was awarded posthumously the Silver Star for his efforts to accomplish his objective and to save his company. His citation states:

> Lieutenant Mars' company while deployed in a sector of mountainous terrain, became the object of an intense enemy mortar attack. Without thought of personal hazard Lieutenant Mars moved among his men adjusting counter-fire and insuring that each man was in protected position. When the severity of the hostile mortar barrage forced the supporting right flank unit to withdraw, Lieutenant Mars' company immediately became chief target for a concentration of enemy machine gun fire. In spite of this he continued to expose himself until he was killed by hostile fire.

Technician Sergeant David Harris, Company L, 371st Infantry, was also awarded the Silver Star for gallantry in action on that day in Italy.

> Under a severe enemy counter-attack, Sergeant Harris's company was forced to withdraw. The Company Commander having been critically wounded, Sergeant Harris took charge of the immediate situation, deployed his platoon into a defensive position and then without regard for personal safety, went back to the enemy exposed area to aid his wounded Company Commander. The officer died in his arms. Sergeant Harris then voluntarily returned to the area four more times, each time bringing back a seriously wounded soldier.

The battalion commander, Lieutenant Colonel Arthur H. Walker, also was awarded the Silver Star posthumously, for his gallantry in action on November 18.

> When one of the companies became disorganized in an attack after its commander was killed, Colonel Walker, the Battalion Commander, im-

mediately went forward to personally reorganize the company and direct its continuation of the attack. All afternoon he exposed himself to intense small arms fire as he encouraged the men to improve their position and adjusted their fire on the enemy. The next day, Colonel Walker, with the aid of an enlisted man, crossed approximately 300 yards of enemy territory under hostile small arms fire, and recovered the body of the Company Commander and evacuated a severely wounded soldier whom they discovered.

Colonel Raymond G. Sherman, Commanding Officer, 370th Infantry, was also awarded the Silver Star. His citation bears stark testimony to the difficult terrain, the stubborn resistance of the enemy and the devastating intensity of the tremendous artillery, mortar and small arms fire directed on his troops:

> Colonel Sherman was personally directing an attack of his regiment against a bitterly contesting foe in mountainous terrain. He was operating in an OP which was under direct enemy observation and subject to intense concentrations of artillery, mortar and machine-gun fire. During the course of the attack, the intensity of this same fire caused the assaulting troops to withdraw but Colonel Sherman remained at this post, without regard for safety, issuing orders for the more advantageous regrouping of his units. Subsequently, Colonel Sherman went to the aid of an officer who had been shot through the neck by enemy small arms fire. He quickly improvised a chair stretcher, and with the assistance of his driver, carried the casualty down the precipitous slopes to safety despite continuing heavy fire.

By 19 November, all front-line companies had completed their reorganization and consolidation of positions substantially as they were before the attack began. For the next few days strong patrolling was resumed and the artillery continued to harass the enemy.

On 21 November the Anti-Tank Company was moved to Vergemoli, where things were quiet until 23 November when large numbers of the enemy were seen approaching the town. It was believed they were preparing to attack, but prompt artillery concentrations broke the formations up, forcing their withdrawal.

On 22 November the Second platoon of the 92nd Reconnaissance Troop joined the provisional platoon under First Lieutenant Montgomery, and the Third platoon dug in about 1200 yards northeast of the First platoon at Bebbio, to provide a security screen.

On November 25, there was not much activity by either the 370th Infantry or by the enemy in the Serchio Sector. In the Second Battalion Sector however (Brazilian Expeditionary Force Sector), the battalion jumped off at 0600 in an attack to seize Mount della Toraccia. All companies were advancing well in spite of stiff resistance during the morning. At 1000, however, Company E was heavily shelled by "friendly" tanks, disrupting and halting the advance, after many casualties. Company F continued to advance until the company was subjected to extremely heavy and accurate mortar fire, causing many casualties and forcing many F Company men to withdraw. Before the day ended, the companies had been reorganized and formed a perimeter defense around tanks of the 751st Tank Battalion, which had been following the advancing infantry. Although the attack was resumed on the following morning, forward movement was slow and difficult and at nightfall the companies dug in and around the tanks in vicinity of Morandella.

The 370th began planning immediately for yet another attack to gain the high ground, with the specific objective still being to drive the Germans from Monte d'Anima. This time the attack was coordinated by 92nd Division with a Partisan force of over 1,000 men, trained and led as a Partisan Division by a British Major Oldham, behind the German lines. A parachute drop from six C-47 planes of arms and ammunition had been made two days before the planned attack, scheduled for 27 November. The plan called for simultaneous drives by the 370th from the south, and by the Partisan Division from the rear of the enemy, the 370th Infantry to drive forward, to the ridges to their front and to generally harass the enemy as a diversionary move. The Third Battalion, 371st Infantry, still attached to the 370th, and still somewhat stripped and battered from its first Serchio attack, and the First Battalion, 370th Infantry, were to drive towards Monte d'Anima, Sassi, and Hill 832.

The 370th jumped off as scheduled at 0700, with a general feeling among line officers and men that with the Partisan Division attacking the Germans from the rear, there was every chance of success in their frontal attack this time.

Unfortunately, the 370th Combat Team had hardly jumped off when it was stopped in its tracks by heavy, accurate fire from all German positions and weapons. The expected heavy attack by Partisans from the rear of the enemy lines failed to materialize. Later reports revealed that spies in Major Oldham's unit had issued false orders directing the majority of the Partisans to return to their assembly area; when the attack jumped off, Major Oldham had only about 60 men. To their credit, they succeeded in getting atop Monte d'Anima at 1000, but were driven off by a heavy counterattack of enemy coming from three directions.[31]

At the end of the day, the lines were the same as in the morning, and Major Oldham's band of Partisans was badly scattered and disorganized.

On 26 November, T/5 Jefferson H. Hilliard, of the reconnaissance troop distinguished himself and was awarded the Silver Star:

> T/5 Hilliard manned a machine gun in a strong point under vigorous enemy attack. For two hours his position was one of two main enemy attacks. During this activity he accounted for at least 12 enemy casualties while he and his assistant were the targets of an intense mortar concentration. When maneuver and superior forces of, the enemy made his position untenable, T/5 Hilliard was ordered to cover the withdrawal of the other men. He removed the machine gun on his shoulder while his assistant

carried the tripod. He fired in this manner until his ammunition was exhausted accounting for at least two more enemy casualties.

On 28 November the 370th Infantry resumed its patrol activities and found the enemy still very alert and making continuous use of his mortars.

On 29 November, the Third Battalion, 371st Infantry, was relieved to return to its regiment. Company A, 371st Infantry remained and was attached to the 370th Infantry, however, and was directed to hold the Calomini Sector and patrol to Hill 1031 daily. The Anti-Tank Company continued to occupy the walled town of Vergemoli, where enemy mortar fire was again active, causing six casualties.

In the Coastal Sector, where the 365th Infantry Combat Team was in line, there was limited enemy troop activity. Patrolling by front line 365th Infantry companies, however continued to be active, particularly along the beach and the Cinquale Canal and the La Foce stream. Interest was high in discovering possible crossing sites. Enemy artillery was not quiet, however, and casualties from that source mounted throughout the month.

During the month of November alone, the 92nd Division had sustained 64 killed, 318 wounded and 115 listed as missing.

The critical impact of these casualty figures lies not only on the *number* of casualties, but in the fact that they included many outstanding officers and enlisted men who had proven themselves in combat. Particularly in small units—patrols, squads, platoons, companies where bold, imaginative leadership and visible courage and initiative were required—these losses were irreplaceable.

The replacement measures utilized were not satisfactory or successful, generally. Transfers were made of officers and/or non-commissioned officers among platoons, companies, battalions, sometimes so often and many times in pitch darkness, that soldiers did not know who was in command. Some replacements came from the East Coast Processing Center where most were AWOL from their *own* units, and were of little use; actually they were a negative influence. Some, those from the 372nd Infantry, a National Guard outfit, were well-trained, but few were available. The basic problem was that the replacement system was not prepared to process trained black infantrymen in sufficient quantities for the needs of a division in combat.

Other problems, dictated, one must assume, by the Allied strategy, began to plague the Division. A series of transfers and attachments of units within the Division, coupled with the transfer of the 365th Combat Team to another sector, combined to shred the front line forces and widen the areas of responsibility for them.

On 30 November the 365th Infantry was withdrawn and by 3 December the entire combat team, including 597th Field Artillery Battalion, Company B, 317th Combat Engineers and Company A, 317th Medical Battalion, moved to the Bologna front and was attached to the 88th Infantry Division, resting on the extreme right of the Fifth Army line.

The 365th Combat Team, which was to be lost to the Buffalo Division until January, 1945, was not the only unit unavailable at that time. The

Second Battalion, 370th Infantry never returned to Division control until 18 December and the Third Battalion remained attached to the South African Division in another sector, leaving the 370th Infantry with only one of its battalions in the Serchio Valley.

This kind of inconsistent command relationships, frequent shifts and transfers, and great distances between units came to be almost routine in the division. In addition to being spread over a front longer than that of other Fifth Army divisions, the development of command control, esprit de corps, and discipline within elements of the division was hampered by the frequent and continual parceling out of units first to one and then to another command.

The 366th Infantry Regiment Enters the Fray

At this time, IV Corps and Fifth Army were determined to try to maintain the numerical strength of the 92nd Division to enable it to continue to contain the enemy in its assigned sector.

The 366th Infantry Regiment, with all black officers and enlisted men was attached to the 92nd Division for this reason. The regiment had arrived in Italy in May 1944, but had been acting as air base security troops for the various Air Force installations in the theatre. As early as September, a few of its officers were exposed to a three-week leadership and battle training program, but when attached to the division, the bulk of its personnel had not trained as infantry for many months.[32]

The regiment reached Leghorn November 26, expecting to have three months of intensive training before entering combat. Instead, Company E entered the line attached to Third Battalion, 371st Infantry in the Coastal Sector, November 30, and other units began to move into the division front lines in quick sequence.

So, instead of bolstering the existing strength of the 92nd Division, the 366th only justified a rationale for giving other units in the Division opportunities to profit from contact with more experienced units; also for 92nd Division units giving relief and rest for veteran white units in the line.

Despite the urgent need for trained black infantry units, there is evidence to indicate the 366th Infantry Regiment was not welcomed with joy by General Almond. The black officers and men found little comfort in his "welcome speech" upon their arrival in the combat zone. Former members of the 366th were asked: "Did you *hear* General Almond's first greeting to the 366th? Was he pleased to have the 366th? Express confidence in it?" Lieutenant Sidney Thompson:[33] "Yes. No, he was not enthusiastic. Said we were assigned not by his wish, was extremely negative and so passed it on to his immediate officers on his General Staff." First Lieutenant John T. Letts:[34] "As I recall General Almond's statement: 'Your Negro newspapers have seen fit to cause you to be brought over here; now I'm going to see that you suffer your share of the casualties.' In my opinion, he was upset because of the high ranking field grade officers in the 366th." First Lieutenant Robert A.

Brown:[35] "Yes. He said to the assembled Regiment that he did not ask for us and he did not need us and that the only reason we were there was because of the Negro newspapers, and since we were there, he was going to make us fight."

Answers by many other former members expressed similar sentiments indicating great apprehension and deep concern about General Almond's obvious displeasure at the assignment of the 366th. Early in December, Colonel Howard D. Queen, Regimental Commander of the 366th, requested relief from command, alleging:[36]

> The treatment the regiment and myself have received during the period of attachment to the 92nd Infantry Division has been such as to disturb me mentally and has not been such as is usually given an officer of my grade and service."

and,

> I have at all times subscribed fully to the policy of higher authority and previously have received the proper courtesy and respect in return.

The initial impressions of mutual dislike, mistrust and misunderstanding between General Almond and the 366th continued, unresolved, throughout the period of its assignment to the 92nd Division.

Four days after its arrival in the front line area, the first of the 366th Infantry units was committed to front line action, and the first eleven days of December, the 366th Infantry units were attached as follows:

Company E on 30 November, attached to Third Battalion, 371 Infantry, on the Coast; the Intelligence and Reconnaissance Platoon (I and R Platoon) on 1 December, attached to 92nd Reconnaissance Troop, First Platoon, now in the Coastal Sector; Company B on 2 December attached to Third Battalion, 371st Infantry; Company I on 5 December, attached to First Battalion, 371st Infantry, relieving Company E of that unit at Azzano; Cannon Company, on 9 December, attached to 370th Combat Team in The Serchio; Anti-Tank Company, on 9 December, attached to 371st Infantry; and K Company, on 11 November, attached to 370th Infantry, in the Serchio. The First Battalion, 366th, operating directly under Division and *not* under its *own* regimental control, relieved the Third Battalion, 371st Infantry in the Coastal Sector 12-13 December.[37]

The Second Battalion, 366th Infantry, less Company E, was attached to 370th Infantry at Barga. Thus, within two weeks, this recently assembled regiment, its commander anticipating a minimum of three months' training and indoctrination before commitment to combat, found itself in the thick of the fighting.

On December 11, the 366th found itself without the leadership of the professional soldier who had led them since 1943. He represented a great loss to all the officers and men of this proud regiment of black soldiers, particularly at such a critical moment in its history. His military accomplishments were regarded as legendary not only by his men but by black Americans familiar with black military history. He had fought and won many battles for them in the conference rooms since the reorganization of the regiment in March 1941, and had preserved, until the attachment to the 92nd Division, the integrity and unity of the regiment. His "Mistreatment" at the hands of the 92nd Division Staff has never been forgiven—even to this day—by most members of the 366th Infantry Regiment, although many of his own officers felt that he was not physically qualified for combat duty and some even expressed the opinion that his successor, Lieutenant Colonel Alonzo Ferguson was a more able regimental commander.

This matter of preserving the integrity and unity of the 366th Infantry was of utmost significance to the officers and enlisted men of the regiment. Throughout the three and a half years of its existence these men had endured many trials and tribulations not common to any other American regiments, and they had survived them all, remaining together as a single fighting unit. They emerged bonded together by pride in its history, and confidence in itself and its capabilities, and with an almost sacred devotion to THE REGIMENT.

The demeaning words in General Almond's "welcome" disturbed them. However, racial animosity, skepticism, doubts—even hatred—all were attitudes and feelings encountered many times before. Indeed, his words led to a feeling they would have an opportunity to fight under command of their own leaders, and as a regiment.

Sadly, it simply was not to be. Sadly, because in this black regiment were officers and enlisted men destined to continue their military careers and to serve with distinction in the Korean and Vietnam Wars. One enlisted man became a major general (James Hamlett) and one officer, Captain Frederick E. Davison, became the first black officer ever promoted to brigadier general during combat operations.

An Abundance of Heroes

October and November saw some hard fighting by the 370th Infantry and the newly arrived Combat Teams of the Buffalo Division. Despite their inexperience, the continuous shifting around of units, the loss of experienced leaders, and the determined resistance of the enemy, the young soldiers acquitted themselves well. Sometimes ordered into situations which were untenable, they fought tenaciously and skillfully to extricate themselves and to try to destroy as many of the enemy as possible. Almost always moving in full view of the waiting enemy, attacking frontally in many instances in the face of overwhelming fire from several directions, they nevertheless plunged forward as ordered.

There was an abundance of heroes in November 1944. How they fought and died is clearly revealed in the words of the citations of men who were awarded the Silver Star for gallantry in action between 16 November and 26 November:

Fred D. Rhodes, Staff Sergeant. 370th Infantry. On 16 November, while proceeding towards the front at night, Sergeant Rhodes's motorized patrol was advanced upon near a village by a lone enemy soldier. Sergeant Rhodes jumped from the truck and as a group of enemy soldiers suddenly appeared, intent upon capturing the truck and patrol intact, he opened fire from his exposed position on the road. His fire forced the enemy to scatter while the patrol dismounted and took cover with light casualties. Sergeant Rhodes then moved toward a nearby building where, still exposed, his fire on the enemy was responsible for the successful evacuation of the wounded patrol members by newly arrived medical personnel. Sergeant Rhodes was then hit by enemy shell fragments but, in spite of his wounds he exhausted his own supply of ammunition then, obtaining an enemy automatic weapon, exhausted its supply inflicting three certain casualties on the enemy. He spent the rest of the night in a nearby field and returned, unaided, to his unit the next afternoon.

St. Clair Gibson, Private First Class, 371st Infantry (Missing in Action). On 18 November, Private first class Gibson's rifle platoon came under increasing, deadly, effective hostile fire in its advance upon an enemy emplacement. Despite withering fire and mounting casualties, Private first class Gibson, with three other men, pressed forward and assaulted the enemy stronghold with hand grenades. His rapid attack inflicted numerous casualties on the enemy, ceasing only when he himself lay wounded by an enemy grenade fragment. Private first class Gibson could not be evacuated when the remainder of his platoon withdrew.

Ernest T. Grice, Sergeant, 370th Infantry. On 18 November, Sergeant Grice commanded a light machine-gun squad in strong-pointing a house on his company's left flank. When the position was attacked by a company of the enemy, Sergeant Grice coordinated all of the machine-guns and individual weapons of his squad and directed 60 mm mortar fire on the approaching hostile elements. His personal direction of machine-gun fire and 130 rounds of mortar fire halted the entire enemy company. Later, in assisting in the adjustment of artillery fire on the remainder of the enemy pocketed in a ravine, he accounted for more enemy casualties.

Eugene A. Graham, Sergeant, 370th Infantry. On 22 November, Sergeant Graham was operating as a radio operator with an attacking platoon which had almost gained a mountain-crest objective when it was met by instense enemy machine-gun fire at point-blank range. This, together with heavy mortar and grenade fire at close range, forced the platoon to withdraw. With intense mortar fire bursting about him, Sergeant Graham calmly radioed for artillery fire upon the enemy and moved up the hill alone. Despite heavy machine-gun fire directed at him and with the pack radio strapped to his back, he moved to a position from which he could observe and direct friendly artillery fire. Alone, he continued crawling under fire well forward of the infantry and successfully directed artillery by radio, silencing an enemy machine gun and several mortars.

From the Arno to the Gothic Line 51

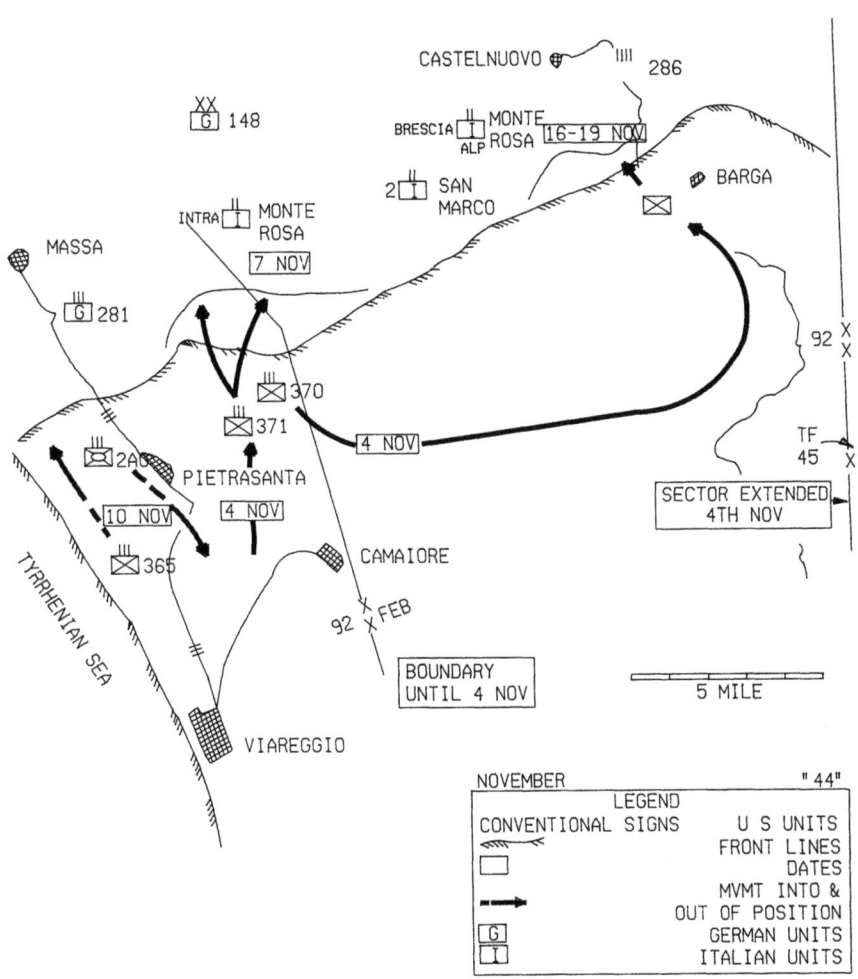

Allied and Enemy Dispositions November 1944

James W. Parrish, First Lieutenant, Infantry. On 22 November, Lieutenant Parrish led a combat patrol with the mission of infiltrating enemy lines. He led his men over an extremely hazardous and steep mountainous route, ambushing a group of 20 of the enemy, and killing five and wounding seven of them. Lieutenant Parrish then ordered his men to change positions, which they did, successfully eluding retaliating enemy machine-gun and small-arms fire. The patrol returned without casualty.

James Taylor T/4, 370th Infantry. On 24 November, the machine-gun section and two platoons of T/4 Taylor were pinned down by enemy machine-gun fire during an attack. Immediately thereafter, enemy artillery landed in the area, killing 2 and wounded 26 men of the company. All of the company except T/4 Taylor withdrew under orders. He remained alone under constant hostile artillery and machine-gun fire, administering first-aid to wounded. He first personally evacuated all of the wounded and then, alone, evacuated all of the equipment, weapons, sleeping bags, ammunition and other material of the two platoons. When all this had been accomplished, he returned, still alone, and evacuated the bodies of the dead personnel.

Wallace H. Hobbs T/5 Reconnaissance Troop (Missing in Action). On 26 November, T/5 Hobbs manned a machine-gun position in a defensive strong-point under determined enemy attack. For two hours, his position received intense mortar and small arms fire. Inflicting numerous casualties on the enemy, T/5 Hobbs was ordered to cover the withdrawal from the strongpoint after it had become partially over-run by numerically superior hostile forces. He held the enemy at bay while the rest of the men withdrew. He exhausted his supply of ammunition, staying at his gun until the position was stormed by the enemy.

Four

The Battles for the Serchio Valley

Probing and Harassing the Enemy

On 1 December, in the Coastal Sector, the badly battered Third Battalion, 371st Infantry, still recovering from its heavy losses in the Serchio Valley, replaced the 365th Infantry, which moved to the Bologna front. With the newly arrived 366th Infantry, with no battle experience, being committed piecemeal throughout the division front, the 371st found itself covering a front of about 15,000 yards. Company B, 366th Infantry moved up, filling the gap between the Second and Third Battalions.

The first four days of December in the 371st Infantry sector were relatively quiet, although aggressive patrolling continued and artillery duels took place at all hours.

It was decided to again attempt to seize and secure Mount Cauala, a part of it nicknamed MAINE by soldiers of the 371st. For several days there had been only slight reaction to patrol contacts, and unusual quiet had prevailed on the mountain top.

At 0400 on 4 December, the Second Battalion, with Major George E. Pinard commanding, moved upward, with Company B, 366th Infantry on the left, Company F in the center and Company G on the right.

Almost immediately, as usual, the enemy was alerted and Company G was deluged with massed enemy fire and, as usual, all movement on MAINE was exposed to hostile observation, and it became impossible for the company to continue its advance. The other two attacking companies moved out under more favorable conditions and made some advances. Soon after Company G withdrew, however, Company F ran into overwhelming enemy resistance and withdrew to its initial position.

Meanwhile by 0715, Company B, 366th Infantry commanded by Captain Walter E. Dabney, moving steadily forward, was on top of ALASKA, one of the several small hills on the left of the sector. They found themselves subjected to heavy enemy mortar, machine gun and small arms fire from the front and right flank. The enemy firing positions could not be located, and Major Pinard, believing the position untenable, requested permission from regiment to withdraw the company. Permission was refused.

Captain Dabney's orders were to hold the position during daylight unless forced back by physical contact. More supporting artillery was called down on the suspected locations of the enemy, relieving the company's situation for awhile.

At 1500, Company F made a demonstration in its area, hoping to divert enemy attention away from Company B. Company B, however, continued to be pounded by unrelenting enemy fire and the company became somewhat disorganized. Captain Dabney moved about valiantly, reorganizing his unit, and accurately directing their fire, even in the face of mounting casualties, and in spite of wounds he received. Several of the enemy were killed including a German officer, and 12 prisoners were captured, and when ordered to withdraw, Company B did so in good order. For his gallant action, Captain Dabney was awarded the Silver Star, the first for the 366th Infantry Regiment.

By 9 December the 92nd Division was positioned from the Ligurian Sea shore at Forte dei Marmi on the west, to the Serchio Valley, on the right flank.

The Third Battalion, 371st Infantry was in position from the sea to Highway #1. In support were a tank company, a tank destroyer company, the 600th Field Artillery Battalion (less Battery A), and units from two British artillery units.

Center positions in front of CALIFORNIA, Mount Cauala, and the villages to the northeast, were occupied by First and Second Battalions. Supporting them were the 599th Field Artillery Battalion and the 371st Infantry Cannon Company.

In the meantime, the Serchio Valley front was manned by the First Battalion, 370th Infantry, at Gallicano, left of the river, and the Second Battalion, 366th Infantry, at Barga, on the right. Flank security was provided by units of the 92nd Reconnaissance Troop. Other supporting units were the 598th Field Artillery Battalion, 366th Infantry Cannon Company, a company of 317th Engineers, Battery A, 600th Field Artillery Battalion (155 MM), and elements of British Anti-Aircraft Artillery units.

In the front line areas for which the 371st Infantry held responsibility, these first days of December were confusing and discouraging. In the center the enemy held all the commanding ground, and the terrain was mountainous, treacherous, and studded at every logical point of attack with almost impregnable man-made and/or natural defenses or combinations of both. Many months had been spent by thousands of technicians, planning, preparing, and improving and arming the intricate network of mine fields, hull-down tanks, tank obstacles, reinforced concrete and steel pill boxes and gun pits for machine guns and snipers, on the coastal plain; and, in the mountains, many tunnels were dug clear through the mountain, leading to connecting steel and concrete emplacements for troops and guns which were impervious to air, artillery and mortar bombardment, and camouflaged so well that often attacking troops found themselves in the midst of groups of enemy before they realized it.

Another discouraging factor was the continuous unimpeded fire delivered on 371st Infantry front line units, by heavy coastal guns located around Punta Bianca and on the hills near the Italian Naval Base of La

Spezia, several miles away. These guns could not be reached by *any* Fifth Army Artillery and, as the war wore on, General Almond, himself, acknowledged that bombardment by naval gunfire and medium bombers was ineffective, and that they would cause much damage to any projected advance.[1]

One tactic by 92nd Division to harass and disrupt the enemy and flush them out of their positions was a program of massing fires of all the .50 calibre machine guns in the regiment, plus all its 57 mm Anti-Tank guns, according to a pre-arranged daily schedule. In addition, supporting artillery joined in harassment, firing "TOT"[2] fires at designated road intersections, known targets, and in concentrating on making MAINE untenable to enemy forces. Despite bleak prospects, unit reliefs and attachments involving the 371st Infantry and the 366th Infantry continued. Aggressive patrolling, however, continued, as did planning to improve positions and gain higher ground.

On 12 December, Company E, 371st Infantry, relieved Company F, which moved to a rest area for a few days. The next night, the Third Battalion was relieved by First Battalion, 366th Infantry and it too moved back to the rest area near Viareggio.

On 14 December, Company B, 371st Infantry attacked toward Pian di Lago. Initially, good progress was made against a surprised foe, and the company doggedly fought its way up the rugged terrain through increasing withering enemy maching gun, mortar and artillery fire. When they reached the crest, the enemy fire from all weapons increased to such intensity and accuracy that further advance was prevented and the Company tried desperately to dig in. From the observation posts on mountains still higher, on that bright sunlit day, the enemy caused an increasing toll of casualties. Supporting artillery fires brought no relief, and Company B was forced to withdraw to a more covered position. Their casualties were evacuated during the night down the treacherous trails, and the next day Company F moved back into the line, relieving Company B.

The harassing of enemy positions via the "Infantry shoots" was increased, with more weapons added, including a unit of British Bofors 40 mm antiaircraft guns. Until 17 December, the enemy failed to react to the harassing fires, but on that date twenty-one shells were received in the First Battalion positions alone. And, in spite of the increased intensity of the 371st Infantry harassing fire, the enemy resistance in the sector did not decrease but rather, became more stubborn. Contact patrols still came under heavy enemy fire and enemy artillery fire increased, markedly, over the entire regimental area that night.[3]

On 20 December, the Third Battalion moved back into the line, in the regimental left sector. Relieved were: Company B, 366th Infantry and part of Company E, 371st Infantry. On the same date Company B, 371st Infantry relieved Company I, 366th Infantry (had been attached to First Battalion, 371st Infantry). On 22 December, Company A rejoined its regiment, leaving it to face the enemy with all its units together again.

For the next few days, enemy front line activity was very limited, and combat patrols made little contact with the enemy. The 371st Infantry Regimental Staff busied itself in formulating plans for its role in the planned division attack which was to jump off on 25 December.

Increased Activity in the Serchio Valley

On 4 December enemy activity began to intensify in the 370th Infantry area in the Serchio Valley. Around midnight five men from Company C were trapped in a house left unguarded, and the enemy killed one and captured the other four. Lieutenant Imes, sent to investigate, was also killed. Later that day, Company C gained some measure of revenge. The Second Platoon caught twelve enemy in a draw, drove them into a house with machine gun and mortar fire, which kept them pinned down. They then flanked the house and again attacked, killing two enemy, wounding two more, and capturing eight, including one officer.

A patrol from Company A raiding Hill 619 was driven off by heavy enemy small arms fire. Another patrol from Company C was blocked from advancing by rushing water when the enemy destroyed an aqueduct from Cascio by demolition.

Still on December 4, the Anti-Tank Company, deployed in and around Vergemoli, was attacked at about 0830 by a full company of Italian Fascist troops led by German officers and non-commissioned officers. Enemy mortar, artillery and small arms fire was intense at the onset and continued throughout the duration of the fighting, with some 300 to 400 rounds of artillery and mortar landing in the vicinity of Vergemoli. The Anti-Tank Company held its positions, withstanding both the heavy fire and the determined attack, and when the fighting ended at nightfall, their positions were still secure. At one time enemy troops had advanced to within ten feet of defensive positions. The enemy suffered an estimated 30 casualties and at the end, had retreated in panic and disorder. The Anti-Tank Company suffered two killed. First Lieutenant Roland F. Fraser was awarded the Silver Star for his remarkable demonstration that day:

> First Lieutenant Fraser was in command of three advanced and isolated strong points outside a village wall around which his company was deployed. A company of Italian Fascists led by German officers and NCO's had launched a strong attack upon the positions with every weapon at their disposal. Under a continuous rain of enemy fire, Lieutenant Fraser constantly exposed himself by moving back and forth between the strong points under his control, directing fire, encouraging his men and replenishing ammunition. His vigorous, aggressive efforts resulted in the absolute repulse of the enemy, who left numerous casualties in fleeing the area.

Further exemplifying the selfless courage of the men who fought in this battle is the citation for the Silver Star, awarded posthumously to Sergeant Sherman F. Powell.

While deploying a defensive position Sergeant Powell's Company was attacked by a company of Italian Fascist Troops led by German officers and non-commissioned officers. As Acting First Sergeant, Sergeant Powell personally went to every position under terrific enemy fire to deliver the company commander's orders. Despite a heavy concentration of enemy fire he brought a new wire line to the company command post. When he left the command post again to administer aid to a wounded soldier, he was mortally wounded while returning.

The next day, apparently stung by the defeat at Vergemoli, the enemy reacted with heavy concentrations of artillery and mortar fire on Vergemoli, Barga, and Gallicano. There was no enemy patrol or attack action on 5 December; however, a patrol to Albiano found it clear of enemy.

During the next few days of December, the German front line of action became relatively quiet. Artillery and mortar fire continued to fall, however. The 370th Combat Team front-line units continued to prepare for a possible enemy attack. Ammunition stocks were replenished and, for the first time, white phosphorous grenades were issued.

On 6 December Vergemoli and Gallicano received light mortar and artillery fire, and one patrol went out—to Hill 1031—and found no enemy there. During the night, however, the enemy fired many flares, obviously trying to induce the troops to fire and reveal their positions; no reaction was made by our forces.

On 7 December, the enemy continued his inactivity in the Serchio except for Vergemoli and Calomini. The Combat Engineers continued to bring forward hundreds of anti-personnel and anti-tank mines, and guards were placed on the bridges already mined. This security was prompted by events of 3 December, when one of the charges on the demolition-prepared bridges near Fornaci was set off by causes unknown at about 0730, blowing a ten-foot gap in it. Repairs were made by the engineers by 2030 and traffic was again routed over the bridge.

Enemy mortar fire was heavy and extremely active again in Vergemoli and Calomini. One 81 mm mortar section near Calomini was hit by a concentration and sustained heavy casualties.

Enemies other than the German troops wreaked much havoc at that time. On 8 December, the cutting of communication lines in the areas from front-line companies back to the First Battalion Command Post and to the regimental command post led to orders to evacuate all civilians from the area north of Gallicano.

The rainy, cold weather continued to be an enemy to be reckoned with. The rains of the past few weeks had brought the Serchio River to crest, and the Bailey bridge near Osteria became endangered. The engineers decided to dynamite the approaches to the bridge and re-route all traffic by way of another concrete bridge in vicinity of Fornaci. In spite of their valiant efforts, the Osteria bridge washed away and was carried downstream, the site badly damaged and now impassable. The engineers were immediately ordered to develop the route on the east bank of the Serchio River, involving several in-place fills and the construction of several more fills before the route became passable.[4]

Quiet again prevailed on 9 December, with the Engineers again battling to repair damage to roads caused by the weather. For a short time the road from Borgo a Mozzano to Lucca was washed out, but the Engineers soon had it back in usable shape. The tempo of evacuation of civilians was increased in the Sector.

The Cannon Company, 366th Infantry, was assigned to 598th Field Artillery Battalion.

On 10 December, the enemy was quiet during the day, except for another artillery shelling of Vergemoli.

In the early morning hours of 11 December, heavy action broke out suddenly. A strong patrol from First Battalion reached their objective on Hill 832, and on a pre-arranged signal, fired a green flare. There, before their eyes, they beheld the enemy in process of making a relief of units into positions on top of the hill. Within minutes, the heavy fire from all weapons by the patrol, augmented by prompt and accurate mortar and artillery fire, routed the enemy. During the next three hours enemy artillery and mortar fire was intensified in reaction to the shelling. Heavily hit were Gallicano and Vergemoli again, as were the Buffalo avenues of approach to Hill 832. A prisoner captured the next morning said, however, that the heavy fire from the assault patrol and the shelling inflicted many casualties on his platoon, causing him to desert.[5]

During the day, the 317th Engineers had opened the road from Barga to Lucca along the east bank of the Serchio River.

On 12 December, the enemy again devoted considerable attention to Vergemoli, shelling the area with some 70 rounds of mortar and artillery throughout the day. A patrol from Company B again entered and thoroughly searched Brucciano, and found no enemy there. The busy Engineers, on this date opened up a new supply route. A long Bailey bridge was completed over the Lima River at Bagni di Lucca, and by midnight they had completed a smaller Bailey bridge over a smaller stream emptying into the Lima, linking up the road from Barga to Lucca down the east bank of the Serchio.

On 13 December, Vergemoli and the Gallicano area again received more heavy shelling. On that night, too, a small enemy patrol slipped past the guard to blow the concrete bridge across the Serchio at Fornaci. Demolition, however, was not properly effected and by morning, Engineers had repaired the bridge.

On 14 December both front line forces were unusually quiet, although 370th Combat Team patrols continued to operate. Promiano received some mortar fire. Some additional .50 calibre machine guns were brought into the lines to join the infantry weapons "shoots."

On 15 December, the enemy resumed heavy shelling of Vergemoli and also shelled Molazzana and Albiano. An enemy raiding party was driven back with considerable casualties by Company C near Cascio. They struck with sudden fury, but the company held its ground and delivered devastating small arms fire against the enemy raiders.

December 17 was another quiet day, with our forces carrying on the usual aggressive patrol activity, with little reaction from the enemy. The .50-Cal machine guns were utilized to fire en mass on suspected enemy positions.

The Anti-Tank Company, still holding tenaciously to Vergemoli, was again subjected to shelling, with some 90–100 rounds falling on the positions in the 24 hours. Active patrolling was the order of the day. A Company B patrol went to Bruciano and again found it clear of enemy, although an enemy patrol had been observed while the Company B patrol was proceeding to its objective. A patrol from Company A, 371st Infantry drew machine gun fire upon approaching the crest of Hill 1031. The enemy set off a flare in front of them at 0330 but no attack developed. Company C received heavy mortar fire on its command post.

On 18 December, the Second Battalion was returned from attachment to the British Expeditionary Force in the Gaggio Montana Sector, and came under 370th Combat Team control again. Early in the morning five Italian Fascist troops wandered into a mine field laid by the Anti-Tank Company in front of positions at Vergemoli. Two were killed, and three captured by the alert defenders and later that morning the company captured two more prisoners. The area near the Regimental Command Post at Fornaci was shelled by the enemy that day.

On 19 December, Company A received considerable artillery and mortar fire, apparently in retaliation to the .50-Cal machine gun and 57 mm gun "shoots." The Anti-Tank Company in Vergemoli endured another customary shelling. The men dug their holes a little deeper and held on.

December 20 and 21 were quiet days, but enemy mortar and artillery fire continued to fall on Vergemoli, Molazzana, and Albiano. Patrols continued to go out and some reported contact with the enemy. Again, the infantry "shoots" brought down retaliatory fire on front line positions. Company G of the just-returned Second Battalion relieved Company A, 371st Infantry, in Calomini, and that Company promptly reverted back to control of its parent regiment in the Coastal Sector. An enemy raiding party hit Company C's right flank platoon at 0500, but they were repulsed with heavy casualties.

On 22 December, orders were received to prepare to attack on the morning of December 25.

Surprise Enemy Counterattack in the Serchio Valley

Early in December, 92nd Division command began preparations to attack along its front, in compliance with Fifth Army's plans to resume offensive operations towards Bologna, and the plans of IV Corps to advance in its zone of responsibility.

At the same time numerous reports led staff to believe the enemy planned an attack in the Serchio area around 10 December. This prompted *some* defensive planning; bridges were prepared for demolition, in case of withdrawal action, and large quantities of mines, barbed wire, and concertina-roll barriers were stored away. Civilians north of Gallicano continued to be evacuated to counter sabotage efforts.

The expected attack did not materialize on December 10, and the Serchio Valley command relaxed its vigilance somewhat and resumed its planning for their own offensive.

Nevertheless, rumors and reports continued to filter through the Division Intelligence network indicating a full scale offensive was still being planned by the enemy; so, the 92nd Division attempted to make minimal preparations for defense of their front, while at the same time, striving to remain in compliance with Fifth Army and IV Corps directives to maintain the offensive. They continued preparations to launch a full scale attack themselves.

Field orders and annexes to them issued in the days prior to 25 December indicated Staff's confusion and uncertainty as to the enemy's intentions.

General Almond issued Field Order Number 4 at 1200 on 17 December from his command post at Viareggio, some 18–20 miles from the Serchio Valley.[6] It states:

> Fifth Army continues offensive operations; IV Corps advance in zone.
>
> 92nd Infantry Division (-365 Combat Team) attacks H-hour, D-Day in zone, seizes objectives, continues pressure on coast towards Massa.

The Intelligence and Artillery annexes make it clear that the main attack was to be made by the 371st Infantry Combat Team in the center with fire support from the 366th Infantry (Second Battalion). The Division Artillery fire plan called for massed fires on MAINE on D-Day and on ALASKA on D-1 Day. Most of the Division and attached artillery was concentrated in the Coastal Sector, and ammunition allocations were heaviest there.

Further instructions and annexes issued as late as 1400 on 23 December make no change except to name D-Day[7]:

> Fifth Army continues offensive operations; IV Corps advances in Zone.
>
> 92nd Infantry Division (Combat Team 365) attacks 25 December at 0800 in Zone, seizes objectives, continues pressure on coast towards Massa.
>
> *Discussion*: Enemy front line units in the Serchio Valley are *not particulary aggressive* at the present time and deserters of 20 December had heard nothing of an attack.
>
> *Conclusions*: The enemy *can* attack in the Serchio with the troops now on line ... at any time. Such an attack could be made anytime after the evening of 24th of December. *At present*, there are *not sufficient indications to favor the capability of attack.*"[8]

Officers in the front line battalions did not agree with these conclusions. Second Lieutenant Sidney Thompson, platoon leader in Company H, 366th Infantry stated, in a postwar interview[9]:

The Battles for the Serchio Valley

It was Fifth Army's fault. All the civilians and most of the front-line troops were aware that enemy activity behind their lines was increasing and that an attack down the Serchio Valley was not only planned, but was the most logical.

Fifth Army was well aware of reports of additional enemy troops in the Serchio Valley Sector: partisan reports of a possible offensive emanating from the Castelnuovo di Garfagnana area; reports confirmed by patrol and reports and air photographs of road and bridge repairs on routes leading into Castelnuovo; and, civilian reports of enemy medium artillery moving toward Aulla and the Serchio Valley.

As early as 22 December Fifth Army Headquarters took steps to move reinforcements to the 92nd Division rear area, as extracts from the G-3 Journal indicates[10]:

1. Move 760 Tank Battalion ... to be attached to 92nd Division.
2. Move two medium companies and Headquarters 755 Tank Battalion ... attached to IV Corps.
3. Motorize 1 RGT 85 Division for movement on 3 hour notice....

The 339th Regiment Combat Team of 85th Division was moved to IV Corps and the 337th Combat Team of the same division was attached to the 92nd Division. The 19th and 21st Brigades of the British 8th Indian Division were placed under "operational control" of the 92nd Division. Other supporting units were ordered to the Lucca area some 15–20 miles south of the lines in the Serchio Valley.

Despite all the activity at the upper command levels attesting to deep concern about an impending attack, no change was made in the plans to attack and *no* reinforcements were added to the thinly-held infantry front lines. Fifth Army was well aware that at least one German Division and two Italian Divisions were in the area and that as many as five German Divisions might be available if needed.

On the morning of 24 December two companies moved out of Barga and into the tiny mountain village of Sommocolonia. Bebbio and Scarpello were each occupied by platoons from the 92nd Reconnaissance Troop.

Word finally came to the 370th Combat Team on the evening of 24 December that the proposed attack against the Germans was postponed. Information that a *German* attack was to be launched in the Serchio Valley on 27 December, prompted the reversal of plans. Captain Samuel Tucker, S-2 of the Second Battalion, 366th, alleged deliberate delay in notifying his unit of the change in plans[11]:

> I believe it was on the night of December 24 when Headquarters 370th Infantry ordered that the company in the vicinity of Sommocolonia under orders to attack would immediately retire from the assembly area and abandon the attack plans.... Early that same day a Captain Schmidt ... appeared in our sector and said to me that his mission was to develop some

"counter-attack plans." I remember that our S-4 Section was ordered to pick up and distribute defensive materials. In retrospect, I can see that higher headquarters *knew* what was about to happen and *knew* that it was *imminent*. We at Second Battalion Headquarters were told nothing. I believe the failure to inform us was deliberate.

All front-line units were notified during the night of 24 December of the change in plans. General Almond's Field Order Number 5 dated 25 December at 1600 exhorted the 92nd Infantry Division to:

> reinforce, organize, occupy and hold present position at all costs. Intensive patrolling; make maximum improvement of existing defensive positions.

At this late stage in the events, it seems strange that the conclusion in the Intelligence Annex to Field Order Number 5 was[12]:

> The enemy will *defend* the present line with units now on line with available support of various elements in the Serchio Valley.

Opening Moves

On the night of December 24–25, anti-tank and 50 cal machine gun fire on enemy positions on the Lama di Sotto–Monte San Quirico ridge line drew a fierce reaction from the enemy on the east bank of the Serchio and the entire ridge was alight with our fire and that of the enemy.

The night of December 25–26 was relatively quiet, although Sommocolonia received some artillery and mortar fire, and considerable long range machine gun fire fell on positions in the east bank of the Serchio. Just after midnight a message from IV Corps requested a follow-up of a report from a priest in Pierpoli that the enemy attack would come December 27. At 0400 the Second Battalion, minus Company G (at Calomini) was withdrawn pursuant to the order to intensify work on a defensive line; it moved back to the high ground west of the Serchio and south of Gallicano with a mission of digging a main defensive position across the mountain mass.

Elements of *two* infantry battalions and *two* platoons from the 92nd Division Reconnaissance Troop were all that remained in front-line positions across nine miles of rugged terrain. West of the river were three companies of the First Battalion, 370th Infantry; east of the river, and in line north of Sommocolonia, were elements of three companies of the Second Battalion, 366th Infantry; two platoons of the 366th Infantry were in Sommocolonia, and the Reconnaissance Troop platoons occupied Bebbio and Scarpello, on the extreme right flank.

At 0414 the First Battalion reported machine gun fire on Companies A and C in vicinity of Molazzano, on the west side of the river. At 0450, reports from the 92nd Reconnaissance Troop platoon at Bebbio on the extreme right, reported hearing small arms and artillery fire in the vicinity of Sommocolonia; simultaneously a red and blue flare appeared in the sky above enemy positions on Lama di Sotto ridge. At 0455, the Second Battalion, 366th Infantry, confirmed this report stating the fire was coming from directly north of Sommocolonia. Our mortars replied and the fire fight died away temporarily. At 0500 all fire on Sommocolonia ceased but heavy artillery, mortar and machine gun fire continued on the Company A and C positions west of the Serchio around Molazzano. At 0530, an enemy squad appeared in the draw north of Sommocolonia and partisan troops met them head-on in a fierce fire fight, driving them off with the aid of small arms and mortar fire from our troops. However, a larger force composed of Austrians and Italians, some dressed as partisans, drove the defending force back into Sommocolonia, and by 0730, they had surrounded them. Desperate, hand to hand fighting, from house to house, took place, spilling into the streets. Lieutenant Graham H. Jenkins sent a radio message that they were being attacked in large numbers and needed help and, at 0730, the battalion commander, 366th Infantry dispatched an additional platoon of Company E to reinforce the platoon already fighting there. Defensive fire was being employed by all weapons against the enemy forces at Sommocolonia, by this time. Meanwhile, enemy artillery and mortar fire continued to fall heavily and accurately on *all* front-line positions on both sides of the river. As the small force of about 60 men fought desperately in Sommocolonia, the 92nd Reconnaissance Troops in Bebbio and Scarpello, on the extreme right flank of the line began to experience heavy enemy pressure. Their alert outposts observed 50 enemy on Lami di Sotto and called down artillery fire on them with good effect. At 0820 a wounded partisan reported 300 enemy in Sommocolonia and fighting their way, house to house.

At the same same, Reconnaissance Troops reported troops with 30 mules attempting to resupply troops attacking Sommocolonia. Again, artillery fire was directed on the mule train with heavy casualties to men and animals observed.

Late in the morning, over 200 Germans from the veteran Austro-German Mittenwald Battalion poured down the sheltered draws between Bebbio and Scarpello, led by Italian guides familiar with the area. Despite the overwhelming odds, the small reconnaissance troop fought bitterly before being forced to withdraw to the Reconnaissance Troop command post at Coreglia, according to plan. The Silver Star awards to Staff Sergeant William Morris and Corporal Jefferson Hilliard reflect the courage and tenacity of these Buffalo soldiers:

> Sergeant Morris commanded several platoon strong points from which he directed artillery fire on two enemy columns, causing at least 35 casualties. When his position was vigorously attacked with heavy mortar, automatic weapons and small arms fire, he quickly coordinated effective counter fire that caused more casualties and repulsed the attack. The enemy then reorganized, attempting to envelope the strong point from all sides at once with a superior force. Sergeant Morris, personally manning

one of his weapons, directed his fire, maintained contact with his company until his radio went out and the enemy had cut off and partially over-run his position from three sides. Then he ordered his men to proceed through the remaining exit to a previously prepared position. During this activity, Sergeant Morris was wounded, but, despite his injuries, he reached his men who had discovered the enemy in the position they now sought. He then safely led his men around the hostile force to a new position where he remained under an intense mortar concentration until recalled by his company.

T/5 Hilliard manned a machine gun in a strong point under vigorous enemy attack. For two hours his position was one of two main enemy objectives. During this activity he accounted for at least 12 enemy casualties while he and his assistant were the target of an intense mortar concentration. When maneuver and superior forces of the enemy made his position untenable, T/5 Hilliard was ordered to cover the withdrawal of the other men. He removed the machine gun from its tripod, and fired from the hip, carrying the belt on his shoulder while his assistant carried the tripod. He fired in this manner until his ammunition was exhausted accounting for at least two more enemy casualties.

By 1200 the gallant band from the 92nd Reconnaissance Troop withdrew to Coreglia according to plan. Captain Tucker comments[13]:

> The Division Reconnaissance Company occupied Mt. Bebbio on our right — the key terrain feature, commanding the entire sector of the Second Battalion. When the Reconnaissance Company was withdrawn we at Battalion Headquarters were not informed that our right flank had been thus exposed.

Bitter, bloody fighting continued within the village of Sommocolonia. The valiant band of 366th Infantry troops fought desperately to try to repel the enemy swarming through the streets. Their task was complicated by the presence among the Germans of Italian soldiers dressed as partisans. This caused split-second delays in reaction by the defenders at times and before they could recover, it was too late. First Lieutenant John R. Fox, Cannon Company, 366th Infantry, was acting as forward observer for the supporting 598th Field Artillery Battalion. His heroic action was described dramatically in the Field Artillery Journal, January 1946[14]:

> One of the forward observers showed unbeatable heroism. Lieutenant Fox and his party had ample time to pull out. They remained on the second floor of a house directing defensive fires until only a handful of defenders remained. As the enemy closed in, Lieutenant Fox called for artillery fire increasingly close to his own position. One of his last requests for fire included a target only 60 yards from him. The enemy continued to press forward in large numbers. When the house ... was entirely surrounded, he called for fire directly on it. He was questioned as to whether the mission

was safe to fire it. He answered, "Fire it! There's more of them than there are of us." He was recommended posthumously for the Distinguished Service Cross.

On 1 April 1982, nearly 39 years later, Lieutenant Fox was awarded the Distinguished Service Cross posthumously for Extraordinary Heroism in Action. The citation concluded:

> ...Later, when a counter attack retook the position from the Germans, Lieutenant Fox's body was found along with bodies of approximately 100 German soldiers, Lieutenant Fox's gallant and courageous actions, at the supreme sacrifice of his own life, contributed greatly to delaying the enemy advance until other infantry and artillery could reorganize to repel the attack. His extraordinarily valorous actions were in keeping with the most cherished traditions of military service, and reflect the utmost credit on him, his unit, and the United States Army.

(The award was presented to Mrs. Arlene Fox, his widow, in a ceremony at Fort Devens, Massachusetts, on Armed Forces Day, 15 May 1982. Major General James F. Hamlett, who served as a first lieutenant in Fox's company at the time of the incident, made the presentation on behalf of the Secretary of War. Present were members of the 366th Infantry Veterans Association, holding their 41st annual reunion.)

As the situation in Sommocolonia steadily worsened, and enemy pressure on 92nd Reconnaissance Troops at Bebbio and Scarpello increased, strong enemy attacks began all along the Second Battalion, 366th Infantry front. All its front-line companies were hit by an estimated two battalions of German Infantry supported by artillery, mortars and machine guns, with the greatest pressure falling on Company G, 366th Infantry. The battalion commander, 366th ordered a platoon from Company E to reinforce Company G, and also ordered the remainder of Company E to move to relieve the beleaguered forces at Sommocolonia. The 370th Infantry Regimental Commander, however, *countermanded* this order and ordered that force to occupy positions on Mount Vano to secure the right flank of the previously selected Main Line of Resistance.

At 1015 a partisan from Sommocolonia reported three enemy companies in the village but also revealed our gallant troops were still there.

Shortly thereafter, the relief platoon first sent from Company E, reached the edge of town, but was immediately swarmed over by the enemy, and was unable to make contact with the platoon already engaged. First Lieutenant Lewis Flagg III, Company H observed[15]:

> The relief should have been a full company, not a platoon. The small group got caught in machine gun cross-fire. The man in front of the Lieutenant and the man behind him were cut down in the first burst of fire and the platoon never had a chance. They tried to fight on, but heavy casualties forced them to retire.

At about 1155, the Germans launched a heavy attack against the ridge southwest of Sommocolonia, and the Second Battalion, 366th Infantry reported the (troops) escape route was rapidly being closed. The brave remnants were finally ordered to withdraw back to the prepared defensive line along the Mount Vano-Barga Ridge. Of 60 Americans fighting in Sommocolonia only one officer and 17 enlisted men were able to withdraw. They did so, fighting every step of the way, still inflicting casualties on the enemy.

The Silver Star was awarded to First Lieutenant Graham H. Jenkins for his gallant actions on that day:

> Lieutenant Jenkins' platoon was on an exposed hill. After a 24-hour artillery and machine gun barrage the enemy launched a deadly offensive at the battalion positions with a numerically superior force. Lieutenant Jenkins, with outstanding personal leadership kept his men in position, without food and with limited amounts of ammunition. Resisting the enemy with fierce determination, Lieutenant Jenkins killed several enemy soldiers who attempted to storm his position during a lull in the artillery fire and exposed himself to help drag three of his wounded machine gunners to comparative safety. Upon being ordered to withdraw, Lieutenant Jenkins refused to leave the unevacuated wounded which now numbered over 50 percent of the platoon unable to walk. He continued to direct counterfire and care for the wounded until his ammunition was exhausted and every man in the platoon but one had become a casualty, and he himself wounded. When the enemy closed over his position he was still trying to comfort a severely wounded soldier. First Lieutenant Jenkins' intrepid valor in the face of overwhelming odds exemplifies the conspicuous gallantry of the American Soldier.

There were many such feats of extraordinary heroism by black soldiers of the 366th Infantry, on that day in Sommocolonia. From the first probing contacts by the German forces at 0414 they fought fiercely and skillfully. Artillery and mortar fire, combined with heavy machine gun and small arms fire, inflicted heavy casualties on the attackers before they were forced to withdraw into the village. Even there, with their numbers growing smaller, ammunition supplies dwindling, and with enemy forces escalating the pressure, they continued to resist. Their leaders, officers and non-commissioned officers continued to lead them, moving men and weapons as threats developed, caring for and comforting their wounded, and exposing themselves time and time again without regard to their own safety. They skillfully directed machine gun and small arms fire, and Lieutenant Fox continued to direct artillery fire until it was right on his own position, killing Germans right at his door. Even in those final desperate moments, he remembered his fellow soldiers. He requested a smoke concentration so that they could withdraw under its cover.

Pressure continued to increase against all positions east of the river. Enemy artillery was extremely active during this time; the town of Fornaci and the 598th Field Artillery Battalion Command Post area received about

113 rounds of enemy artillery between 0810 and 0918; also all roads leading to forward elements were continually shelled. At one time, the Air Observation Post observed five enemy batteries firing at once.

A series of reports added to the evidence that the point of greatest danger from the enemy was from the right front and flank. And so, the remainder of the Second Battalion, 370th Infantry, in reserve on the west bank, was directed to assemble for movement to the front east of the river.

The Second Battalion, 366th Infantry, and the 92nd Reconnaissance Troops were ordered to form a defensive line hinged on Mount Vano.

At 1245 a civilian reported that four companies of Germans were moving down from Bebbio towards Barga.[16] A little later, three civilian refugees reported to Reconnaissance Troop that they had escaped from a column of an estimated 1000 Germans at 0300. They stated the column had divided into two groups—one headed for Mount Vano, the other for Renaio—also that they had asked for routes to Pedona. As a result, at 1445, the remaining platoon of tanks were positioned along the Fornaci-Barga road, where they could cover the ridge above Barga to Bebbio and the draw leading to Pedona. This represented the last reserve immediately available to the 370th Combat Team.

At 1400 the enemy attacked Second Battalion, 366th Infantry positions around Barga with a large force preceded by a massive artillery shelling. The assault units hit Company G, 366th Infantry with pulverizing force accompanied by heavy, and accurate artillery and mortar fire. Although the company resisted stubbornly, inflicting heavy casualties on the advancing enemy troops, it became disorganized, leaving a gap on the east bank of the Serchio to the Barga Ridge.[17] A German company poured through the gap and moved unopposed—for a time—to the south. Other elements of the Second Battalion, 366th withdrew to avoid being outflanked.

At about 1630, Reconnaissance Troop reported an estimated two enemy companies in Tiglio, on the extreme right flank.

At 1730, the Second Battalion, 366th reported Company G on the left was reeling under the heavy pressure and after four hours of pounding from continuous assault units and heavy artillery and mortar fire, was withdrawing. At 1800, it was reported that the enemy had forced its way through the company along the river road and was heading for the Regimental Command Post at Fornaci. All command post personnel were organized in defensive positions, the platoon of tanks south of Barga was shifted over and the platoon of Company F, 370th Infantry moved in. Battery C, 598th Field Artillery Battalion, in process of executing the most difficult of artillery movements in battle, a retrograde movement, joined in with orders to fire 100 rounds of 105 mm shells per gun straight down the road just west of the command post. Their performance is described[18]:

> First Lieutenant Davidson, the battery commander, had no communications except to his guns. 400 rounds remained at the position. With the help of the battalion commander he prepared fixed concentrations. All were for Charge I. The first, for a zone of 1,830-1930 yards, dislodged a

German formation, which despite depleted numbers, started to advance. The next concentration was fired at 1700 yards and again inflicted heavy casualties on the enemy. Further concentrations were fired at 1,900 yards and 2,300 yards.

The enemy attack did not reach the command post. At 1840, the platoon of tanks and the platoon of Company F, 370th Infantry, plus elements of regimental Headquarters Company, moved to the north end of Fornaci and set up defensive position.

There was no further enemy contact that evening on the east side of the river. By nightfall the regimental line of defense extended generally from Coreglia to Barga, then sharply south to the north side of Fornaci, and across the river along the high ground south of Trasillico.

The Regimental Command Post moved back to Osteria and the 598th Field Artillery Battalion had completed displacement of its command post, and its vital Fire Direction Center, as well as all its firing batteries to the new positions, all without interrupting any fire missions.

The battered companies of Second Battalion, 370th Infantry and 92nd Reconnaissance Troop reorganized as the German attack slowed down during the night and no further ground was lost.

Despite being forced to withdraw by an overwhelming enemy force, Company G, 366th Infantry, had fought stubbornly throughout the day. The exploits of Pfc Trueheart Fogg are described in his citation for the Silver Star:

> A determined enemy force counter-attacked and penetrated to the platoon squad area of Fogg's battalion. From his position, Pfc. Fogg observed a hostile raiding party of 25 enemy soldiers armed with hand grenades, machine guns, and "burp" guns approaching his platoon area. When an enemy machine gun squad proceeded to set up its weapon, Pfc. Fogg moved out under heavy artillery and mortar fire and killed all of the four-man enemy crew with his Browning Automatic Rifle. Immediately thereafter another enemy machine gun opened fire from his left front and pinned him down. Then, as a squad of enemy soldiers advanced on his position with concentrated small arms fire, Pfc. Fogg with utter disregard for his own safety, boldly stood up and fired on the second machine gun crew, completely wiping it out. His action in single handedly destroying the enemy weapons resulted in saving his platoon from almost certain annihilation.

Action on the Left Bank

As stated previously, the first enemy action was at 0414 when Company A, 370th Infantry, reported machine gun and "burp" pistol fire supported by mortar fire on their positions at Molazzana, west of the river. This fire continued on Company C, 370th Infantry positions there, and as the morning moved on, it increased in volume.

At 0400 the enemy was reported in Promiana.

At about 0530, after a lively fire fight at Molazzana, and during a lull that followed, some of the enemy tried to surrender, but the skeptical Buffalo soldiers felt that was a deception that had been tried before and blasted away at them. At 0606 the enemy increased the frequency and intensity of their attacks on both companies, firing rifle grenades now and increasing the mortar and artillery fire on the positions. At about 0650 the enemy fired heavy concentrations across the entire sector, with particular attention to the Molazzana area, and enemy assault troops in force began to move from north of Molazzana in the attack. Throughout the morning Companies A and B beat off attack after attack successfully, with heavy casualties to the enemy.

At about the same time, Company G, 370th Infantry, in positions in Calomini, had to fight desperately after the enemy, by infiltration, occupied a church at the east end of the hill where Company H's supporting machine gun section and mortar section had been stationed. The enemy captured these vital units and weapons, but despite that and their presence in the village, Company G fought bitterly and regained possession of Calomini, inflicting heavy casualties on the enemy in the process. They did this in spite of heavy attacks from front and rear.

By 0830, with Calomini surrounded, Promiana occupied by the enemy, and Companies A and C heavily engaged in repelling repeated attacks, coupled with the heavy volume of artillery and mortar fire, all led to a mistaken assumption that the major enemy thrust was developing on the west bank of the river.

Accordingly, Company F, 370th Infantry (less one platoon) part of the flimsy reserve available, was ordered attached to the First Battalion. By 1045, however, the Buffalo soldiers' situation on the west bank had so improved that Company F was ordered to the assistance of the Second Battalion, 366th Infantry on the *east* side of the river.

By 1400, that company was in position in vicinity of Mount Vano, under Second Battalion, 366th control. The rest of the reserve, the Second Battalion, 370th Infantry (less Companies G and F) had been ordered at 0800 to report to its assembly area at Correglia.

So, the First Battalion was left, alone, to defend the west bank, with no reserves immediately available.

By 1500, the enemy who had captured the church at Calomini, had been pinned down by machine gun, mortar and artillery fire, and retreated, and the positions and all of Calomini were re-occupied by Company G immediately.

Throughout the battles during the morning, enemy artillery and mortar fire fell continuously on First Battalion positions in Calomini, Molazzana and Vergemoli. In spite of the constant barrages, however, the Buffalo soldiers dug further into the ground, or found cover in the debris of fallen buildings, and repelled attack after attack sometimes from two, sometimes three sides. Repeatedly, defensive artillery and mortar fire was called down on the onrushing enemy, as the Buffalo soldiers raked them with machine gun and rifle fire, and hand grenades. In addition, mines laid by first battalion companies along all draws, trails, roads leading to their positions, were responsible for many casualties among the enemy, and broke up some assaults before they could gather momentum. Usually, these minefields were laid just the night before and in some cases the job was not completed at daybreak. The determined men of First Battalion, 370th Infantry continued the job in most cases, and under most hazardous conditions. Such was the case as is shown in the words of the citation for the Silver Star awarded to Second Lieutenant Irving F. Dickerson:

> Under threat of an impending enemy attack, Second Lieutenant Dickerson was ordered to supervise the laying of anti-personnel mines across certain terrain on his Company's left flank. The area was under continuous hostile artillery fire, and the bright moonlight made direct enemy observation certain. Nevertheless, Lieutenant Dickerson worked on his task for the rest of the night, and unsatisfied when daylight came, and now in full view of the enemy, he continued working until hit by a sniper. Despite his wounds, he stayed until he had satisfactorily completed his assignment, then went unaided to an aid station.

The *Resume of Events* by Captain Kelly accurately sums up the situation up until noon December 26[19]:

> After beginning the attack in Calomini by infiltration around 0400, the enemy then moved assault units where ever possible to attempt to surround defensive positions; at about 0800 he shifted to formal methods, attacking in force preceded by heavy artillery preparatory concentrations moving all along the front rather than at selected points. The command posts of both front line battalions, of regiment and the Field Artillery, previously ignored, were shelled constantly all day, disrupting communications and causing casualties. It was obvious the enemy had excellent information of key installations and after daybreak visual observation from the mountain peaks was available continuously.
>
> Nevertheless, the results of the enemy's efforts at noon were that *west* of the Serchio, *no* positions had been overrun except for some installations in rear of Calonimi. The enemy had been pinned down and subjected to heavy shelling and mortaring, and his efforts in this sector were slackening and continued to slacken.

Heavy shelling of First Battalion, 370th units continued; however, in the afternoon of the 26th Company A's request for reinforcements at one point was denied as they were more urgently needed on the east side of the river. At 1655, the commanding officer, 370th Infantry, realizing that the First Battalion obviously must depend on its own resources, though severely strained because of the day's heavy fighting, moved to have the battalion draw in its defenses. Anti-Tank Company at Vergemoli was to move back to

Trassilico, to better protect the flank; Company A with one platoon of Company B attached was to maneuver laterally, thus abandoning positions under observation and fire by the enemy in Promiano and strengthening the C. Rio positions which were under some threat.

When the enemy broke through on the east side near the river the Second Battalion, 366th Infantry was ordered to withdraw to a new line. In order to prevent a dangerous gap in depth from occurring, First Battalion, 370th Infantry was ordered to occupy previously reconnoitered defensive positions on the south side of the Gallicano stream, under cover of darkness. All positions were to be occupied by dawn.

So, after battling the enemy to a standstill, despite constant ground attacks all day, under continuous heavy artillery and mortar barrages, and tenaciously clinging to their positions, inflicting heavy casualties on the enemy in the process, the troops of the First Battalion left these positions in a disciplined manner and under orders. The next morning they were again prepared to face the enemy, proud of the previous day's work.

Delays in Support Dispositions

At about 1500 General Crittenberger, IV Corps Commander, with his Chief of Staff and other staff members, reached Colonel Sherman at the command post, still in Fornaci. He reviewed, then approved the defensive plans, then announced that reinforcing troops from the British 8th Indian Division would take up defensive positions behind the 370th and 366th Infantry positions. At this time, the 370th, sure that it could stand fast, asked only that a motorized battalion of the 19th Indian Brigade be used on its right flank, from positions previously occupied by 92nd Reconnaissance Troops, to prevent further encirclements. On corps order, the combat team had sent trucks to pick up the Indian Battalion near Marlia at 1100. About 1230, 92nd Division Headquarters informed 370th Infantry that the battalion was available, and at 1455, Lieutenant Rhodes went to the appointed meeting place and found the battalion not yet arrived. However, the battalion commander of the Indian Battalion informed him he was under the command of the commanding officer of the 19th Indian Brigade, *not* the commanding officer of the 370th Combat Team or anyone else. The British Commanding General was finally located and he flatly stated such a plan as proposed could upset his entire defensive scheme and refused to act until he had telephoned IV Corps. He further stated his battalion would not arrive until after dark. In a telephone conversation with IV Corps Chief of Staff, the arrangements were amended so that troops would remain under control of 19th Indian Brigade, but the mission of the brigade would still be reinforcing the right flank.[20]

While all this dialogue and confusion as to the status and use of these desperately needed supporting units was going on, the black soldiers at Sommocolonia were fighting desperately to hold, as ordered, *at all costs*, that tiny village; the valiant, but small forces from the 92nd Reconnaissance Troop, were doing the same thing, high on the mountain, on the crucial right

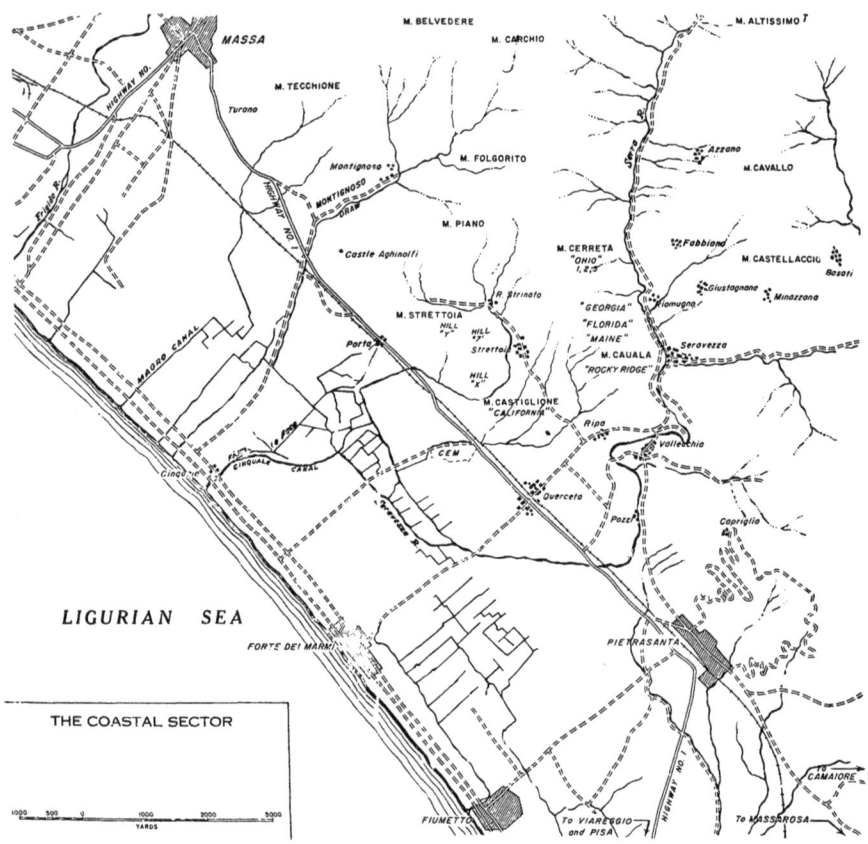

The Coastal Sector

flank at Beggio and Scarpello. Company G and Company F of Second Battalion, 366th Infantry near the river, faced savage ground assaults.

By this time it had become clear that the main thrust of the enemy attack was to be directed down from the over-run flank and straight down the Serchio Valley following the east bank of the river.

It is likely that if the entire Brigade of the 8th Indiana Division had been committed that afternoon, the enemy attack would have been halted.

As it was, the Indian troops did not arrive until after nightfall. One company of the 21st Brigade was ordered to hold a sector on Il Colle to link up with 92nd Reconnaissance Troops in Coreglia, on the right, and Second Battalion, 366th on the left. The commanding officer, 370th Combat Team *personally* instructed the company commander that night. At about 0900 the next day, it was discovered that in spite of the specific instructions from the Combat Team Commander, the Indian company was *not* in position in Colle, but on the hill in rear of Colle. About the failure of the Indian Company to move into position on Colle Ridge, Captain Tucker says[21]:

Late in the afternoon—after dark—my battalion commanding officer received an order to withdraw. A line running generally east and west, had been drawn on a map crossing several ridges and draws, stopping at a hill marked "Colle." The order said: "The Indians will anchor their left at (or by) midnight." I (and others) went back to reconnoiter by moonlight. The assigned line was tactically unsound; but, hastily, we developed the best defense we could, consistent with the order, and our units withdrew to it. *All through the night* we had patrols out from Company E, trying to make contact with the Indians on our right.

The battalion of the 19th Indian Brigade and the one company of the 21st Brigade were attached to the 370th Infantry as soon as they arrived. The 19th Brigade went into previously reconnoitered positions on the Pian di Correglia.

Action on 27 December—East of the River

By midnight, communication was out to all units because of continuous enemy shelling, and movement of command posts.

At 0400, Second Battalion 366th reported that they were in assigned positions, and later reported they were in urgent need of engineer tools, but none were available at the time.

At 0700 after it was learned that a tank platoon left in Fornaci had pulled back through error, the commanding officer of 370th Combat Team ordered it back and refused to release them as long as he held responsibility for the sector. After some dispute with the British, this was agreed to.

The Reconnaissance Troop was still in Coreglia and the platoon of Company F, 370th Infantry, was still in Fornaci.

At 0940 a liaison party from the Air Corps reported to the Command Post.

At 1000, tanks from **Company B, 760 Tank Battalion,** reported hearing small arms and burp gun fire, and seeing troops in vicinity of Seggio. A few minutes later, Second Battalion, 366th Infantry reported Company G had withdrawn to the battalion command post at Pedona. The Battalion Commander and his staff at this time had two platoons of Company E and many others who had become lost or confused during the night under control. Some men from Company F, 370th Infantry, who had been at Fornaci, were also gathered up. The heavy enemy pressure started coming at about 1000 from Barga towards Pedona and struck the Second Battalion, 366th with overwhelming power, forcing their grudging withdrawal.

At this point Lt. Colonel John J. Phelan, 370th Regimental Executive Officer, took to the field and, he was able to reorganize the troops and finally establish a firm defensive line on the bluffs just in the rear of Pedona. The citation for the Silver Star award illuminates the magnitude of his actions on that day:

Lieutenant Colonel Phelan, the Regimental Executive Officer received word at the command post that the entire regimental right sector was in imminent danger of collapse under repeated and deadly determined hostile attacks. Lieutenant Colonel Phelan immediately proceeded to the sector and under a continuous barrage of all enemy arms, he re-grouped his troops in a new defensive line establishing a defense which held. During this time, he was at all times under direct or partial observation of the enemy and in constant threat from enemy artillery, mortars, and small arms.

The bold leadership and defensive action exhibited by Lieutenant Colonel Phelan inspired both the officers and men with the offensive spirit necessary to successfully check the enemy.

Meanwhile, further to the east, at 1000, German Mountain troops, clad in white uniforms, descended in force on Tiglio Alto and Tiglio Basso, both only a few kilometers from Coreglia. Mortar fire fell on positions of 92nd Reconnaissance Troops. The Second Battalion, 370th Infantry, less Company F, with a company of the 19th Indian Brigade attached, moved eastward to cover this threat. However, by the time the main enemy thrust had been stopped at Pedona, Coreglia had been abandoned by remaining 92nd Reconnaissance Troops.

At about 1300, Major General Dudley Russell, Commander of the 8th Indian Division, assumed command of the sector.

He divided the original sector of the 92nd Division into approximately two equal parts, with the 92nd Division taking the area on the coast. He immediately directed that all troops of the 370th Infantry and attached units, withdraw to the west bank and join the First Battalion, 370th Infantry. The move was to be completed before dawn and Colonel Sherman's forces were given the responsibility for holding the high ground south of Gallicano. The 370th Command Post was moved to Pian della Rocca. At 1530, necessary orders were issued and 370th and Second Battalion, 366th Infantry troops were assembled in vicinity of Calavorno, marched to new positions on the west side of the river, which were completely occupied before dawn on the 28th.

At 1243, fighter bombers attacked **Sommocolonia**.

At 1359, our fighter bombers attacked Barga.

At 1520 our fighter bombers attacked Vergemoli.

Air support pounded the German front line troops with over 200 sorties on that day.

The 598th Field Artillery Battalion, was ordered to remain east of the river and continue to fire as direct support battalion for the 8th Indian Division.

On the west side of the river, the Anti-Tank Company and attached partisans were in position at Trasillico at 2400.

The situation of the First Battalion 370th Infantry throughout the day was difficult to ascertain because unit command posts were moving in

The Battles for the Serchio Valley

mountainous terrain. Its forward areas were cleared about 0300 and the troops were in their positions by daylight.

The First Battalion held fast during all day of the 27th.

By the evening of December 27, the air strikes, coupled with the added fresh troop strength, had stopped the German drive. It is believed, too that the stubborn resistance by the greatly outnumbered and thinly-spread Buffalo troops at Bebbio, Scarpello, Barga and Sommocolonia, accompanied by accurate and continuous defensive fire continuously delivered by our artillery and mortars, exacted considerable casualties among the attacking forces. The records do not indicate any particularly heavy fighting by the troops of the 8th Indian Division. It was as if the Germans had decided to withdraw — according to plan. Within two days the Germans were out of Barga. On 28 December, the time was spent organizing and improving the new positions and re-equipping the Second Battalion, 366th Infantry. The First Battalion, 370th Infantry was positioned along the high ground south of Gallicano from Verni to the hills overlooking Gallicano, then south to a point across from Fornaci. The Second Battalion, 370th Infantry was placed in depth in the same position.

The Second Battalion, 366th Infantry relieved the anti-tank company at Trasillico, and dug positions on the mountains to the rear as far as Mount Albano. The I and R platoons of the 370th and 366th formed a protective screen on the first flank from Mount Bicacca to Mount Croce, south to Mount Baldorie. The Regimental Command Post was moved to Trebbio.

By 29 December, the entire situation was becoming quite stable. A patrol from Company C, 370th Infantry, went to Verni, found no enemy there, but were fired on when they probed into Gallicano. The anti-tank company was relieved by Company E of 366th Infantry, and moved into Fabbriche.

At 1100 the 370th Infantry came under operational control of 8th Indian Division. At 1515 a patrol from First Battalion, 370th reported no enemy in Gallicano.

At midnight, Second Battalion, 370th Infantry, less Company G, moved into Fabbriche; Company A moved into Bolognana, about 3 kilometres north, and Company C moved up to the ridge south of Gallicano.

All during the day of 30 December battalion commanders and company commanders reconnoitered the left flank of the regiment, and ordered anti-tank company to reconnoiter positions for road blocks between Bolognana and Gallicano; these were established after dark.

Patrols to Gallicano and Molazzano met very feeble resistance.

The I and R Platoon and the Mine Platoon of the anti-tank company patrolled the left flank, and the I and R Platoon of the 366th Infantry linked up with the Reconnaissance Troop near Camaiore, Company A spent the day maneuvering into position.

At dawn, 31 December companies E and F moved forward and dug defensive positions along the new line, working feverishly most of the day. Company G rested in Fabbriche, where the 370th Infantry Command Post was also established.

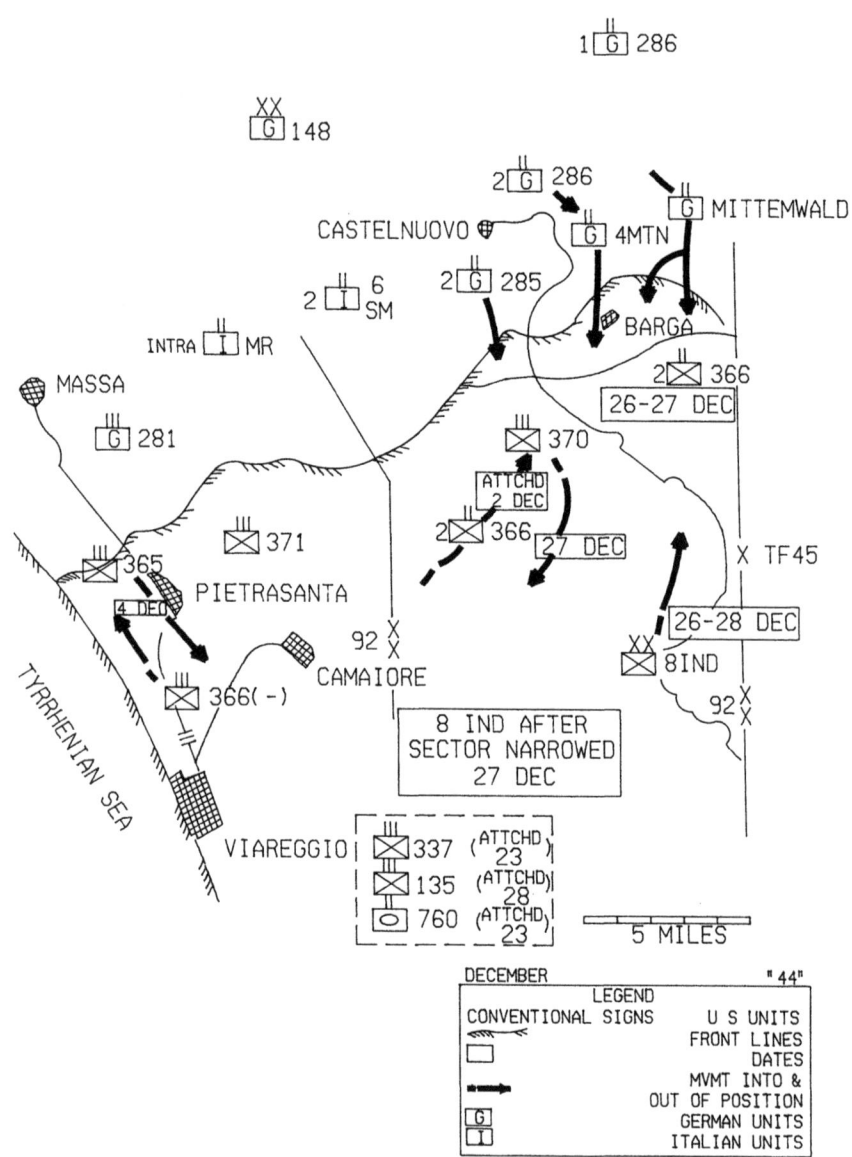

Allied and Enemy Dispositions December 1944

By the end of December, enemy troops had fled or been driven out of Barga; Sommocolonia was reoccupied, strong Allied patrols boldly entered Bebbio, Gallicano, and Molazzano against only feeble enemy resistance. Heavy and accurate mortar and artillery support was given these patrols, as well as strong air support.

By 1 January, the so-called "German threat to Fifth Army's supply lines," was ended.

By this time the Second Battalion 366th Infantry, and the First and Second battalions of the 370th Infantry, had been reorganized and re-equipped, and, from firmly established positions on the west side of the Serchio River, had begun to send power patrols into enemy positions.

On 10 January, the Indian troops were withdrawn from the Serchio Valley, the 370th Infantry again reverted to 92nd Division control, and the 92nd Division resumed control of the Serchio Valley with Brigadier General John Wood in command.[22] The same day, the 365th Infantry, which had been attached to the 88th Division on the Bologna front, since December 2, returned to 92nd Division control. The 365th promptly relieved the 370th Infantry east of the Serchio River, with the First and Second battalions going into positions in the vicinity of Barga, and the Third Battalion in reserve in the vicinity of Coreglia. The Regimental Command Post of the 365th was located in Ghivizzano.

Operations in the Coastal Sector

While elements of the 370th and 366th were preparing to attack in the Serchio Valley on Christmas day, the 371st Infantry with the First Battalion, 366th Infantry attached, was preparing to attack in the Coastal Sector towards Massa.

On 22 December, its A Company was returned from attachment to the 370th Infantry (from 24 November); companies B and I, 366th Infantry rejoined their parent regiment, and, for the first time since entering combat, the entire regiment was intact — but not for long.

The First and Second battalions, 366th Infantry were positioned from the Ligurian Sea to a line Pietrasanta — Massa.

Replacements were sent to all front-line units to bring them up to strength. A company of tanks was attached and ordered to move back and forth noisily, so as to be seen and heard by the enemy, and hopefully, to convince him that a large tank force was involved. Strong combat patrols were sent out but little contact was reported. As the hour of attack neared, the tempo of artillery fire was stepped up.

Then, at 1715, on 24 December, word was received that the attack was postponed and the commander of the 371st ordered that, "for the 24 hour period beginning at midnight, December 24, not one shot was to be fired except in self defense or upon orders from higher headquarters."[23]

When word was received of the enemy penetration in the Serchio, all units had been alerted for possible offensive action in the 371st sector. Mine fields were hastily laid, tactical wire lines re-laid, and shifts of units occurred all along the line into positions deemed more advantageous for covering the wide front. Additional wire and other obstacles were suitably placed.

Counter-attack plans were hastily made. Company F was pulled out of the front lines and moved back to an area near Pietrasanta. The Third Battalion was relieved by elements of the First Battalion, 366th Infantry on 26 December, and was moved into position as regimental reserve.

The enemy made no offensive effort in the Coastal Sector, except for sending a strong patrol against Company E, which was driven off. Many enemy flares went up on the mountains but no further aggressive action occurred.

The division ordered that each battalion send out patrols for the specific purpose of capturing prisoners. On 29 December, Company I, commanded by Captain Ezekiel C. Smith, operating as a "power" patrol, passed through the Second Battalion, climbing up Mount Cauala. Finding it difficult to control his entire company over the treacherous mountain terrain in the darkness, Captain Smith left one platoon halfway up the mountain, in support, and continued on. He reached the top without drawing any fire from the enemy. Within minutes, burly Private First Class Milton Hall literally "snatched" a surprised German soldier bodily from his fox-hole, and Captain Smith led his company back down the mountain, dragging the PW with them.

The company suffered no casualties.

On the coast, patrols of the 366th Infantry were active, and for the most part successful against a sensitive enemy who, although not offensive-minded, reacted strongly to patrol probes.

Aftermath

Recriminations and accusations came quickly from Army Command Headquarters. Both Generals Clark and Truscott concluded that the German attack had caused serious disruption of Fifth Army troops dispositions and thus tended to cast blame upon the 92nd Division for the abandonment of plans to renew the winter offensive.

There were other reasons for postponing such plans, however, and the action in the Serchio only served to confirm the necessity to delay the offensive until spring. It convinced Allied commanders that conditions all along the front were definitely unfavorable for it. The enemy made it clear they intended to hold fast in their Gothic Line positions. The weather, the unfriendly terrain, the depleted ammunition stocks, and the physical and emotional condition of the troops — all dictated postponement of the attack.

General Clark, in a postwar book, stated[24]:

> It (92nd Division) did not come up to the test, and when the Germans struck down the Serchio Valley, the Regimental Commanders were unable to exercise sufficient control over their troops in an emergency.

General Truscott stated[25]:

> The Germans launched several limited objective attacks in the Serchio Valley, with forces involving five or six battalions which struck the First Battalion, 370th Infantry and the Second Battalion, 366th Infantry, both of which "melted away" — term which was to be frequently used in describing actions of colored troops.

General Almond agreed with the assessment of his superiors and offered nothing in defense of his soldiers. Neither he nor his staff, nor the 370th Regimental Commander, Colonel Sherman or *his* staff were blamed or criticized for the "defeat." All the blame was heaped upon the junior officers and the enlisted men, many of whom felt they were thrust into an impossible situation because of inadequate preparation and planning by command staff.

General Almond could have offered a sound military rationale for the defeat had he chosen to do so. At his order a special report was submitted to *him* by the commanding officer, 370th Infantry on 4 March, 1945, parts of which are quoted herein[26]:

> There were several factors militating against a really sound defensive set up against a major enemy effort.
> (a) Due to the small number of troops available and large frontage assigned, both flanks of the position were open except for a reconnaissance screen.
> (b) The Combat Team was itself under orders to launch an attack as part of a larger effort on December 25. The planning for this effort and the consequent disposition of troops naturally limited defensive preparations. Word that this attack was postponed did not reach Combat Team 370 until the evening of 24 December, 1944.
> (c) The mission of the Combat Team at all times had been to maintain constant offensive pressure against the enemy to prevent the shifting of more troops to the Bologna front. Accordingly, the Combat Team had pushed forward to the lower slopes of ridges held by the enemy. This mission had been further amplified by a directive that in the event of attack the Combat Team was to *hold* its present position at all costs.

As to events as the battle developed, the report indicates:

> The positions on the west side held firm; those on the east side were outflanked and pushed back, and in the case of G Company, 366th Infantry, penetrated. The Regimental reserve was simply insufficient to hold the line.

And, as to the utilization of the Indian troops:

> Confusion arose as to the exact status of the Indian units. Co-ordination with them does not seem to have been very satisfactory. This seems largely

due to vague and somewhat conflicting orders and instructions given to both parties by Higher Headquarters. So much of the information was given or received over the telephone in conversation between commanders that it is difficult to follow the exact progress. Apparently neither side was sure just who was in command and what the sectors of responsibility were. Also it seems that a unified command should have been established earlier to avoid the confusion as it developed, 370th Combat Team was led to believe it would have Indian Troops attached and planned accordingly only to find those troops unavailable.

As to the amount of actual fighting the Indian troops engaged in:

> As the action later developed, the Germans did not exploit their initial successes. As a matter of fact, east of the river, the enemy *retired to his original line*."

Captain Tucker, in his letter of July 1980 (previously cited) expressed conclusions similar to those in the report[27]:

> I met Colonel Robinson (Battalion Commander) near Pedona, leading his troops. There was no panic. I do not doubt that there was some disorganization, but I do not recall not knowing, generally, the location of 3 rifle companies. The suggestion of a rout is news to me. I do not recall seeing Lieutenant Colonel Phelan.

Lieutenant Edward Peeks wrote in a letter 20 April 1980:

> The Second Battalion (366th) Staff functioned intact throughout the entire action. (Colonel Robinson, Captains Tucker and Pratt, and Lieutenant Robert Brown). The withdrawal was mostly orderly.

The comments of General Fretter-Pico, Commander of German Troops in the Serchio attack, in a post-war interview are quite revealing[28]:

> The weakness of your deployment in the Serchio Valley at the time of my attack on 26 December 1944, was that your troops were deployed on a front which was too long for the number of men available, and your reserves were too far in the rear areas which prevented their being deployed immediately. I stopped my attack in the vicinity of Fornaci because I did not have a sufficient force to allow me to push on to Bagni di Lucca or Lucca.

The German commander and the 370th Infantry commander appear to have reached similar conclusions.

There were other heroic acts honored by award of the Silver Star during this period:

William E. Porter, First Lieutenant, Infantry. Lieutenant Porter's platoon was attacking a strong enemy position. The enemy's automatic weapons fire pinned down the platoon. Lieutenant Porter alone, advanced on an enemy machine nest, killed the German officer in charge and forced the enemy to surrender, thus facilitating the advance of his company. Later in the day, after his platoon had been completely surrounded by superior enemy forces he constantly exposed himself to hostile fire in moving back and forth between platoon positions maintaining contact, directing fire, encouraging his men, and leading them in fighting their way out of the enemy trap.

(Posthumous) John A. Williams, Staff Sergeant, Infantry. On December 26, 1944, when the enemy counter-attacked and infiltrated a town held by our troops and forced a withdrawal, Sergeant Williams, a platoon guide, was ordered to take a squad of men to cover the withdrawal. The squad encountered a sniper while moving into position and Staff Sergeant Williams personally maneuvered to an advantageous point and fired upon the sniper thus enabling the squad to proceed. Subsequently, when the enemy fired an intense concentration of artillery on the entire area, Sergeant Williams and two other men became separated from their squads. Finding a soldier in OD uniform guarding a house, they went to inquire the whereabouts of their unit. As they approached closer they discovered that the soldier was one of the enemy dressed in American uniform. The enemy attempted to fire upon them, Sergeant Williams made a blind tackle, the enemy wounded him mortally but his grappling with the German enabled his companions to escape to safety. Sergeant Williams' aggressiveness and self-sacrifice was a heroic exemplification of the fighting spirit of the American soldier.

Melvin W. Walker, First Lieutenant, 366th Infantry. On December 30 1944, the raiding party of which First Lieutenant Walker was a member, was assigned the mission of crossing an enemy-observed canal, penetrating enemy lines, capturing prisoners and locating and destroying hostile installations. First Lieutenant Walker proceeded under cover of smoke across a heavily mined beach and through icy water while subjected to intense enemy artillery, mortar and automatic weapons fire. After crossing the canal, he assisted in directing the fire fight and, in spite of finding that his own weapon would not fire because of exposure to water and sand he repeatedly exposed himself to draw enemy fire. When the company returned from the raid, he assisted in the evacuation of the wounded at the canal and led the group through withering hostile fire back to safety.

Five

February Attack in Coastal Sector

Plan Fourth Term

In January 1945, high level Intelligence reports indicated German intentions to withdraw from Italy and to replace German troops with Italian troops. Even then, elements of three Fascist divisions were operating in the coastal sector and in the Serchio Valley. These were the Monte Rosa, the San Marco, and the Italia. In at least one instance it was believed that such a relief was already in process. Colonel Donald M. MacWillie, G-2 of the 92nd Division reported[1]:

> The introduction of the Second Battalion, Bersaglieri Regiment of the Italia Division to *replace* the Second Battalion, 286th Regiment (German), east of the Serchio, *seems* certain now.

Plan "Fourth Term," developed by General Almond and the 92nd Division staff was designed to explore the extent of enemy withdrawal plans. It was not designed as a full-scale, long-range offensive action, but as a limited objective attack. It was believed that it would have the following results.

1. Provide more complete information about the enemy dispositions and strength in front of the 92nd Division;
2. Cause transfers of enemy troops from other fronts;
3. Disrupt the enemy supply system and;
4. Cause dislocation of artillery positions.

It was also anticipated that, if successful, the high morale of the troops would be restored after the unfavorable results of the Serchio Valley action during the month of December.

In the first phase of the attack, the objective was along the line Magro Canal–Montignoso–Mount Folgorito.

If that first phase was successful, the second phase was along the line Frigido River–Massa.

The IV Corps Commander approved Plan Fourth Term, but limited the operation to the first phase *only*.

February Attack in Coastal Sector

The five mile sector from the sea to the mountains east of Highway #1 was to be the battleground. First, the enemy was to be driven from the Strettoia Hills, and the higher peaks along the Mount Cerretta–Folgorito Ridge line. Thus, the troops attacking on the coastal plain and along Highway #1 would be protected from observation and fire from these hills and peaks. Hopefully, this would open the way for the drive to Massa, and enable Allied artillery to be positioned within range of La Spezia, the Italian Naval Base.

Prior to the main action a major diversionary operation was to be made in the Serchio Valley. In addition to drawing enemy reserves from the coast, holding the maximum troops in the Serchio Valley, it was hoped to clear the Lama di Sotto Ridge of enemy, thus assuring direct observation to Castelnuovo di Garfagnana the huge German Supply and Communications Center.[2]

A crossing was to be made at the Cinquale Canal, near the sea.

Under Plan Fourth Term:

1. Brigadier General John Wood, Ass't Division Commander, would continue to command troops in the Serchio Valley Sector.
2. Two Brigades of the 8th Indian Division would be in reserve, one for the Serchio Sector and one for the coast. (Never used.)
3. One battalion of medium tanks and two companies of light tanks would support assaulting units, with the principal effort being made at the Cinquale Canal crossing.
4. In addition to the 92nd Division Artillery, two battalions of reinforcing medium artillery and one battalion of heavy artillery were to be provided.
5. Air support was to be provided by two medium bombardment squadrons and two light bombardment squadrons. "Rover Joe" and "Horsefly" were to be utilized whenever possible.[3]

The plan itself acknowledged two significant disadvantages; the first was that "the enemy position is heavily mined, fortified and, from a terrain standpoint, very strong. Secondly, offensive actions in the directions indicated would not be decisive and would cause only small immediate difficulties to the enemy."[4]

The 371st Infantry was to attack on the right through the high ground in a column of battalions; the 370th Infantry in the center in column of battalions, and the Third Battalion, 366th Infantry was to make a combined Tank-infantry effort around the mouth of the La Foce (Cinquale) canal. The goal was to reach Phase Line #1 on the afternoon of the second day.

Diversion in the Serchio Valley

The 365th Infantry Combat Team, with the 366th Infantry, minus its Third Battalion, attached, launched the attack in the Serchio Valley on both sides of the river, on 4 February.

West of the river, Company C, 366th Infantry, occupied Gallicano and pushed patrols forward to probe enemy dispositions. On the east side, second battalion units moved into Albiano and Castelvecchio, at the foot of the Lama di Sotto ridge, some 3000 feet high.

The main attack began the next morning. It represented the first major offensive action for the 365th Infantry.

At 0645, on 5 February, the third battalion, 365th Infantry attacked to the north with the mission of seizing and holding Lama di Sotto, Mt. Della Stella, and Hill 906.[5] Companies I and L, with I on the right, attacked abreast simultaneously. By 0750 Company L was on Hill 906, after some very bitter fighting in which the company suffered some 30 casualties; Company I also encountered intense resistance from small arms, machine gun, mortar and artillery fire, but drove the enemy from Lama di Sotto, capturing four Germans and eight Italians in the process. At 0750, a platoon from Company K was on Mt. Della Stella.

The enemy suffered heavy casualties from the Buffalo soldiers' assaulting units and their supporting mortar and artillery fire.

Meanwhile, Company C was alerted and motorized for use as a mobile reserve, and at 1400, Company A, less one platoon, was ordered to move to **Sommocolonia** at once.

Considerable mortar and artillery pounded the newly taken positions throughout the day, and enemy counter-attacks were launched against them, some in considerable strength and armour. At 1400, one platoon of Company A was sent to reinforce the Company K platoon on Mt. Della Stella which was being heavily counter-attacked. Company I received a strong counter-attack at 1810, and although the enemy penetrated the perimeter defenses, the Buffalos of Company I beat them off after vicious hand-to-hand fighting. The enemy fled in panic and disarray. Another platoon of Company A was then sent up to reinforce Company I.

During the first day's action, the Third Battalion suffered 54 casualties. Thirty-five enemy were taken prisoner, and their casualties were estimated as heavy, from the various fire fights, and accurate and heavy artillery and mortar fire. As a result of the action of the Third Battalion, the front lines were advanced 2000 yards to the ridge Mt. Della Stella–Lama di Sotto–Albiano–**Castelvecchio**.

During the day, the Second Battalion sent three patrols of platoon **strength to forge far north of Trebbio, Castelvecchio, and Albiano,** to determine enemy dispositions in the battalion zone preparatory to a probable advance by the battalion on the next morning.

The 365th Infantry, with its determined, well-coordinated and swift attack had achieved complete surprise and was able to reach initial objectives quickly. However, the German resistance became increasingly stubborn, because of the importance of Lama di Sotto Ridge. The enemy simply could not afford to permit the loss of that important position.

On 6 Feb, the Second Battalion, 365th Infantry attacked at 0645 with companies F and G abreast and Company E in reserve at Albiano. At 0850, Company G reached its objective on Hill 608, but Company F encountered fierce enemy resistance, resulting in heavy casualties. When the Company was about halfway to Lama di Sotto Ridge, Captain Bernard Yolles, the Company Commander, was killed, and the attack stalled. Company E with Captain William S.M. Banks, Jr. in command, was ordered to continue the mission of Company F and to seize the objective before dark. At 1600 Company E began moving up to pass through Company F and attacked through Company F at 1730. Company F was moved to Albiano as battalion reserve. Captain Banks led Company E in several hard-hitting assaults, and by 1945, it was on its objective and busied itself in consolidating its position.

At 1400, the First Battalion, less Company A, moved near Barga, to relieve the Third Battalion on 7 Feb.

At 1530, Company G was counter-attacked; it rejected it with considerable casualties to the Germans.

At 1615, Company K's platoon was counter-attacked by an estimated 30 man force, and this attack was driven off by small arms, machine gun, and artillery and mortar fire.

At 1815, Company I was counter-attacked by an estimated company, and this attack, too, was beaten off with heavy casualties to the enemy; the enemy troops advanced doggedly through the American artillery and mortar concentrations but the remnants were routed when the men of Company I rose from their fox holes and fought them hand-to-hand.

Immediately, Company C was sent to reinforce I Company.

During the afternoon of the 6th, the Third Battalion, 366th Infantry, less Company F, was attached to the 365th Infantry at Fornaci.

By the end of the day, the 365th Infantry had captured four PW's, and had suffered an estimated 58 casualties. Enemy counter-attacks, ranging from 20-30 men to a full company, had been successfully repulsed.

Enemy casualties were high.

Elements of the Second and Third Battalions were astride or near the Regimental Objectives — Lama di Sotto-Mt. Della Stella-Hill 906.

On 7 Feb, most of the day was spent in effecting the relief by the First Battalion. By 0800, Company C had relieved Company I, Company A had relieved Company K. The two relieved companies then moved to an assembly area near Barga. As Company B was relieving Company L, heavy enemy mortar and artillery fire descended on the positions, causing the relief to be delayed until after dark. By 2300, the First Battalion was firmly in positions previously held by the Third Battalion.

That same day, the 365th Infantry Command Post moved forward from Ghivizzano to Fornaci, and Second Battalion, 366th also assembled nearby.

Seventeen PW's were captured and 35 casualties were reported.

Shortly after midnight of 7-8 Feb, the German troops of the 386th

Grenadier Regiment began a series of fierce counter-attacks levelled at the First Battalion troops on the ridge. The first one, in company strength, came at 0100 and was repulsed with heavy casualties to the enemy, with the help of artillery fire. During the afternoon, Companies B and C received three counter-attacks, the third coming at 1715 by an estimated force of one battalion. The attacks came on three sides of the companies and they were finally forced from Lama and Mt. Della Stella, and withdrew about 500 yards to positions north of Sommocolonia. The withdrawal was made in good order, with the enemy continuing to suffer many casualties from small arms, machine gun, mortar and artillery fire.

At 0910, Company G was counter-attacked by an estimated enemy company. Artillery defensive fire aided in repulsing the attack, causing substantial enemy casualties.

Enemy pressure continued to increase on 9 Feb. At 0720 Company G was counter-attacked on the left flank and at 0810, Company E received counter-attacks on their front and left flank. After fierce fighting, by 0830, the counter-attack on Company G had been stopped and the attack on Company E had been slowed. At 1125, Company E was again counter-attacked, but by 1150 the enemy had been beaten off. At 1950, Company G successfully drove off another counter-attack.

On 8 and 9 Feb, ten enemy counter-attacks had been thrown against the 365th Infantry, and 75 casualties had been sustained, but heavy casualties were also inflicted on the enemy.

That night, the Regiment was ordered to re-capture and consolidate the Lama di Sotto Ridge.

At 0630 on 10 Feb, the 365th resolutely moved forward with three battalions abreast; the Third on the right, the First in the center, and the attached Second Battalion, 366th Infantry (minus Company F), on the left. The Second Battalion, 365th Infantry, was on the extreme left of the sector busily improving their positions.

The enemy was ready. Their defensive artillery and mortar fires was heavy and accurate, but the 365th Infantry troops forged ahead relentlessly. Company B seized Hill 906 and began to dig in. Company A was unsuccessful in attempting to retake Hill 1048, and after vicious fire fights, withdrew to Sommocolonia. Companies E and G, 366th Infantry, suffered heavy casualties in their advance and were stopped short of their objective.

The advance of Third Battalion, 365th Infantry slowed down near the end of the day due to savage resistance by enemy troops and heavy concentrations of artillery and mortar fire. After gaining more ground, they were ordered to pull back and at 2125, the Third Battalion occupied and began organizing on Mt. Della Stella.

At 1730 Company A launched its final unsuccessful attack to gain Hill 1048.

The following day the Germans continued to pound away at the lines. Company B fought off two counter-attacks before 0810, sustaining several casualties while scoring heavily against the enemy; at 1600, the Company was assaulted from the front and flank. The enemy was held off until 1835 at which time it was forced to withdraw to vicinity of Sommocolonia. At this point, Company I, which had been ordered up to aid Company B in holding Hill 906, was caught in the open and was subjected to heavy artillery, mortar and machine gun fire and was forced to halt. After re-organizing, Company I took up defensive positions on Trebbio ridge. At 1920, Company E received its eighth counter-attack which was driven off with small arms, machine gun and artillery and mortar fire.

It is ironic that the operation by the 365th Infantry and elements of the 366th Infantry in the Serchio was, on the whole, a well executed and extremely effective attack, but went relatively ignored because it was only intended as a diversion for the main effort near the coast.

Even though the Lama di Sotto Ridge remained in enemy hands, their hold on it was tenuous, and it continued to be subjected to attacks, strong patrol actions, and continuous artillery and heavy weapons' fire from the American forces.

As a result, outposts of the 365th Infantry had advanced about a mile and in general, the positions lost in December 26-28 German attack were retaken.

Although exposed to enemy observation throughout the sunlit days, and subjected continuously to accurate and heavy enemy artillery and mortar fire—which was never completely neutralized despite excellent American artillery support—the black Buffalo soldiers advanced steadily. Taking advantage of what cover they could find they slipped through draws and behind ridges to close with Germans and Italians and blasted them from their secure positions on the mountain tops with small arms, grenades, and machine guns. Once they occupied the enemy positions, they quickly consolidated them, and repelled at least twenty counter-attacks, some as large as an entire battalion. Several counter-attacks were repelled after hand-to-hand fighting only a few steps away from their positions.

Artillery and mortar support fire was excellent, and during some of the fighting "Rover Joe" Air Force planes delivered many telling blows on the enemy front line troops as well as enemy artillery positions and supply and communications installations.

There were countless instances of great courage and intelligent leadership by many of the Buffaloes—both white and black—of the 365th Infantry, as well as the black officers and enlisted men of the 366th Infantry.

A total of 288 prisoners were taken during the period, and one entire battalion, the Second Battalion, First Bersaglieri Regiment, Italia Division, were completely neutralized. Heavy casualties were also inflicted on the First and Second Battalions, of the 286th Regiment, 148 Division (German).

American Casualties

Wounded in Action	241 Enlisted Men	8 Officers
Killed in Action	52 Enlisted Men	1 Officer
Totals	293 Enlisted Men	9 Officers

The exact number of casualties suffered by the enemy was difficult to discern. However, some idea of the extent can be ascertained by some messages recorded in the S-1 Journal of messages from front line units.[6]

Time	Date	Messages
1015	4 Feb 45	Six–seven enemy personnel fired on 0912-0923. Effect Good Observed 35 enemy at Trippignano. Were fired at by Dixie Red from 1330 1405. Buildings hit and time fire used. Excellent effect.
1415	8 Feb 45	Company C receiving counter-attack, enemy being held off by artillery and mortar fire. Lama di Sotto being heavily shelled from north. Dixie Red will fire counter-battery.
0830	9 Feb 45	Counter-attack on G Company has been stopped with 10 enemy casualties. Counter-attack on E Company slowed down.
1027		E Company is being counter-attacked from Hill 461.
1613		Now have artillery on a probably mule train at 178071.
1658		Junior officer reports mule train and enemy personnel at 178071 also enemy personnel in Trippignano.
2035		Counter-attack beaten off. Casualties and damage unknown.
0813	11 Feb 45	Baker Company engaged in fire fight, at 1715 called for defensive fires which were fired and adjusted until 0750.
0927	11 Feb 45	Jerries seen wearing British uniforms, shot.
2128	11 Feb 45	Baker has closed in Sommocolonia at 2000 (Estimated they killed 20 Krauts).
2104	12 Feb 45	At 2000 George Company engaged with 60 mm mortars a combat patrol at 181067. Enemy machine gun with patrol was silenced.
1725	19 Feb 45	A party searching for an observation post saw 16 decomposing bodies of 16 German and 9 Poles and Italians outside a house vic 176063.

These messages add credence to the estimate of heavy casualties dealt to the enemy. They also underscore the determination and aggressiveness of the Buffalo soldiers in their unceasing effort to dislodge the strong enemy forces from their well defended, strongly fortified fixed positions.

While the diversion was winding to a close, the main effort was in progress on the other side of the mountains in the coastal area.

The Main Attack Begins — 8 February

The positions held by the enemy in the Serchio Valley and along the jagged Mt. Folgorito–Mt. Cauala Mountain Ridge, as well as the flat coastal plain, were among the most formidable defenses in the entire 200-mile-long Gothic Line. German loss of these positions would clear the way for American Fifth Army forces to capture the naval base of La Spezia, and then permit a wide open drive to key enemy installations in mid-northern Italy and the wide Po valley.

The enemy demonstrated just how important these positions were to them and how determined they were to repel any attempt to dislodge them, by their stubborn resistance against the Buffalo division in four days of bitter fighting 8-11 February 1945.

The American units attacked at 0600 all along the five mile front, moving straight forward towards their objectives. The early morning darkness blanketed the advance across the Initial Point and the Line of Departure (Jumping Off Point). However, by the time the troops drew closer to their objectives they came under cool and deadly scrutiny from enemy observers; these included soldiers on the mountain tops, as well as those sitting securely behind concrete and reinforced steel emplacements on the sides of the lower hills and close to the ground on the coastal flats.

A slight mist prevailed, with low scattered cloudiness and the haze still permitted visibility to six-eight miles in the mountains, and up to 12 miles in the coastal area.

On the skyline to the north, the Buffalo Soldiers could see the Castle Aghinolfi, ominous, threatening, sinister, towering above the battle area.

The 370th Infantry Attack on Strettoia Hills

The 370th was to attack over its narrow front (200-500 yards), in a column of battalions, with the Third Battalion leading the assault, followed closely by the Second Battalion; the First Battalion was held in reserve, to be committed only on Division order. These formations were intended to facilitate exploitation of any momentum gained by the leading battalion, in its assault on Hill "X" by having the Second Battalion drive through the Third Battalion and force the enemy from Hill "Y," then seize the high ground around Castle Aghinolfi. If initial success was achieved, the First Battalion was to be held in readiness to continue the forward thrust by passing through the Third Battalion to capture the high ground overlooking Montignoso.

As the 370th Infantry was advancing through the hills, another regimental strike force of volunteers, labeled the "Raiders" was to move up Highway One. The 60 enlisted men and three officers were supported by two tank companies, one from the 758th (light) Tank Battalion and the other from the 760th (medium) Tank Battalion. A tank destroyer platoon, a company from the division's 317th Engineer Battalion, and the Regiment's Anti-Tank Mine Platoon completed the make up of the force.

The "Raiders" had been carefully selected and had been in special training for two weeks. The intent was to take enemy attention away from the main attack of the 370th Infantry and to capture and control a portion of the Montignoso Road overlooking the Magro Canal west of Highway One.[7]

These hills to the immediate front of the 370th Infantry designated: "X," "Y" and "Z," and Aghinolfi, were part of the Strettoia mountain mass overlooking the town of Strettoia.

Hill "X," the lowest, was 450 feet high, and somewhat round, but it was ridged with a series of flat platforms of earth and rock rising each above the other. Hills "Y" and "Z" were similar in appearance, but were higher — 600 feet — and were beyond and looked down on Hill "X" from two sides, "Z" to the east and "Y" to the west.

All these hills were studded with a series of enemy strong-points, which included interlocking and mutually supporting steel and concrete fortifications for machine guns, mortars and observation posts. Barbed wire abounded throughout the hundreds of carefully planted mines covering all anticipated approaches.

The mountain leading to Castle Aghinolfi was particularly strongly fortified from its base to the four-foot thick mortar and stone fences which circled the Castle at different levels. Minefields, concrete and re-inforced steel bunkers and dugouts, inter-connected laterally and some accessible through man-high tunnels extending from the north side of the mountain, provided protection and flexibility of movement for the defenders. Heavy and light machine guns were placed so as to deliver devastating mutually supporting cross fire. These emplacements also hid artillery and mortar observation teams, who had an unobstructed view of the frontally advancing 370th Infantry and the Third Battalion, 366th Infantry, now advancing on the Coastal Plain, as well as the 371st Infantry, even now reaching for the dominating peaks of Cerreta Ridge only a few hundred yards to the east. Snipers abounded in single-man concrete pits all along the front.

The thick, centuries-old fences and walls around the massive castle were impervious to pounding by bombing from Allied planes, and all types and calibres of artillery and mortars. Here too, the barbed wire entanglements and extensive minefields, covered by trip-wires which released flares, bathing any attackers in brilliant light for several minutes, and simultaneously sending signals to previously sited mortars, machine guns, and artillery. These barriers blended into the mountain side to effectively channel any attacking force into the established fire lanes.

H-hour was 0600 on 8 February.

The attack was preceded by a tremendous artillery preparation by all 92nd Division and attached artillery batteries, amplified by all supporting infantry weapons, tanks, tank destroyers and planes. For ten minutes all fire was concentrated on previously identified or suspected enemy strong points, machine-gun, mortar, and artillery positions, observation posts and communications and transport installations. Chemical mortars and artillery smoke-shells pounded the immediate front of the advancing troops to cover the movement of the tanks and infantrymen towards the objectives.

When the earth-shattering artillery fire was lifted, the black infantrymen moved foward quietly through the grey dawn, silent and numbed by the sudden and ominous silence and their thoughts about the dangerous and formidable enemy lying in wait for them ahead.

By 0650, with engineers clearing the way through the mine fields under small arms and mortar fire, Company 1 and Company K had moved swiftly through the outer German defenses. By 0705 Company L was a half-mile into the hills but was temporarily held up by increasingly heavy machine gun and small arms fire; the Forward Observer with the company called down artillery and the battalion's mortars sang out, neutralizing the enemy machine guns and by 0930 the west half of Hill "X" was cleared of the enemy. In the heavy fighting, two machine guns were captured and several Germans were taken prisoner. The company dug in at once.

Company K, overcoming increasing heavy enemy resistance from small arms and automatic weapons fire, advanced to the right of and slightly behind Company L towards the top of Hill "Z." By 1093 they reached the objective, and began to dig in.

The advance of the leading companies of the Third Battalion was aided by heavy and accurate supporting fires by the artillery, coupled with bombing and strafing missions against enemy positions in the hills and on the distant coastal batteries at Punta Bianca.

At this juncture, Company I was ordered to pass through Company L and secure Hill "Y." By 1500, the objective was taken, the company capturing nine prisoners, destroying several machine gun positions, and inflicting heavy casualties on the enemy.

In one quick violent thrust, a group of the enemy was driven into one of the caves and fired on with bazookas when they refused to surrender.

By this time the entire defensive systems of the German defenders had become completely aroused and operative all along the fronts of all attacking units. The coastal gun batteries began to fire on all positions, and it is significant to note that, despite continuous attacks by Air Force bombers and fighters, these heavy calibre guns fired without interruption throughout the four days of the fighting. The same was true of enemy mortars and artillery, which was devastatingly accurate, heavy in volume and almost always timely, despite all counter battery efforts of the American artillery. As the battle progressed it became evident that the Intelligence Reports relative to that fact issued daily up the 8th were woefully inadequate. A special report subsequent to the operation admits[8]:

> Enemy artillery positions previously "inactive" were exposed. 21 active gun positions were located on the first day (8th) of the action.

Field Order #7, contains a Photo Interpretation Report dated 7 December 1944[9]:

> The information from this report is from aerial photographs taken between 15 Nov and 15 Dec 1944

and,

> Few new defenses have been noted.

This miscalculation proved to be a major cause of the difficulties that followed on that first day.

At 1600 Company I, in the midst of organizing its position on Hill "Y," was counter-attacked by an estimated 60–80 enemy troops; after vicious, close-in fighting, the enemy fled in disarray.

First Lieutenant John Madison, now in command of Company I, resolutely remained on the hill throughout the shelling, ready to fight to the death against the enemy counter-attack expected to follow.

Company K, on Hill "Z," was counter-attacked also and, despite valiant efforts was forced to withdraw to the lower portion of the hill. Here, they made their stand under heavy machine gun fire from both flanks. Throughout the four days, Company K stood fast against all enemy assaults.

Meanwhile, the Second Battalion had been ordered to occupy a position on Hill "Y" to the left of Company I. Company F had cleared Hill "X," and were fighting their way up to Hill "Y" just as Company I was in the midst of repelling the German counter-attack.

At 1730, forward observers of the 598th Field Artillery reported a "Shattering, inferno-like mortar barrage on the Company I position." Second Battalion reported[10]:

> At this time the Third Battalion received a tremendous barrage of mixed heavy mortar and artillery fire estimated to be between 400 and 500 rounds.

This thunderous barrage caused heavy casualties in Company I.

Two officers were wounded and the Company Commander was killed; many enlisted men also became casualties, and in the immediate terror and panic, many men began to leave the hill. A few withdrew to Hill "X," but many more scattered back to the original Line of Departure.

Companies F and G, of the Second Battalion reached Hill "Z" just in time to be hammered by the same barrage. Company F proceeded towards the objective, but came under heavy machine gun fire which pinned them down just as they arrived on Hill "Y."

Company G, meantime, discovered that due to the mortar barrage, the rear half of the company was completely disorganized, but 50–60 men remained on Hill "X."

Shortly after the barrage, Lieutenant Madison with the remnants of Company I, was ordered to withdraw. Company L was ordered to secure the eastern portion of the Hill, but as they advanced, they met some Company F and men from Companies I and L coming off the hill. In the confusion of continuing heavy machine gun, small arms, and mortar and artillery fire, Company L became disorganized and started off the hill.

By 2000, no 92nd Division troops were left on Hill "Y."

The Second Battalion, however, hung on stubbornly on Hill "X," despite their depleted ranks due to heavy casualties and disorganization among all units.

Company K was still intact on the eastern slope of Hill "X."

Companies G and F and part of Company E dug in on Hill "X" in an all-around defense. The enemy shelling never ceased, and caused many casualties from tree bursts. Lieutenant Miles, commanding Company F and Captain Thayer commanding Company G reported that they had run into mine fields on Hill "X," and on the reverse slope of Hill "Y," also causing many casualties.[11] Mines there were laid in no definite pattern, and that factor, coupled with the heavy shelling, made it difficult for the mine clearing units to do a good job of clearing the mines. The extensive mine fields caused great difficulties in evacuation of wounded and movement of supplies. Because of them, only one trail was cleared for use in moving up and down Hill "X," and this route was subjected to continuous shelling through the night, hampering the reorganization of men back into position.

Throughout the night, officers and non-commissioned officers worked at reorganizing the 370th Infantry units to be prepared to resume the attack on Hill "Y" at 0600 on the next day. For his courageous leadership that day and night, Lieutenant Aurelius Miles was awarded the Silver Star. The words of his citation portray vividly the action:

> Silver Star, Aurelius A. Miles, First Lieutenant, Infantry, U.S. Army, for gallantry in action on February 1945, in Italy. The enemy launched a counter-attack against Lieutenant Miles' Company as it moved into a new position on a hill under cover of darkness. The pressure of the hostile at-attack forced his company to withdraw and brought much confusion to 5 other companies which then occupied the hill. Lieutenant Miles, realizing the situation, gathered all the men he could see and led them under withering enemy fire and over heavily mined terrain to defensive positions along the base of the hill. All night he personally checked the positions and re-arranged the lines. During the next day, the constantly exposed himself in keeping control of his sector of the hill. He left the safety of his fox hole during an artillery barrage to personally supervise the evacuation of two casualties and maintained his command post in a fox-hole, 20 yards from the front line until he was wounded.

During the day, the Raiders and their supporting armor met with little success in the diversion action down Highway #1.[12] The engineers and a mine platoon were to clear three obstacles on the highway north of Querceta. Porta was to have been shelled, then reduced by tanks and tank destroyers beginning at 0500. After completion of the operation during which the Raiders were to provide local security, they were to wipe out all resistance in vicinity of Porta. Supporting medium tanks would then be mounted for the drive to the Montignoso Canal.

A tank was knocked out near the first by-pass. After some delay the force proceeded up Highway #1. However, the now fully aroused enemy stopped them short of Porta with heavy machine gun and small arms fire from their front and from protected positions on the forward slope of Hill "X." The enemy kept them pinned down most of the day under this fire, augmented by artillery and mortar fire.

The 371st Reaches for the Higher Ground

At H-hour, the 371st Infantry crossed the Line of Departure, on the right, aiming for the high ground of Mt. Cerretta and Mt. Folgorito, where some of the crests along the rugged ridge rise to 4500–5000 feet. The First and Second Battalions advanced abreast; the Third Battalion waited in reserve near Pozzi while K Company protected the right flank.

The terrain and the German defenses along the Mt. Folgorito Ridge were among the most formidable in the Gothic Line. Towering Mt. Folgorito peak itself was over 4500 feet high, providing visual observation over the entire coastal plain, and all the hills, valleys and draws in the 370th Infantry Zone; artillery and mortar observers from its high point could look almost straight down at every mountain, every road or trail, every valley, and ravine or draw leading to objectives in front of the 371st Infantry.

The first of the mountain barriers along the Ridge was Mt. Cauala, less than a mile northeast of the lower hills of the Strettoia mass, where the 370th Infantry was fighting valiantly. Mt. Cauala was 1200 feet high, and looked down upon the village of Seravezza, as well as all approaches to it. It was rocky and rugged and bare of cover except for some occasional shrubs and small trees. Any trails were narrow and winding and well identified and defended by the enemy. ROCKY RIDGE, so named by the Buffalo Soldiers, was a sort of platform about 400–500 feet almost straight up on the south and eastern side of Mt. Cauala. ROCKY RIDGE was exceptionally well-defended.

Rising successively higher, towards Mt. Folgorito were several sharp-topped mountains, code named MAINE, FLORIDA, GEORGIA, and, approaching Mt. Ceretta, three connected peaks called OHIO 1, 2, and 3.

In addition to the advantage provided by the terrain, the Germans had built an excellent system of fortifications all along the Ridge line. Weapons of all kinds—mortars, machine guns, cannon, anti-tank guns—were concealed and protected by concrete and steel bunkers or were emplaced in positions blasted out of the solid rock walls of the mountains.

Enemy bunkers were very elaborate, well furnished and comfortable. Revetments and extensive digging made them impervious to direct artillery and mortar fire, and all but the most accurate of direct tank fire. In one instance the bunker proper was reached by way of a 20-foot tunnel.

All defensive positions were mutually supporting and connected by lateral trails, trenches, or tunnels. In all firing positions, the weapons had been sited and prepared to fire on *any* targets approaching them. Barbed wire was cleverly placed throughout, with warning devices attached, and extensive minefields were carefully planted before all avenues of approach. In some cases the mines were placed haphazardly, but they always restricted movement and maneuver. Tank barriers and demolitions impeded and channeled the movement of tanks and motorized units below.

By the time the 10-minute preparation by the 599th Field Artillery Battalion and other supporting weapons was completed, the First Battalion was advancing towards MAINE, its first objective; the Second Battalion moved on ROCKY RIDGE, on the left of the zone.

February Attack in Coastal Sector

At 0615 reports indicated that 370th Infantry elements, to the left, were receiving automatic weapons fire from OHIO 1. The 4.2 Chemical Mortars, augmented by 75 mm howitzers, shifted their fire and delivered smoke and high explosive shelling on that point.

Assaulting units of the First Battalion moved quickly up the vertical approaches to MAINE, overpowering enemy resistance quickly. Other units struck at FLORIDA and GEORGIA, and by 0855, Company A had a platoon near the peak of GEORGIA, but was held up by a mine field, and small arms and machine gun. The troops tried to work their way out of the minefield, while fighting off snipers and the steady enemy fire from Germans on the hill, and the OHIO hill. Finally, at about 1015 Company A, now under intense heavy artillery and mortar fire, moved back slightly to the northeast edge of a wooded area. Company B, by this time had advanced to a point 100 yards north of the woods, while Company C was passing around the mountain to the left of Company B; all three companies now were on GEORGIA, near the top by 1040.

The Second Battalion attacked formidable, well-defined ROCKY RIDGE with two companies abreast. Company E, with Captain Winston D. Wetlaufer in command, was on the left and Company G led by Captain William E. Cooke, was on the right, while Company F, led by Captain Edmund Essholm, was in reserve.

The assaulting companies made steady progress, seizing their initial objectives by 1000 hours despite finding the zone heavily mined, and overcoming small arms, machine gun fire as well as increasing and accurate mortar fire. Company E, shortly after jumping off, discovered it was in the midst of an extensive minefield in which the mines had been laid in a haphazard, non-patterned manner. Almost immediately the stalled company became the object of heavy concentrations of artillery and mortar fire, and small arms, machine gun and sniper fire, causing many casualties. Nevertheless, the Buffalo Soldiers began clearing paths and maneuvering through the minefield, meanwhile fighting off several enemy attacks, and continued their advance.

Shortly after 0800 another incident occurred which adversely affected the events of that first day and which blunted the momentum of the 371st Infantry attack, at the very beginning. "Rover Joe" was called to bomb and strafe OHIO 1 and 2, in the First Battalion Zone. Smoke was accurately placed on the designated targets, but instead the planes bombed and strafed Company G as it was struggling up the steep sides of ROCKY RIDGE on Mt. Cauala, in the face of heavy enemy opposition. A number of casualties resulted, included the company commander. Two enlisted men were killed.

The misguided air attack, in full view of the men of the 370th Infantry, fighting their way up the Strettoia Hills and those of the 370st Infantry, just beginning to assault their objectives along Folgorito Ridge, aroused feelings of frustration and animosity among them that remained throughout the rest of the Italian Campaign. The very sight of comrades killed and wounded because of a mistake by their own planes left deep emotional scars.

The immediate result was panic and some disorganization; however, Company F was committed and moved in to maintain the momentum of the attack and to cover the reorganization of Company G. Company F, fighting desperately and with great determination, captured twenty-five prisoners, much enemy arms and equipment, and inflicted heavy casualties—dead and wounded—on the enemy.

Shortly after 1030, enemy resistance increased all along the lines, and the tempo of enemy artillery and mortar fire increased notably, and the advance of the Second Battalion was slowed.

Company E, meanwhile, was intact, and still clearing its way out of minefields and fighting enemy off defenders simultaneously. Heavy enemy small arms fire was being received on its left flank.

With its units holding their own and clinging tenaciously to positions near the summits of their objectives, and with enemy resistance increasing, the Regimental Commander halted the advance to permit reorganization all along the line. After a brief respite, he ordered a resumption of the attack at 1400. Heavy artillery and mortar concentrations were dropped on MAINE, FLORIDA, GEORGIA, and OHIO 1, and 2, and air strikes hit those and rear objectives. At 1400, all units resumed the advance. At 1410 two red flares went up on GEORGIA (German signal: "Being Attacked").

By this time, heavy enemy artillery fire was falling on MAINE. The Regimental Advanced observation post observed Buffalo Soldiers destroying an enemy machine gun position and another unit throwing TNT into an enemy bunker while under the heavy fire.

Shortly thereafter, heavy enemy artillery and mortar fire was falling on all other positions in the First Battalion zone. Machine gun fire was being received by Buffalo troops on one hill from enemy forces on other hills. The enemy supporting fires and the resistance of front-line elements was so great that the battalion's attack was again halted.

At 1350, Company E had cleared two minefields and was again moving forward. Company G, again in action, moved to the northeast to contact First Battalion elements and to resume the advance.

At 1425, Company E ran into another minefield and was receiving heavy machine gun fire from the upper reaches of ROCKY RIDGE. The company again held its ground, repelled a counter-attack, and continued to advance. The citation for the Silver Star award to Captain Wetlaufer tells the story of the heroic action of Company E on that day.

> In personally leading his company in an attack on a heavily fortified position, Captain Wetlaufer came under heavy enemy artillery, mortar and machine gun fire which failed to stop his advance. Despite mounting casualties he maneuvered his company through a dense minefield and captured his objective after personally directing the assault platoon in the removal of mines. When the enemy later launched a determined counter-attack, Captain Wetlaufer continually exposed himself to enemy fire in repulsing the attack. He captured eight enemy soldiers, killed and wounded many more, and withdrew only when so ordered.

Captain Wetlaufer had previously received the Bronze Star for heroic achievement in action on 4, 9, and 11 January.

Throughout the rest of the afternoon, it became evident that ROCKY RIDGE and GEORGIA were exceptionally strong points in the enemy defense line, and supporting enemy artillery, mortar, machine gun, and sniper fire was so coordinated as to ensure maximum fire power on call on our forward positions on these strong points. Despite continous pressure by attacking elements, and heavy and accurate American artillery and mortar fire on these mountain bastions, and bombing and strafing by planes, the Buffaloes were unable to dislodge the Germans completely.

At 1800 all elements were ordered to dig in and plan to continue the attack at 1630 the next morning with GEORGIA and OHIO 1 as the objectives.

At 1912, redoubtable Company E, still fighting out of minefields, reported capturing two more, killing nine, and taking two machine guns.

During the first day, the 371st lost some of its finest officers and enlisted men. One, Lieutenant Theodore O. Smith, was awarded an Oak Leaf Cluster to the Silver Star for his action on that day:

> Lieutenant Smith was the leader of a squad committed to assist in taking his company's initial objective. Passing through one platoon which had suffered numerous casualties, he seized his objective under heavy enemy artillery and machine gun fire. Using the balance of his platoon he then captured nine enemy soldiers from well fortified positions which commanded the ridge of approach. Still under increasing enemy fire, Lieutenant Smith then used another squad to capture a second enemy position which yielded numerous small arms threatening the entire left flank of the company's objective. His intrepid determination in his desire to close with the enemy and destroy him exemplified the highest gallantry of the American soldier.

Lieutenant Smith was revered by his men and was widely known throughout the Buffalo Division. He had won his first Silver Star for gallantry in action on January 11, 1945. His intelligence and courage are illuminated in the words of that citation:

> Lieutenant Smith led a patrol on a mission to capture enemy prisoners. At daybreak he moved his patrol forward so effectively, through in full view of the enemy and on mined terrain, that he was able to surprise and capture an enemy sentry. Lieutenant Smith then entered an enemy-held house where he captured an unattended machine gun. The enemy in the house, alerted by the noise of the patrol, rushed toward their gun positions, throwing hand grenades at the patrol. The patrol quickly killed all of the enemy with hand grenades and sub-machine gun fire. Then, as hostile mortar and machine gun fire opened up outside the house, Lieutenant Smith withdrew all his men without a casualty.

His loss on that first day of battle was sorely felt by his comrades.

The 366th—Ordeal on the Plains

Task Force #1 attacked in the coastal sector at the same time the 370th and 371st reached for the hills and mountains to the east. From the very beginning it became obvious that the German defense plan was to deny the mountain positions to the Americans, and then concentrate maximum pressure on the troops struggling to advance across the marshy, treacherous and heavily defended coastal area.

One of the many mistakes in the plan by General Almond's staff quickly became clear and glaring to junior officers. It was in attacking frontally and simultaneously along the three fronts, instead of utilizing sufficient forces to first rout the Germans from their mountain defenses, and occupy and hold them.

It became evident quickly that as long as the Germans controlled the mountains, it would be *impossible* for our forces to drive them from their coastal positions. It should not have come as a surprise that the most determined resistance developed in that coastal sector. Arrayed against them were Italian troops and German troops from the 148 Fusilier Battalion, supported by dozens of previously inactive or unknown enemy artillery batteries, self-propelled guns (88 mm) and mortars and, most devastating of all, several coastal batteries of heavy, long range guns emplaced in the rocky cliffs at Punta Bianca.

The crushing effect of these guns on the attack along the coast was not even mentioned in General Truscott's subsequent negative report.[13] Nor did General Almond or his staff in their subsequent public evaluations truly assess the effect they had on the outcome of the operation. No mention of them has ever been made in any media references either.

However, later, in planning for the April 1945 offensive, General Almond states in a letter to General Truscott, subject, "Air Bombardment of Coastal Guns."[14]

1. The Coastal batteries on Punta Bianca are among the enemy's chief harassing agencies in the coastal sector, and is one of the threats against our advance—These guns are accurately registered on all key points along the coast and have proven their ability to deliver extremely effective fire on our positions without fear of retaliation. the positions are—beyond the maximum range of the available artillery—have been attacked repeatedly by light bombers without any apparent effect.
2. It is urgently requested that these guns be attacked by Heavy and Medium Bombardment aviation beginning 1 April 1945, and that this form of attack be continued until the batteries are put out of action.
3. These guns present a serious threat to any contemplated operation. *In the recent operations of 8-11 February, these guns caused heavy casualties among our troops in the sector just North of F. la Foce (Cinquale Canal)* (underlined by author). They are causing damage to front line positions now.

A report attached to General Almond's letter, by the acting chief of staff of the 92nd Division confirmed that these guns had conducted registrations on the outskirts of Massa and Carrara, and on all the main road systems and on critical bridge sites from Canale Magro to Marina Di Carrara. The report describes the guns:

> The guns are strongly emplaced and well protected.
>
> Two guns, 152 mm, are two towers of a former naval cruiser, and have regular revolving turrets. These towers are located in a tunnel which is approximately 20 mm west of a large white house.
>
> Four guns, 152 mm, are in very heavy concrete bunkers connected by tunnels.
>
> Four guns, 152 mm are emplaced in a bluff.
>
> These guns are protected by mines, light and heavy anti-aircraft guns, wire, and emplaced machine guns, and it is not believed that raids on the positions could be successful.

He too, admitted the effectiveness of these guns on the action of 8–11 February:

> Many diver-bomber missions have failed to impair the effectiveness of these guns as was particularly evident during the action of 8-11 February, *when their fire was singularly effective* (underlined by author). These guns are causing damage to our front lines—now, and if not destroyed, will cause damage to any advance we make. The registration ... and can affect any advance on our part seriously.

These guns, designed for coastal defense against sea attack by naval elements against the once-great Italian Naval Base of La Specia, were used against the black foot soldiers of the 366th Infantry, and were *never* silenced during the four days of the battle. To many of the survivors the continuous fire from these guns was one of the most terrifying and destructive factors in the enemy's defense.

Said Lieutenant Dennette Harrod, 366th Infantry[15]:

> The sound of gunfire from Punta Bianca never ceased and the sound and the sight of the heavy shells falling and exploding among us was terrifying, but we stayed there until ordered back.

Even effective fire support from Allied Naval Forces was nullified in this attack because destroyers had to stay over 30,000 yards from these coastal defense guns, which out-ranged them.[16] As a result, the enemy ground forces were able to move reinforcements and mount counter-attacks using the coastal roads quite freely.

In addition to these defenses the terrain along the coast lent itself to maximum defense capabilities, which were expertly exploited by the Germans. Dozens of natural canals, and creeks, and man-made drainage and irrigation ditches criss-crossed the sector, generally running parallel to the front lines. As a result, inland from the wet, sandy beach, to the hills in the 370th Zone, the ground was soft and mushy, creating problems for tanks and other vehicles to maneuver, except on the two north-south hard roads. Thousands of mines were laid on roads, trails, paths, ditches and other routes of advance making it necessary, when these could not be removed, for attacking units to attempt to select alternate routes. All such routes of approach had been anticipated and were covered by previously registered artillery, mortars, and machine guns, as well as the coastal guns at Punta Bianca. The effect was to literally force the attacking troops to advance directly into areas where most effective and destructive firepower could be brought to bear against them, day or night.

Enemy strong points were strategically located and offered maximum - protection for the occupants. Inter-connected concrete bunkers and pill boxes, built close to the ground, sometimes containing 10-20 men, were not only impervious to artillery and mortar fire, but some were so well camouflaged that they could not be seen from as close as 20 feet away. Many were not even revealed in the intelligence air photos produced for the division.

Enemy snipers were in emplacements, dug-outs, and in many locations along the narrow front and were active throughout the three day operation.

The beaches were heavily mined even out beyond the surf and up to the coastal road, and were under constant shelling and long range machine gun fire.

The 317th Engineer Battalion's companies, assigned to each of the three attacking forces, attempted, always under enemy fire, to remove and clear routes through the thousands of mines, but it would appear that the task was too massive for them alone.

On the night of 6-7 February, a platoon of engineers glided stealthily along the beach to clear mines from a wide lane to the sea for the tanks to be able to move up past the mouth of the Cinquale Canal. On the following night, to make double sure the lane was clear, a different platoon of engineers re-checked the route for mines and declared the path clear.

On the morning of 8 February just as the 370th and 371st Infantry were moving up, on the right, Task Force 1, under command of Lieutenant Colonel Edward Rowny, the commanding officer of the division's 317th Engineer Combat Battalion, stood poised and ready to move. The infantry strike force was the Third Battalion, 366th Infantry, commanded by black Major Willis D. Polk; supporting units were the 27th Armored Field Artillery Battalion (less Company C), of the First Armored Division; Company C, 760th Tank Battalion; First Platoon, Company B of the 701st Tank Destroyer Battalion; the First Platoon, of Company A, 984th Chemical Mortar Battalion; and the First Platoon, Company B, of the 317th Engineer Combat Battalion.

The plan called for infantry and engineers, mounted on medium tanks, to move forward along the sea's edge and across the mouth of the knee-deep, 90-foot wide Cinquale Canal, under cover of the artillery preparation. Once past the Canal, the troops were to dismount, with the engineers proceeding to clear mine fields and other obstacles ahead of the tanks, and the infantry to fan out under supporting fire of the tanks, to protect the engineers. Then the tanks, closely followed by the foot soldiers, were to forge ahead and lead the attack towards Montignosa. Meanwhile the Tank Destroyer Battalion was to deliver fire when needed from positions on the south side of the Canal against flank attacks or enemy crossing attempts.

At 0545 the 27th Field Artillery Battalion began firing its thunderous concentrations, muffling the roar of tank engines as they moved along the shore of the sea, around the mouth of the Canal and, mounted by troops from Company L, 366th Infantry, and engineers.

At 0555, the weight and din of the other artillery batteries and all other supporting weapons was added to that of the 27th Field Artillery Battalion, as they opened fire on all known or suspected enemy close-in and long range positions and observation points. As the 10-minute preparation wound down to a close, the chemical mortars and the artillery dumped smoke shells all along the front to mask the forward movement of the Third Battalion soldiers; and, as they advanced, artillery fire was dropped on machine gun positions, located and reported by artillery Forward Observers moving along with the infantry.

The tanks, with Company L and the engineers aboard, moved up the beach and around the mouth of the Canal as planned and turned inland at 0730, at a point about 500 yards north of the Cinquale Canal.

However, difficulties were developing and mounting quickly.

The Task Force Commander reported that his command force of ten persons followed the first wave across the Canal, and he noted that the job of clearing mines in the gap to the sea had been done well by the engineers on the nights of 6 and 7 February.[17] However two of the tanks were disabled right at the Canal mouth; one had hit a mine and the other was drowned out in the Canal waters. All the other tanks had continued forward, however. These two tanks, although disabled, continued to fire covering fire for troops moving across the canal throughout the day.

By 0700 the enemy reaction to the attack began to accelerate. Heavy artillery and mortar fire began to fall on the advancing elements, and on canal crossing points and machine gun, automatic weapons, and sniper fire signalled the beginning of determined resistance by the well-entrenched enemy. The coastal batteries at Punta Bianca began to fire all along the front, and several shells landed on the mouth of the canal. Colonel Rowny reported[18]:

> The first one hit squarely in the middle of my little command group and when I looked around there were only two others who had not been hit. The shell had killed seven. The entire mouth of the canal appeared to turn red with blood.

By this time (1000), the heavy artillery and mortar fire had cut the wire lines in many places and radio communication facilities had been seriously damaged, causing tenuous problems in contact and control.

In only a short time, six more tanks were lost because of mines as they began to turn inward toward the coastal road running north-south, west of Highway 1. Artillery, mortar and small arms and machine gun fire added to the difficulties. By 0820, elements of Company L, advancing aggressively through the heavy fire, reached its objective near the Magro Canal. Company I, at the same time, was reaching forward for its position in the line.

By 0930 all the forces committed, including the Task Force Commander and his group, had crossed and were involved in heavy fighting north of the Cinquale Canal.

By 1000, eight of the ten tanks involved in the crossing had been disabled. They blocked the lanes which had been cleared by the engineers and this necessitated the clearing of mines for a by-pass.

By this time, too, the thoroughly aroused enemy was delivering heavy and accurate artillery and mortar fire on all elements of the attacking force all along the area of advance. Despite the artillery concentrations fired earlier on observed enemy machine gun positions, the Buffalo infantrymen found themselves receiving heavy and accurate machine gun, and automatic weapons and small arms fire from untouched and cleverly concealed, mutually supporting strong points. Added to the fire was the continuous, devastating, and accurate shelling from the coastal guns at Punta Bianca. Snipers, too, began their pesky and deadly tasks, with demoralizing effect.

As the tanks halted, and the engineers dismounted and began clearing mines for the by-pass, they came under the heavy fire, suffering heavy casualties. Two tanks managed to turn off of the beach area, one reaching a point some 25 yards away, and the other only 15 yards. The task force commander describes the situation vividly[19]:

> The enemy had brought small arms fire on the point of break-through, and I noticed a half-dozen engineer soldiers laying dead or wounded at this point. Artillery and mortar fire were falling on the dispersed tanks and it was obvious that their exposed position was the worst possible place they could be.

Many of the infantrymen and engineers had dismounted and were trying to dig-in around the tanks. Lieutenant Colonel Rowny says[20]:

> I gathered together a handful of engineers and had them prod for mines with bayonets. Then I instructed the commander of the second tank to try to pass the first tank. It worked. We now had one disabled tank — 25 yards in from the beach, and a good one about 60 yards from the beach.

During the next half hour, ten dead and about thirty wounded men were moved away from the cleared lane and the view of the troops, and the Buffalo Soldiers began to again move forward.

By this time, none of the tanks was moving; the hard-pressed infantry, who were trying to fight their way inland, found themselves having to do so without the promised close tank support which was considered so vital to the success of the mission. However, despite their immobility now and throughout the four days of the operation, many of the tank crews remained with their stationary iron monsters and delivered telling artillery fire on close-in targets identified for them and coordinated their machine gun fire to aid in breaking up several enemy counter-attacks, and to support local small unit attacks by the Infantry and engineers.

Company L, commanded by Captain Wejay S. Bundara, made good progress as he pushed forward the First Platoon, the Weapons Platoon and Company Headquarters close to the battalion objective and began to organize a defensive position just south of the Magro Canal. Company I, commanded by First Lieutenant Melvin Walker (earlier winner of a Silver Star for heroism in January) was supposed to pass through positions occupied by Company L and place its eastern-most elements about 700 yards inland. However, Company I, in its bold advance across open and exposed terrain was caught in heavy artillery and mortar concentration and their advance to their objective was delayed. Some elements of Company I moved in on the right of Company L and some, under the company commander, moved to its left. Casualties in both attacking companies were heavy during the advance.

Company K, also subjected to heavy artillery and mortar fire, moved east and began to organize a position behind Companies I and L, about 350 yards north of the Cinquale Canal.

First Lieutenant Dennette Harrod, commanding the First Platoon, Company I, describes the furious action of that day[21]:

> The tanks had stopped on the beach, some hit by artillery, some knocked out by mines. Heavy shells from Punta Bianca and La Spezia were falling on us all over the area. I don't know how we did it, but we kept moving up, through all that shelling and mortar and machine gun fire, losing killed and wounded every step of the way. We had advanced about 400 yards beyond the Canal, when I got hit in both legs by artillery shell fragments, and I went down. Company L had about 50 prisoners lined up against a farm house. I don't know how I came out of it alive. Lieutenant Walker (commanding officer of L Company) was also wounded about the same time and was carried out. The fire from Punta Bianca came at us all morning.

First Lieutenant John T. Letts, acting S-2, was also seriously wounded, and the battalion commander, Major Willis D. Polk and his S-3, Captain George Welch were both killed. The words of the citation for the Silver Star reflect the inspiring leadership and courage of Major Polk:

> Major Polk was in command of an infantry battalion participating in a task force operation of infantry, tanks, and engineers in an offensive against the enemy. During the planning of the attack he displayed great

initiative and zeal, and had his men in a high state of willingness to close with the enemy before jump-off time. Shortly after launching of the attack the battalion sector was subjected to intense enemy artillery and mortar fire. Major Polk then personally went out to encourage the troops and while doing this was hit by artillery fragments. Despite his wounds, he refused to be evacuated, and remained with his troops. As he personally led them toward their objective, he was hit and killed by an enemy sniper.

Captain Raymond A. Diggs, Executive Officer of the Third Battalion, was ordered forward, took command and after making a quick estimate of the situation he ordered all units to continue the advance. The attack was immediately accelerated under his inspiring leadership, as is confirmed in the citation for the Silver Star awarded him:

> Captain Diggs was acting Executive Officer of an infantry battalion that was part of a task force of infantry, armor, and engineers. When the battalion commander and S-2 were killed, Captain Diggs, without a supporting staff, assumed command of the battalion. Under pressure of vigorous enemy counter-attack he rallied his company into defensive groups that repelled the enemy and subsequently moved off offensively.

At about 1030, the enemy launched a strong counter-attack straight down the beach where the tanks of the 760th Tank Battalion sat stranded like beached whales. The Tank Commander, however, called for artillery fire, which in a matter of moments, was falling directly on the advancing enemy, and the tanks raked their front ranks with devastating machine gun fire at point blank range.

Meanwhile, First Lieutenant Thomas Johnson, of the 317th Engineer Combat Battalion, with 25–30 men had established and organized a strong point on a hump overlooking the beach and delivered devastating small arms and automatic weapons fire into the flanks of the enemy. The enemy suffered heavy casualties and the remnants fled in complete panic.

Efforts to move tanks and foot troops inland into a wooded area continued and by 1500 most of Companies I, K, and M were into positions in the woods.

At 1700, Captain Diggs ordered Company B to organize a defensive position to the left of Company L from the east to the outer Coastal Road using its First and Second Platoons, and to send the Third and Fourth Platoons to protect the battalion forward command post. Despite the disorganization caused by the shelling, and many casualties, Company B managed to establish the line as ordered.

Several small counter-attacks were launched by the enemy during the day, and were repulsed by Companies L and I, and other elements of Task Force One. The night of 8-9 February brought three counter-attacks, each succeeding attack increasing in force and intensity. Shortly after dark, enemy flares appeared above the frontline area, immersing the east-west road and buildings in persistent bright light. A strong force firing "burp" guns swept forward towards the sea. Protected from enemy bazooka fire by 366th infantrymen dug in about 75 yards in front of it, the tank farthest east opened fire with cannon and machine gun fire; the combined tank and small arms and machine gun fire from the infantry repelled the counter-attack with heavy casualties to the enemy.

Two hours later, another strong counter-attack was launched by the enemy and it was repulsed, but not before they had advanced past the battalion command post.

The third counter-attack found the enemy advancing all the way to the beach with desperate fighting in the darkness with small arms, automatic weapons and hand grenades taking their toll of the enemy.

By 0400, the battalion command post represented the east limit of the Task Force One line.

Throughout this first day of fighting, the Engineers valiantly went about their functions under accurate and heavy artillery, mortar, small arms and machine gun fire, suffering many casualties in the process. It became necessary several times, to operate as infantrymen to repel counter-attacks in their immediate sectors, and to seek out and eliminate snipers. Their road clearing units, the bridge building units, mine clearing details and units removing obstacles, were constantly interrupted in their efforts by the heavy enemy fire.

At 1115, efforts were made to operate an infantry support raft across the Cinquale Canal near a demolished inner coast bridge. Heavy, observed mortar fire directly on the site prevented construction of this raft. All day, the beginning of any attempt to build it brought an immediate reaction from enemy mortars, artillery, and machine gun fire.

In attempting to clear a path for tanks across the beach from the surf to the woods, difficulty was encountered in locating mines, and the task was made much more difficult as tank after tank ground to a halt and the engineers had to seek cover as best they could from the heavy fire rained upon them in their exposed position on the beach.

Attempts to clear the lateral road from the outer coast road to the inner coast road was stalled when the beleaguered infantry was unable to clear out all snipers firing on the engineer mine party.

That night, at 2130 IV Corps ordered its 337th Engineer Battalion (IV Corps) to construct a pneumatic treadway bridge across the Cinquale Canal at the inner coast road. Commencing at midnight, Company B, 317th Engineers, moved the bridge equipment to the site. The 337th were made into "true believers," because at 0235, the S-3 of the 337th Engineers reported that his unit had been driven from the site by heavy mortar fire, and that construction of a bridge under existing conditions was impossible. The Chief of Staff was immediately notified.[22]

During the day the entire 317th Engineer Battalion was in action in the Coastal Sector, leaving the 365th Infantry Regiment and the Second Battalion, 366th Infantry with no engineer support in the Serchio Valley. Engineer elements removed mines and cleared jeep supply roads on the south slopes of Mt. Cauala for the 371st Infantry. Company A, attached to the

370th Infantry and working behind the Ranger Company opened and swept Highway 1, at times in clear view of the enemy. They repaired a crater to open the way for tanks of the 760th Tank Battalion to pass. When enemy resistance increased, the engineers and the Ranger Company were pinned down by small arms and machine gun fire coming from the high ground on the forward slope of Hill "X," east of Highway I. A tank was disabled by a mine, and the force was unable to move for several hours. The company commander of Company A remained in contact with the 370th Infantry and fought *as infantry* until recalled later that day. Elements of A Company also breached mine-fields and barbed-wire entanglements on Hills "X" and "Y" and "Z."

Several awards for gallantry were awarded members of the 317th Engineers for their deeds on that first day of the attack:

> Second Lieutenant Warren B. Stevens' platoon was pinned down in an advance area by intense enemy mortar fire and snipers. Aware of the fact that he and his men would have to stay in this position all day, Lieutenant Stevens deliberately exposed himself to draw fire that would disclose the exact location of the snipers. He then directed rifle and grenade fire on the hostile position until the snipers were silenced.

The Silver Star citation for Private John Q. Mitchell pinpoints the dangers and difficulties engineers encountered in accomplishing their mission.

> Private Mitchell, a Combat Engineer attached to a rifle company, was assigned the mission of blowing hostile barbed-wire entanglements that impeded the company's assault. Under withering small arms fire, he crawled to the wire, placed his bangalores and blew the entanglements. Additional enemy machine gun and sniper fire then held up the infantry assault by pinning down the Company Commander. Private Mitchell spotted the sniper's position, moved to a more advantageous point, and killed the enemy soldier. From that position, he spotted a machine gun nest, and, wounding the enemy gunner with his first shot, he then rushed the position and captured the enemy. The machine gun and the sniper thus silenced, the infantry was enabled to advance.

All other Task Force One positions known to the enemy and, approaches to them, continued under heavy artillery and mortar fire even during this night. Constant shelling of the Cinquale Canal, particularly at the crossing point near the beach, disrupted all normal supply functions. With no bridge available supplies had to be carried by men across the canal and they, being under direct observation from high points on the mountains, were immediately fired upon by all types of enemy weapons. Machine gun fire played along the length of the Canal, constantly further interrupting supply functions. Most units had to do without critical supplies such as ammunition, water and food on the first day. Some attempts were made to press tanks into service to transport men and supplies across the Canal, with some success.

North of the canal, as previously stated, extensively laid minefields limited tank movement; mines were laid at different depths and many times, after several tanks had passed over a route, one of them following would hit a mine.

It was almost impossible to keep wire lines intact and operative due to continual breaks by the constant shelling, and the harrassing fire delivered by the enemy on wire crews working in the open. Major Richard G. Tindall, Division Signal Officer, was sent forward to discover a means of getting the wire in and keeping it in. Officers and men questioned later were of the opinion that he and others from Division Headquarters did not believe it was as bad as it really was. He insisted on moving forward along the beach in his vehicle and was killed instantly by an artillery shell burst.

Excerpts from the Division G-2 Periodic Report for the period from 1200 on 8 Feb to 1200 on 9 Feb give stark testimony to the vicious nature of the fighting by our troops in the Coastal Sector, and to the heavy continuous enemy artillery concentration fired on our forces during the period[23]:

> Five short-lived, local counter-attacks were successfully broken up by our defensive artillery [with the help of infantry machine gun, small arms, and grenade and mortar fire].
>
> At 1420 the enemy was repulsed on Strettoia.
>
> An undetermined number of type of tanks were reported—Porta this morning.
>
> In the afternoon, 325 rounds of enemy artillery landed between Forte dei Marmi and the Cinquale Canal with the most intense concentrations around the mouth of the Canal. During the night, 99 more rounds of artillery fell north of the Canal.

This heavy and accurate volume of artillery fire from all calibres of guns was augmented by extremely heavy and accurate fire from enemy mortars, tanks and machine guns, all falling on the front-line elements of the Buffalo Soldiers struggling to advance through a maze of hundreds of mines.

The Second Day of Battle—9 February

The weather, combined with the formidable terrain and the increasingly stubborn German resistance presented more discouraging problems for the American Forces on this second day of battle.

The bad weather prevented the operation of aircraft and the loss of this support was sorely felt by all commanders. Also, although the Division artillery continued to support the attack, very poor visibility hampered observation from both ground observation posts and air observation posts.[24]

The night of 8-9 February was a night of travail for the 370th

Infantry. During the day the devastating enemy artillery, mortar, and machine gun fire and repeated counter-attacks had finally driven the companies off Hill "Y" and part of Hill "X," and most of the night was spent in reorganizing their companies.

The Division classified missing men as "stragglers." Events would indicate they were not all "stragglers."

Many men were separated from their squads, platoons, companies, and leaders during the confusion of battle and in the frantic search for cover and protection from the fierce uninterrupted enemy fire which blanketed their positions with flying jagged fragments of steel. As the daylight fled, the confusion and fear mounted as they searched for one another in the darkness, sometimes blundering into minefields, tripping wires and bringing more mortar and machine gun fire cascading down their ranks. Men lay wounded in minefields or in fully exposed positions for hours and evacuation was nigh impossible. Men of the A and P Platoons of the Second Battalion had been designated as stretcher-bearers, but only one dangerous trail could be used for evacuation and supply.

Because of heavy battle casualties among officers and non-commissioned officers, men wandered, leaderless, down the treacherous slopes, joining others who had found cover in houses, caves, and cellars.

Mine fields, laid in irregular patterns, severely limited maneuverability and restricted the area in which troops could be assembled and organized. Therefore, company areas near the base of the hills were selected, and as men were located, they were organized into squads and platoons. All officers not in positions on the hills assisted in locating the men.

Initially, as they were organized into sizable strength, they were sent up to rejoin the dug-in troops. However, the enemy shellfire on the single route used resulted in further casualties and more confusion. As a result, in some cases, only a small number reached the positions on the hills. Finally, these efforts were delayed while the 598th Field Artillery Battalion fired 438 rounds on all unobserved avenues of approach to interdict any further enemy attacks against the troops holding Hill "X."

All Third Battalion troops still on Hill "X" were attached to the Second Battalion. Captain Thayer assumed command of all troops located and began to assemble them near Querceta in the early morning hours of the 9th. Most of the day was spent in this effort, while the depleted troops on Hill "X" doggedly fought off enemy counter-attacks and remained in place despite accurate and concentrated mortar and artillery fire. They paid a heavy toll for their efforts, and some further disorganization occurred.

At 0430 Captain Thayer reported that he had only 40-50 men in position representing officers and men from companies of the Second Battalion. The attack set for 0600 against Hill "Y" was then delayed after consultation with the Regimental Commander, and a secondary defense line was established near the base of Hill "X." Elements of G and E Companies went back into positions on the hill during the day.[25] Company K, still holding out on Hill "Z" but under enemy machine gun fire from both flanks, was attached to the Second Battalion.

The Third Battalion, continuing its reorganization, reported that "by the evening of the 9th, Company I had 113 men, Company L 136 men; Company M was "intact," and its Company K was still in position on Hill "Z."[26]

Throughout the day, Second and Third Battalion troops had made limited gains and managed to hold them against several enemy counterattacks.

Company I, with limited resources made a move towards Hill "Y" but again was battered by enemy artillery, mortar and machine gun fire and was unable to advance.

At 1500, however, the Third Battalion, in reserve at Querceta, was ordered to move to Hill "X" during the night in preparation to attack Hill "Y" the next morning. In addition the Third Battalion of the 371st Infantry, was attached to the 370th Infantry to reinforce the attack.

The Line of Departure was the positions on Hill "X," now held by the Second Battalion. Company I was to seize and secure the left half of Hill "Y"; Company L was to attack through the Second Battalion and take the right half of Hill "Y." Company K meanwhile was to infiltrate men into the houses on Hill "Z" during the night and at H-hour they were to attack and seize the north portion of Hill "Z" and to protect the Battalion's right flank. The Heavy Weapons Company (M) was to support Companies I and L, and the 50 calibre machine guns were to fire on the enemy right flank.

During the night, the 371st Infantry's Cannon and Anti-Tank Companies were attached to the 370th Infantry with the mission of securing Hill "X" and relieving the Second Battalion the next day.

That night, too, Lieutenant Miles, commanding Company F was seriously wounded and evacuated, leaving that hard-hit company without an officer, as three of its officers had been killed and one wounded. The First Sergeant had also been killed. Captain Thayer was then ordered to absorb Company F troops into his Company G.

During the day, some other significant attachments and adjustments were made by Division Headquarters, which did little to aid the Second and Third Battalions of the 370th Infantry.

Company C reverted to Division reserve; one platoon of tanks from the 760th Tank Battalion was attached to the regiment; and at 1345 Lieutenant Colonel Harold R. Everman, Commanding Officer of the First Battalion, 370th Infantry (in Division Reserve) was ordered to relieve the Commanding Officer of Task Force One (Lieutenant Colonel Rowny), and to move Company A into the Task Force One sector with him.

No reason has been stated for the relief of Lieutenant Colonel Rowny after only one-and-a-half days. In General Truscott's report it states, however,[27]

> The substitution in command and the employment of two additional rifle companies failed to produce the results desired.

Throughout the night of 9-10 February efforts to reorganize and increase the forces in position on Hill "X" continued. The 370th Infantry had suffered heavy losses in the two days of fighting, and these losses included some very effective officers and non-commissioned officers. As in all military engagements, the courageous men, the key men, always seem to find more than their share of maiming and death. Companies, platoons and squads are demoralized by the removal of experienced and trusted officers and NCO's. Battalions become unbalanced when companies have to combine because of heavy casualties. Even with rest and reinforcement, many units do not fully recover because the necessary experienced leadership remaining is insufficient.

The 370th Infantry casualties for the two days were[28]:

Officers	*Enlisted Men*	*Non-Battle*
13	170	33

In spite of their losses, the 370th Infantry strove valiantly to prepare for resumption of the offensive in the morning.

The 371st Continues the Attack

At 0600, on the second day of battle, the heavy rainfall and the terrain made the going more difficult and uncomfortable, as the First and Second Battalions of the 371st Infantry prepared to continue the attack in the mountainous sector.

The First Battalion continued its assault on the well established and fortified German positions along the jagged peaks, while the Second Battalion prepared to resume the effort to dislodge the enemy in their formidable defenses on ROCKY RIDGE.

The Anti-Tank Company had dug in during the night but had not yet made contact with the 370th Infantry on its left.

Company E had maneuvered its way through a mine field and found itself in another, suffering further casualties, but struck out at the enemy with well-coordinated small arms and automatic weapons fire.

The 598th Field Artillery Battalion fired a 225 round preparatory barrage on the enemy-held objectives and at 0630, assault elements of both battalions moved forward.

The First Platoon of B Company, 760th Tank Battalion, took positions near Ripa to give direct fire support to the Regiment.

Enemy artillery, accurate machine gun and small arms fire came down on Companies A, B, and C of the First Battalion from strong points on GEORGIA, OHIO 1 and STONY POINT. At 0720, Company A attacked GEORGIA, drawing heavy machine gun fire, slowing their advance; Companies B and C moved ahead, by-passing GEORGIA strong points, continuing northwards. Companies B and C then turned and moved to assault the German positions from the rear. A mine field delayed their advance, but by 0845, it had been cleared, and their attack continued, but slowly.

Tanks, artillery and assault guns were firing on STONY POINT.

Enemy mortar and artillery fire became more intense as the First Battalion troops began tightening the ring around GEORGIA, and enemy activity around that area became more pronounced, as they added at least two platoons from their local reserves. As the Buffalo Soldiers advanced slowly through the minefields, some of which included Teller mines rigged as antipersonnel, the enemy abandoned several bunkers and was ferreted from others. Deserters from the First Company 281st Regiment, 148th Division, reported later that on the 9th, their Second platoon on GEORGIA suffered heavy casualties during this assault.[29]

In the Second Battalion zone, by 0745, Company E was still engaged in a fire fight from the minefield. Company G pulled back temporarily to permit the artillery, tanks, and Tank Destroyers to blast at the enemy positions to their front. In dropping back, only one platoon of Company G remained in position at that time.

The battalion commander then decided to commit Company F between the Company G platoon and Company E with a mission of taking ROCKY RIDGE. The plan was coordinated with the First Battalion, which was preparing to assault GEORGIA, jump off time to be at 1200.

Company E had driven off the enemy in its fire fight by 1000 but it was still in another minefield, and due to casualties in its left platoon, *it* was withdrawn and the support platoon brought in.

Although battling through minefield after minefield, Captain Wetlaufer's valiant Company E retained its battle order and control, and delivered vicious, well coordinated small arms and machine gun fire against enemy assaults in spite of continuing casualties.

Because of the minefields, Company E was not in position to maneuver very well, however, which imposed some limitations to the planned assault on ROCKY RIDGE by Company F. Then, just before 1200, Company E suffered four more casualties from mines. The First Battalion had pulled off the upper reaches of GEORGIA and was pounding the hill with all available weapons. At 1128 the regimental advanced observation post reported seeing First Battalion troops crawling towards the top of GEORGIA.

The jump-off time was moved up to 1230 to permit all units to improve their lines.

At 1205 both battalions signified readiness, although Company E was receiving heavy machine gun fire from both flanks.

By this time enemy defensive fire was intensified from all positions along the entire ridge line, and enemy artillery concentrations were drumming relentlessly at all front line positions of the regiment. Nevertheless, the troops moved forward resolutely into the enemy fire.

Company E quickly captured an enemy machine gun and crew, as did Company F. A smoke screen was laid on GEORGIA by artillery and mortars, and the First Battalion, supported by a barrage from 4.2 chemical mortars, the 598th Field Artillery, assault guns, tanks, and its own 60 mm and 81 mm mortars, began moving towards the objective.

The steep embankments were almost as formidable a barrier as the enemy minefields, small arms, and machine gun fire, and the mortar and artillery fire of the enemy.

The loss of air support was sorely felt.

At 1350 the First Battalion was forced to halt the advance due to heavy casualties, and dug in, planning to resume the attack after reorganizing. Company F of the Second Battalion had made significant progress against ROCKY RIDGE.

At 1700, another preparatory artillery and mortar concentration was delivered on GEORGIA, and Company B attacked the peak with two platoons moving against it from the north. After a violent close-in fire fight, Company B continued its advance and by 1930 was digging in on the north and west slopes of the hill, while Company A occupied the south side of it.

The platoon from Anti-Tank Company, on the left of the sector, had made contact with the right element of the 370th Infantry, and during this assault, was subjected to heavy and accurate shelling. Twice it was forced to leave its position but by 1930, it was reoccupying. The regimental commander then ordered the troops to dig-in and prepare to continue to attack in the morning. The 4.2 chemical mortars, artillery, assault guns and tanks were directed to coordinate harassing fire missions from 0600 to 0625, and concentrations on OHIO 1 and 2 from 0625 to 0635, the next morning.

That evening, too, the Third Battalion of the 371st Infantry, in reserve, was attached to the hard-pressed 370th Infantry to reinforce the attack on Hills "X" and "Y" the next day.

Casualties

	Battle		*Non-Battle*	*Total*
	Officers	*Enlisted Men*		
8 Feb:	2	44	16	62
9 Feb:	1	19	26	46
Total:	3	63	42	108

The 366th Fights On

The 9th of February brought no pause in the stubborn resistance by the enemy in the coastal sector against the Second Battalion, 366th Infantry. The struggle continued in an area extending 1000 yards north of the Cinquale and about 600 yards inland. The intense enemy shelling of the previous day had continued throughout the night, with some 100 rounds of mixed calibres falling in the battle zone and the enemy pressing several strong counter-attacks against the foot troops and tanks struggling to regain position and cohesion in their attack.

During the night, a platoon of Company A, 370th Infantry was ordered to move to the Canal area. Company B from the 370th had already joined in the battle and had been quickly bloodied as they advanced north of the canal towards the left front of the sector.

The tanks remaining on the beach took up defensive positions to enable them to repel any enemy counter-attacks along the beach by either enemy foot troops or armor. Three medium tanks at the junction of the Montignoso–inner coast road positioned themselves to ward off any enemy counter-attacks or patrols which might by-pass friendly troops and come from the direction of the Cinquale Canal to the south. The tanks in the vicinity of the Task Force Command Post were prepared to reject any attacks on the command post. In at least two attacks that night, the enemy was driven off with heavy casualties by the defending troops, largely through the support of devastating machine gun and cannon fire delivered by a section of tanks.

At 1510 the task force commander ordered that the attack be resumed at 0630 to accomplish the mission using the *original* plan.[30] Helmuth O. Froeschle, Executive Officer of the 760th Tank Battalion, was appointed Task Force Executive Officer, and came forward on foot to the Task Force Command Post.

Efforts were made to reorganize the men who had become scattered during the night; to place troops back into positions under proper leaders; getting infantry supporting weapons into position. This proved to be a difficult accomplishment.

Neither the 317th Engineers, nor the 337th Engineers (from IV Corps) had been able to complete construction of two bridges, determined to be vital to the success of the operation, because of accurate heavy and medium artillery observed fire on the canal, as well as the heavy machine gun, mortar, and small arms fire—and sniper fire, which increased in intensity every time working parties tried to do their job. The loss of bridges contributed to the difficulties in treating and evacuating casualties, as well as hampering communications and supply efforts.

Nevertheless, the attack was launched at 0640.

The Third Platoon of Company K, 366th Infantry, jabbed forward but was forced back by hostile machine gun and accurate sniper fire from the right flank, suffering heavy casualties, despite support from tanks. The tanks then withdrew to previously occupied positions just forward of the L D of the attack.

The remaining tanks on the beach then attempted to break out of the beach area and up onto Montignosso road, but their advance was again stalled when two tanks hit mines. The remainder of the tanks then remained on the beach.

As the attack of the Third Platoon of Company K was being repelled, enemy smoke shells landed on positions along the beach and the woods near the coast road.[31] Company L then reported that a strong enemy counter-attack had begun, that their ammunition supply was depleted and that they were having problems with functioning of their weapons. Defensive fire was called for, and the furious artillery concentrations, combined with heavy machine gun and cannon fire from tanks and the fire from the infantry in position broke up the counter-attack. The company was reorganized, and moved back into the line.

At 0800, another counter-attack again drove 366th units on the left back and considerable time was again spent in re-organization.

On the "hinge" of the line along the beach from the sea to the outer coastal road, elements of Company B, 370th Infantry, struggled against strong enemy resistance to firmly establish their position. Three patrols were sent up from the company to clean out enemy who had reoccupied the left of the line originally held by Company I in order to allow the reoccupation of the line by Company B. Approximately one-half of the patrol members were killed or wounded in this mission which was doomed to failure from its inception.[32] In the din and confusion of shellfire, mortars, machine guns, small arms, these patrols were ordered to advance on open exposed ground with little space for maneuver, and with no attempt at deception, straight in the face of the determined enemy.

They followed orders and were cut down.

While enemy resistance was increasing, the First Battalion, 370th Infantry, was in process of moving to the Cinquale Canal area. Lieutenant Colonel Harold R. Everman, its commander, prepared to take over as Commanding Officer of Task Force #1 from Lieutenant Colonel Rowny.

Company C, of the First Battalion remained at Pozzi as division reserve.

Three medium tanks and ten light tanks were dispatched to meet Companies A and D, whose troops were to mount the tanks near Querceta on Highway #1 and be transported first to Forte dei Marmi. From there, the tanks were to carry the infantrymen across the Canal near its mouth.

The report of Headquarters 760th Tank Battalion sounds disarmingly routine[33]:

> As the three mediums reached the mouth of the canal, the column came under artillery and mortar fire and the infantry on the light tanks dismounted and sought cover. The three medium tanks were successful in crossing the Canal and deposited the infantry there before returning to the south side. Several more trips were made during the day to carry infantrymen across but, in one crossing in the afternoon, three light tanks became submerged in craters in the mouth of the canal and had to be abandoned.

According to the report of the First Battalion, 370th Infantry, the operation was far from "routine."[34]

> Commanding officer, 760th Tank Battalion stated infantry (Company A) straggled and would not accompany tanks. Officers of Company A stated tanks had proceeded along wrong road, had tried to turn around, had jammed up, a heavy enemy artillery concentration had fallen in the area and that infantry had left area and taken cover.

and further,

Executive Officer, First Battalion, contacted commanding officer, 760th Tank Battalion and requested tanks to take Company D across canal. Request was denied, *Tank Commanding Officer saying it was impossible to cross the canal.* (Underlining by author.) D Company started to cross the canal on foot. Suffered casualties. D Company took cover. Executive Officer received written orders via S-1 that the *balance* of the battalion would be moved across the canal. He contacted commanding officer, 760th Tank Battalion, told him that he, the Executive Officer, had written orders from First Battalion Commanding Officer that the tanks *would* take Company D across the canal. Ex was then given 6 tanks. Company D and 1 platoon of Company A were put on tanks and taken across canal. Tanks returned. Ex then requested tanks to take balance of Company A (A Company now reorganized). Executive was told that four tanks had been bogged down in carrying D Company across. Company A was then ordered by Executive Officer to cross canal on foot.

While all this confusion in orders was taking place the men of Companies A and B sought whatever cover they could from the dreadful enemy shelling and waited for someone to give some orders that made sense to them. During that period, the commanding officer of Company A was evacuated for "battle-field neurosis" and only two lieutenants were left in the company. Feverish efforts were then mounted to "reorganize" the companies.

The report indicates that the difficulties continued[35]:

> Ex received order that some tanks would be available to carry supplies across the canal. Looked for tanks, found them, but was informed by Tank commanding officer that they would *not* be used to carry supplies across the canal. Executive Officer telephoned G-3 (Division Headquarters) who said: "Contact Tanks Again." Returned to Tank commanding officer who reiterated statement that tanks would *not* cross. Ex then organized carrying party of two officers and 41 men to carry supplies across canal.

Lieutenant Henson and Lieutenant Harris set about reorganizing Company A and what men of Company B that could be located and dug in along the beach and extending towards the coastal road. One squad of Company B, along with elements of Third Battalion, 366th Infantry, were located in and around the forward Task Force #1 Command Post.

Difficulties for the First Battalion continued in its efforts to establish wire communications to the forward command post across the canal. Late in the afternoon orders were given to lay a wire across the canal. The commanding officer reported to the executive officer that wire could *not* be laid due to heavy enemy artillery and mortar fire. The commanding officer was given another order to get wire across the canal and was given extra men. The wire was laid across the canal but was shot out in 10 minutes and never replaced.[36]

During the morning, over 300 rounds of artillery fell in the Coastal

Sector.[37] The 152 mm coastal guns on Punta Bianca were active despite repeated bombings by our fighter bombers. At 1430, Colonel Everman arrived with written orders to assume command of all troops north of the Cinquale Canal and ordering Lieutenant Colonel Rowny to return to the Division Command Post.

The next morning, Lieutenant Colonel Rowny assumed command of troops south of the Cinquale Canal, to organize a line south of the canal with the added mission of reorganizing and aiding communications and supply for the First Battalion, 370th Infantry.[38]

During the night of 9-10 February heavy mortar and small arms fire was received in the coastal sector. The command post received bazooka and small arms fire from the woods 50 yards east and it was reported that one tank was knocked out.

The Task Force Commander issued an attack order at 0400 for an attack at 0600 the next morning. Nineteen medium tanks of the 760th Tank Battalion, 8 light tanks from the 758th Tank Battalion, and 8 Tank Destroyers were moved up the Montignoso Road to Highway #1. Two companies of engineers and one platoon from the Division Reserve Company, Company C of 370th Infantry were also included in that force.

The Third Day of Battle — 10 February

On the morning of 10 February, the 370th Infantry resumed the attack on the heavily mined Strettoia-Sera sector, after spending the night regrouping and reorganizing. Elements of Companies G and K were dug in on Hill "X," which had been largely cleared of the enemy.

The First Battalion had been sent to relieve elements of the 366th Infantry in the coastal sector north of the Cinquale Canal, and the Third Battalion, 371st Infantry, commanded by Lieutenant Colonel Arthur H. Walker, was attached and held in an area near Pozzi.

Companies I and L, jumped off at 0630, with Company I headed towards the left with the objective of seizing and securing the left half of Hill "Y," and Company moving to seize the right side of Hill "Y." As they advanced in the early daylight, enemy observers again triggered heavy concentrations of accurately placed artillery and mortar fire directly on the formations. No escape was possible from the hail of thunderous, screaming shell fire and the troops suffered heavy casualties.

While the Third Battalion, 371st Infantry began hurriedly moving forward to continue the drive to Hill "Y," courageous Lieutenant John Madison was ordered to take over a detachment made up of men of Companies I and L. Three line officers from the 371st, in response to the orders from Division Headquarters, arrived and were assigned to Lieutenant Madison's group, two going to Company I and one to Company L.

The Third Battalion, 371st Infantry attacked at 1000 through Company G, still firmly dug in on Hill "X," and by 1025, they had secured a foothold on Hill "Y" as well as part of the west slope of Hill "X."

During their advance, they were guided through the mine fields by guides from the battered Second Battalion, 370th Infantry, and after they were on the objective, the A and P platoons of the Second and Third Battalions, 370th Infantry, cleared and taped two paths through the mine field up to the 371st troops, now under heavy enemy fire.

By 1300, the troops from Companies I and L had been formed into a command group under command of Lieutenant Madison. He was ordered to proceed to a woods west of Hill "Y" to provide left flank protection for the Third Battalion, 371st Infantry, on Hill "Y."

The companies of the 371st Infantry did not find it easy to advance through the badly hit troops of the 370th Infantry and up, over, and beyond Hill "X" to Hill "Y." They moved out in good order about 0915, with artillery Forward Observers moving with the attacking companies. They moved through the smoke and shelling and crossed the Line of Departure on time. Company L, leading, encountered some small arms and sniper fire from the flanks, but through the aggressiveness of the company commander they drove through the enemy resistance and continued to press on. Company I moved quickly following and eliminated several enemy snipers harassing the flanks. At approximately 1100, Lieutenant Colonel Walker, the battalion commander, who was forward with the leading elements was killed by enemy mortar fire. The Battalion Executive Officer and S-3 immediately went forward and took command. An enemy counter-attack was launched against the advancing Company I, which halted them and caused some men to leave their positions. They were quickly re-grouped and rejoined their comrades, and, with the help of accurately placed defensive artillery fires from the 598th Field Artillery, repelled the counter-attack.

By 1500, Lieutenant Madison's detachment had proceeded up Hill "X" and from there to Hill "Y" where they made contact with the left flank of the Third Battalion, 371st Infantry, and began to dig in, determined to stay. By 1525, Lieutenant Madison's detachment had captured seven prisoners, two machine guns, and two enemy dugouts.

At 1600 a strong enemy force of 50 to 60 men, several with automatic weapons, attacked against the exposed left flank. Company L stood fast and after an hour the enemy withdrew after suffering heavy casualties from the Buffaloes' accurate and sustained small arms and machine gun fire and heavy artillery and mortar fire.[39]

At 1800, the Battalion position on Hill "Y" was well organized, with the flanks strengthened by three (3) sections of heavy machine guns; both wire and radio communications were functioning.[40]

Company E of the Second Battalion, 370th Infantry, was ordered to proceed to clean out snipers and small pockets of resistance in the rear of the Third Battalion, 371st Infantry. When this company reached Hill "X," it was held up and ordered to dig in and be prepared to continue on the mission at daybreak on 11 February.

At 2045, all elements of the Second Battalion, 370th Infantry, except Company E, were relieved by Anti-Tank Company, 371st Infantry.

During the night of 10-11 February, heavy rains fell and the front line troops stirred fitfully under heavy and persistent mortar fire, waiting for the morning battle—sure to come.

The 371st Continues to Reach Forward

During the night of 9-10 February heavy enemy artillery and mortar fire continued to harass the 371st troops as they maneuvered in the black of night around the enemy positions high on the several peaks, preparing to renew the assault in the morning. Re-supply of ammunition, food and equipment, evacuation of wounded, organization and improvement of positions, replacement of key leaders—all were extremely difficult, uncomfortable, and fraught with peril on the slippery slopes in the pitch blackness.

During the early morning hours the Division G-2 section warned the regiment of a possible enemy counter-attack. All units were promptly alerted.

At 0423 the First Battalion Commander decided he preferred to arrange for his own supporting artillery fire through his artillery liason officer. He planned to leave a small holding force to contain the enemy occupying FLORIDA, then have Company A strike out for the summit of GEORGIA and attempt a juncture with Company B, now poised to move against GEORGIA from positions near the peak. If not able to capture GEORGIA by this maneuver, he planned to leave a small force to hold the positions, then to push forward with the rest of the battalion.

Some problems plagued the battalion before H-hour. Supplies, badly needed, had not been moved forward, hampering the ability to coordinate its offensive with the Second Battalion, preparing again to attempt to dislodge the stubborn, well-entrenched enemy from ROCKY RIDGE and MAINE. Too, despite feverish efforts of all commanders throughout the night, the battalion strength was quite depleted. Casualties from the shelling during the night, men stumbling around the mountainside searching vainly for their units or seeking warmth from the bitter cold or protection from enemy fire—all such factors contributed to the incomplete organization of the battalion by morning. Then, at 0600 the Division Commander directed the Regimental Commander as follows[41]:

> 371st Infantry will push towards its objective. The Third Battalion minus Company K will be attached to 370 and 370 will have *priority* on *all* artillery. If 370 does not go forward the attack will be called off. 371 will transfer three line officers to 370 immediately.

So, on the brink of launching the attack, the 371st Infantry learned it must move without assurance of maximum artillery support, and seriously handicapped by having already lost key line officers as casualties, now was ordered to transfer three officers to the 370th Infantry. The removal of the Third Battalion left the 371st with only two depleted battalions to go against the fully aroused enemy.

Nevertheless, at 0600, both battalions reported they were ready, and

February Attack in Coastal Sector

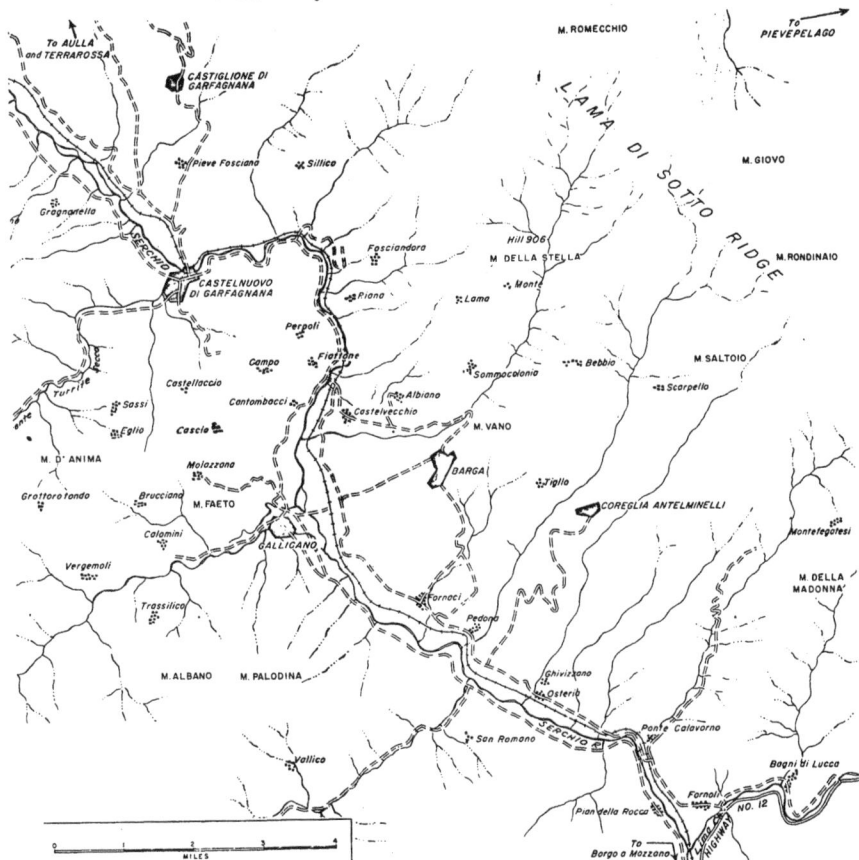

The Serchio Valley Sector

at 0630, after the 599th Field Artillery Battalion and the attached support weapons had fired the preparatory concentrations on OHIO 1 and 2 and the other targets specified on the previous evening, they jumped off. By 0640, Company A was moving around to the left of GEORGIA. The re-organized Company G constituted the regimental reserve along with the two remaining platoons of the Anti-Tank Company. Company B drove straight up onto GEORGIA from the north and west, while Company C was facing north into the GEORGIA woods, to protect the flanks.

Anti-Tank Company reported that it no longer had contact with 370th Infantry, on the left; its third platoon captured two prisoners of war.

In the Second Battalion, by 0730, they ran into a minefield and withdrew slightly, while a mine-clearing detail attempted to clear a path.

Company E, still in mine fields, was being fired on by three enemy machine guns, but continued to fight back while endeavoring to clear paths.

All over the 371st Sector, enemy forces resisted fiercely every attempt to reach the summits of the mountains they appeared determined to hold at all costs. Firing accurate and heavy machine gun and small arms fire from well dug-in positions and emplacements, they were able to coordinate their fire so that a continuous stream of bullets flowed to every point of advance by the Buffalo Soldiers. Fire from OHIO 1 and 2 pelted the troops attacking GEORGIA from the north, despite heavy artillery, cannon, and mortar fire directed on those two hills from supporting units of the 371st Infantry. Enemy forces on GEORGIA, while fighting off attacks by the three companies of First Battalion, were also firing down on American troops on FLORIDA and MAINE.

Enemy artillery and mortar fire continued to fall on the Buffalo troops, in full view as they clambered up the precipitous sides of the mountains, slipping and sliding on the rock and shale, clawing and grabbing at scrub brush and big rocks. Routes of supply and evacuation, as well as draws and gullies containing American mortar positions or used to concentrate and organize small attack units, were continually being searched out by heavy enemy barrages.

Around every mountain objective were laid massive minefields, cleverly placed to channel attacking forces into the deadly lanes of fire, and so extensive that the courageous 317th Engineers simply could not cover them all, adding to the fear and confusion engulfing the soldiers.

Despite the fanatic enemy resistance, Companies B and C pressed their assault on the GEORGIA strongpoint.

They advanced to within a short distance of the top, but had to pull up because of the heavy enemy small arms, automatic weapons and machine gun fire, augmented by artillery and mortar fire. By 1055, the First Battalion halted the assault on GEORGIA and was by-passing the hill, leaving a small, well armed and strongly positioned force to continue to lay heavy fire on it, as other assault groups from the companies moved forward to pass each other alternately towards the OHIO hills. Mines and heavy fire turned them back. The battalion then was ordered to double back and attempt another assault on GEORGIA from the north. There they ran into another large mine-field.

By this time, the First Battalion had given up trying to take OHIO 1, and, while working its way out of the mine-field, moved to secure one of the saddles between OHIO 1 and GEORGIA.

In all these movements and maneuvers, despite casualties to key personnel, the 371st units, fighting on the upper slopes of the hills, retained their integrity and cohesion and inflicted heavy casualties on the enemy.

Resistance on the enemy's left flank was extremely strong in the sector, but heavy pressure on his right flank by Second Battalion troops was causing him to withdraw, albeit slowly. At 1345, Company F reported a strong enemy counter-attack, and heavy artillery concentrations were placed on the area by supporting units and the reported attack was completely neutralized. It was felt that part of the sector had completely collapsed, since no sustained action was pursued by the counter-attacking force.

Company E, still in a minefield, captured another machine gun. Toward the middle of the afternoon a prisoner stated that his unit, which had been left to defend GEORGIA, had evacuated the hill.[42]

Top: Kitchen scene, 25th Infantry, 1880–1881, Montana; middle: squadron, 9th Cavalry, 1889, Nebraska; bottom: Company B, 25th Infantry, 1888, Montana. (Courtesy Fort Huachuca Historical Museum.)

This page, top: Noncommissioned Officers, 10th Cavalry, 1914; bottom: 366th Infantry in World War I (from left: Lt. Col. L. Abbott, Capt. Joseph L. Lowe, Lt. A.R. Fisher, Capt. E. White), 1918. Opposite, top: nine 369th Infantrymen, with French Croix de Guerre, Feb. 1919; bottom Sgt. Joe Louis, heavyweight champion, visits Fort Huachuca (Ariz.) troops, July 1943. (Courtesy Fort Huachuca Historical Museum.)

Opposite, top: Gen. George C. Marshall inspecting 600th Field Artillery Battalion mess hall, Fort Huachuca, Ariz., 1943 (courtesy Fort Huachuca Historical Museum); bottom: 370th Infantry troops advance towards Arno River past destroyed German tank, near Ponsacco, Sept. 1, 1944 (Dept. of Defense). This page: Across the Arno, toward German positions, 370th troops slog up steep muddy bank near Pontederra, Sept. 1, 1944 (Dept. of Defense).

Opposite: Tired Buffalo soldier rests from battle near Lucca; only babies and infantrymen sleep like this; Sept. 5, 1944. This page: 92nd Division medics make their way up the trail to rescue surviving members of the 100th Battalion after mortar shells killed six on OHIO Ridge, April 4, 1945. (Dept. of Defense.)

Opposite: 370th Infantry wire section lays wire in Ponsacco area, Aug. 28, 1944. This page: Sgt. Henry Grice, 370th Infantry, with German prisoner of war, after the action that earned him a Silver Star, Nov. 18, 1944. (Dept. of Defense.)

Opposite: Gun crew of Battery B, 598th Field Artillery, preparing to fire at the enemy across the Arno, Sept. 1, 1944. This page: T/5 Charles Jones, 92nd Division medic, tends the wounds of Pfc. Thomas W. Skayhan, 1st Armored Division, near Lucca, Sept. 5, 1944. (Dept. of Defense.)

Above: Lt. Gen. Lucian K. Truscott, Jr., Fifth Army commander, chats with troops of the 92nd Division after their heroic stand in the hills above Viareggio, Dec. 1944. Opposite, top: Italian prisoners of war guarded by 365th Infantry soldiers, in Calavorno area, Feb. 4, 1945; bottom: ammunition-carrying troops of Company A, 365th Infantry, pinned down by enemy sniper in Sommocolonia area, Jan. 10, 1945. (Dept. of Defense.)

Opposite: 3rd Platoon, 92nd Cavalry Reconnaissance Troop, moves through La Spezia on the day of its liberation, April 24, 1945. Above: Buffalo soldiers enter newly liberated Genoa, April 27, 1945. (Dept. of Defense.)

Two walking wounded Buffalo soldiers going to aid station, Italy, fall 1944. (Dept. of Defense.)

As night closed over the dark hills, the 371st Infantry Battalions were within reach of the top of their objectives and were improving and consolidating their positions and replenishing needed supplies in preparation for expected counter-attacks on the morning of 11 February. It was learned that the artillery allocation for the 0600-0635 preparatory fire would be limited to a total of only 100 rounds, which would create a severe handicap to attacking soldiers. However, the combined fire of 4.2 chemical mortars, a British 44 mm gun unit, assault guns and tanks, was committed for firing on target areas during the preparatory fires period.[43]

Casualties

Battle		Non-Battle
Officers	*Enlisted Men*	
5	30	49

The Last Battle for the 366th

On 10 February in the early hours, after a night of heavy artillery and mortar shelling, Task Force I, now made up of the First Battalion, 370th Infantry, with the Third Battalion, 366th Infantry, now attached to it, moved to resume the attack.

With the mountains still not fully taken on the right, no one could *move* even in the dim daylight without being seen from the German observation posts still dug in on the many peaks. Throughout the night heavy concentrations of artillery and mortars, already ranged in on the Cinquale Canal, fell on the narrowing beachhead. As dawn broke over the bare coastal plain, it laid bare the troops of Task Force I under the eyes and guns of the enemy, still firmly established in the fixed defensive fortifications at the tops of the mountains.

Heavy and accurate fire from the heavy guns at Punta Bianca and La Spezia, continued to fall on the infantry soldiers; added to this, was the concentration of fire directed on them from enemy positions in the hills. There was no cover to hide them and no room to maneuver. The only "strategy" offered them was to wage another series of frontal attacks.

During the night, efforts were again made to establish wire communications and to move badly needed supplies to front line units. Shortly after midnight a wire party reached some elements across the canal, but did not get to the battalion command post. While one carrying party attempted to cross the Canal, three amber flares and one blue flare burst high in the air, illuminating the attackers, caught without cover in the open ground. Enemy machine guns swept them with interlocking bands of fire and mortar shells thumped wickedly into them.

The 317th Engineers, during the night, continued to try to build a foot bridge across the canal. Shortly after midnight Company C, using one platoon for security and one platoon carrying bridge equipment, moved boldly to the crossing site, where it came under enemy fire and halted. The security platoon returned the fire and neutralized the enemy; however, after the work party had launched two bays, heavy enemy mortar fire forced them to abandon the area.

The 337th Engineers (IV Corps) had abandoned its plans to build a treadway bridge at the inner coast road, as ordered, after being at the site only three hours. The 317th Engineers, in total darkness, continued its efforts to open and sweep routes for movement and tanks behind the Task Force as well as north of the Canal.

The entire force was subjected to several counter-attacks, also. The battalion command post received mortar and small arms fire, and, at one point, bazooka fire from a wooded area some 75 yards east of the command post knocked out one tank. Early in the morning, Lieutenant Bracey, Company B, 370th Infantry successfully led one squad in an assault on two houses near the command post which were occupied by the enemy.

At 0400, Lieutenant Colonel Everman ordered the battalion to attack at 0600 along the Montignoso road to Highway #1, the force to consist of a Tank-Engineers and Infantry assault. Five tanks from Company A, 760th Tank Battalion, along with two companies of engineers and one platoon of infantry from Company C were to jump off together. Communication was not completely established in the two hours, however, and at 0600 only one platoon of engineers and a total of one platoon of infantrymen from Company A were ready.[44]

At 0600 as this force moved out, it was immediately met by a strong enemy counter-attack supported by heavy artillery, mortar and machine gun fire and enemy infantry anti-tank weapons. The infantry and engineers were immediately pinned down, and forced into a limited withdrawal, as the tanks assumed defensive positions in the vicinity of the command post and fired on enemy troops. The fighting continued throughout the morning, enemy small arms fire finally being silenced at 1330.

At 0730 an enemy counter-attack by 50–60 enemy troops were driven off with heavy casualties.

At 1100 another strong enemy counter-attack was repulsed by combined fire of infantry engineers and tanks, with all defensive fires of the field artillery and mortars. One group of 30 enemy were fired on by artillery at 1130 with heavy casualties.

Another attack was ordered for 1630 with one platoon of Company A and one platoon of Company B, supported by tanks and artillery. Artillery time fire was directed at enemy troops off-shore near Company B's positions just as the attack was launched; other Allied artillery joined in the firing. Unfortunately, much of the friendly artillery fire fell on Company B, causing several casualties.[45]

The tanks, though stationary, continued to strike out with cannon fire and heavy machine guns. One tank near the battalion command post, detected enemy movement in a bunker some 200 yards eastward, and poured heavy cannon fire into it. Company B withdrew slightly after the misguided artillery bombardment.

Company K, 366th Infantry, north of the battalion command post, reported a heavy counter-attack at 1730 and withdrew towards the command post. By 1800, after enemy pressure continued to increase, with a strong enemy counter-attack reportedly coming south on the coastal road, the attack was called off and all efforts were directed at stabilizing the forces along a new line. Lieutenant Colonel Everman was then ordered to withdraw south of the Cinquale Canal. He directed the order of withdrawal to be covered by Company B, and details were set up to assist in the evacuation of the wounded. He and his staff reached the rear command post at Forte Dei Marmi at about 0300, 11 Feb 1945.

Throughout the day, supply routes and troop assembly areas south of the Canal were openly exposed to hostile enemy observation; heavy artillery fire from the heavy guns at Punta Bianca, and pin-point accurate mortar fire fell upon the men and machines just as it fell upon those north of the Canal.

Despite these difficulties and resultant casualties, supplies began to flow forward by hand-carry and on tanks, in increasing quantities as the day unfolded. By 1430 an artillery liaison party riding on a tank was able to deliver supplies to the battalion command post; these supplies included communications materials, ammunition, food, clothing and medical supplies. After unloading, the tank returned for another load.

The task of re-organizing the units of the 366th Infantry south of the Canal proceeded despite harassing enemy fire. As men from Companies I and L, of the 366th Infantry, were identified, they were sent to small group concentration points, where they were re-equipped with clothing, new rifles and ammunition, and assigned under control of Company L. By 1500, they were preparing to return to the fray when reports were received of an enemy counter-attack south of the Canal, and they were immediately moved to a reserve position instead.

Before this re-constituted force, again ready and able to fight, could be committed, the order to withdraw was issued. All of the armored forces still south of the Canal were also ordered into defensive positions to repel the enemy forces "reported" to be crossing the Canal.

One of the engineer reconnaissance parties engaged in a short vicious fire fight with an enemy patrol crossing the Cinquale Canal and heading west. The enemy patrol was driven back with considerable casualties.

The 371st Clings to the Ridge Line — 11 February

At 0600, the Commander of the First Battalion reported, "We have taken GEORGIA and are occupying the bunkers."[46]

During the night enemy shelling from artillery and mortars continued. Field Order #8, from Division Headquarters, had been received and the two battalion commanders began making preparations to "consolidate their present positions and re-constitute their reserves."

Some much needed supplies were hand-carried to the troops still digging in on or near the summits. Wounded were evacuated down the precipitous trails to treatment facilities — and relative safety.

At 0745, Company E reported an undetermined number of enemy moving towards them. Though still in a minefield, their coordinated fire and movement, augmented again by prompt fire of supporting artillery and all available organic weapons of the company drove the enemy back reeling from the ferocity of their resistance. One prisoner was captured by Company E, and at 0845 the routed enemy were reported as fleeing north.

They took refuge in some houses beyond a ridge and the supporting artillery and tanks began pounding the buildings. Our tanks then moved closed to the front.

By 1120, the 370th Infantry troops were pulling back below Hill "X" on the left, and was merging its Company K in with the 371st's Anti-Tank Platoon.

At that time, the 371st Regimental plan was to set up defensive positions on the OHIO RIDGE *if* the First Battalion could capture OHIO 1. If not successful in that effort, the force was to pull back and establish its main defensive line on the GEORGIA ridge.

By 1230, Company E had taken five more prisoners.

As night fell, the First Battalion, unable to dislodge the stubborn defenders on OHIO 1, outposted the line of the pimple north of GEORGIA. Company B, encountering only mines, sat on top of GEORGIA. The Main Line of Resistance thus ran over and around GEORGIA and west along the entire ridge. The two platoons of Anti-Tank Company were attached to the First Battalion and occupied already dug-in positions on FLORIDA, constituting the battalion reserve.

The Second Battalion outposted its existing positions with platoons from Companies E and F, and at 1910, it was reported that they "were holding despite withering enemy barrages on their positions."[47] Company G was ordered into the regimental reserve south of Ripa.

The remainder of the Second Battalion drew back slightly and established the Main Line of Resistance on GEORGIA Ridge, tying in with the First Battalion on the right, and the 370th Infantry on the left.

As the four-day battle subsided, the 371st Infantry's two battalions stood fast on the high ground. Goodman describes the 371st aptly[48]:

> Throughout the 4-day operations, most of the troops performed skillfully and courageously. Straggling was negligible, and although all objectives were not reached, an advance of 800 yards was made and held against stubborn resistance.

Elements of 370th and 371st Give Ground

On 11 February, in the pitch darkness of the after-midnight hours, the Third Battalion 371st Infantry, now under new leadership, and now also charged with responsibility for the Central Sector, moved to consolidate positions held and to re-constitute reserves, as ordered.

Company L of the 371st was on Hill "Y" and a "Task Force Sturtevant, under Major Sturtevant and composed of elements of its Anti-Tank and Cannon Companies, took over the position on Hill "X." Company E, Second Battalion, 370th Infantry, also remained on the hill, while the remainder of the Second Battalion converged on the assembly area near Ripa, to reorganize.

Elements of Companies I and L, Third Battalion, 370th Infantry, under dauntless, indomitable Lieutenant John Madison, protected the left flank of the 371st Infantry troops on Hill "Y."

Elements of Company I, 371st Infantry, and Company K, 370th Infantry held tenuous positions on Hill "Y."

By 0300, all units were in place and digging in furiously or reorganizing furiously.

Enemy artillery and mortar fire continued to fall throughout the night, with flares brutally shattering the darkness from time to time bathing the Buffalo Soldiers in brilliant, revealing light to expose them to the incessant fires of the enemy.

In the early morning hours a strong enemy counter-attack was launched against Company L on Hill "Y." At first the troops held fast, but when artillery defensive fires did not come quickly, the determined German troops drove them back from their positions toward Hill "X."

At the time the counter-attack came, the artillery forward observer was out of contact with his battalion, as his wire lines had been cut by enemy shell-fire and his radio was inoperative. The observer's fire commands finally reached the guns through the infantry's radio channels, but by the time the 598th Field Artillery Battalion fired in close support and had also called on the reinforcing battalion, division artillery and corps artillery, it was too late to help the men on the hill.

The units on Hill "Z," seeing Company L withdrawing on its left, began to withdraw also. Lieutenant Madison and his stubborn band remained in position until the last possible moment, inflicting heavy casualties on the enemy. When the order for general withdrawal came, his men fell back. He himself was mortally wounded.

He was a magnificent officer. The citation for the Silver Star reflects his courage and fighting spirit:

> Silver Star (Posthumous). John M. Madison, First Lieutenant, Infantry. For gallantry in action on 8 and 10 February 1945, in Italy. Lieutenant Madison's company had taken its objective against light enemy resistance. Immediately thereafter, the enemy subjected the position to terrific artillery and mortar fire, which killed or wounded all officers except First Lieutenant Madison. Extremely heavy casualties and the lack of leadership disorganized the company and it sought to withdraw. Lieutenant Madison gathered the remaining fifteen men and regardless of continuing enemy fire, put them into position to hold the hill. By sheer personal courage and

disregard for his own life, Lieutenant Madison inspired his men to repulse three separate enemy counter-attacks aimed exclusively at their position. He withdrew only upon orders. Two days later, he captured seven enemy soldiers while leading his company in an attack through an extensive unmarked minefield.

Company K was still in position on Hill "Z," but regimental headquarters ordered their withdrawal. Under cover of smoke, they moved back in good order and by 1020 were in position on the newly established defensive line, extending from Highway #1.

While the troops of the Third Battalion, 371st Infantry and the Second and Third Battalions, 370th Infantry were withdrawing; the combined artillery batteries continued to fire heavy concentrations. Throughout the day, the 598th Field Artillery Battalion continued normal harassing fire.

By the end of the day, the Third Battalion, 371st Infantry, had been relieved and reverted back to control of its parent regiment.

The 370th Infantry, minus its First Battalion, organized positions near their jump off point on the first day of the attack.

The enemy, surely because of heavy losses in men and material, made no attempt to occupy Hill "X" or to engage the 370th's front lines.

Results of the Attack

1. The enemy proved, again, that he had no intention of giving up key terrain features considered necessary to their defense scheme, except under extremely heavy pressure.
2. Identifications and dispositions that were exposed indicated that the enemy found it necessary to commit his division reserves and reinforcements from higher reserve groups.
3. A large number of enemy artillery positions, many previously considered "inactive" by 92nd Division Intelligence Staff, were exposed.
4. All enemy dispositions—troops and artillery—were, in fact, fully exposed. The German command itself, regarded the operation as a reconnaissance in force, to determine the strength of the German defenses, and the Buffalo Division, by testing those defenses to the utmost, accomplished that mission.[49]
5. Because of the Buffalo Soldiers' vigorous assaults against front-line positions the enemy was forced to maximum use of *all* arms and as a result large, critical reserves of ammunition considered vital to future operations, was expended.[50] Even the coastal guns at Punta Bianca, despite being under constant air attack, continued to deliver devastating fire on front-line troops, particularly along the Cinquale Canal, throughout the entire operation without interruption.

February Attack in Coastal Sector

6. Serious material losses were incurred by the enemy. Prisoner of war and civilian reports confirm that aerial bombardment and the artillery shelling was very effective.
7. Enemy personnel losses were heavy. In the Coastal Sector enemy casualties were estimated at 36 percent; in the rest of the Division front, losses were at 21 percent, and along the entire front, they were 275 percent. Total enemy casualties was estimated at 423 killed and wounded.[51] Most enemy casualties occurred in close contact encounters, and resulted from rifle and carbine, machine gun, grenade, 60 mm and 81 mm mortar fire, and mines, all weapons of infantrymen and engineers; supporting artillery and Air Force planes also contributed.
8. Among enemy losses were 254 Prisoners of War, taken in front-line actions, 145 in the Coastal Sector, and 109 by the 366th and 365th in the Serchio Valley.
9. The repeated frontal assaults on the enemy's critical strong points, and the stubborn resistance to his counter-attacks, seriously depleted his front-line strength as the battle wore on. In fact, consideration was given to withdrawal from some front-line positions.[52] The German commander, in a post-war interview, stated[53]:

    > A plan of withdrawal was not undertaken at the time of your attack on 8–11 February 1945. I would have done so if your attack had continued.

    Significantly, at the end, the enemy was unable to mount an effort to drive the 92nd Division back from the original Line of Departure.
10. All along the front, gains of from 800 to 1800 yards were made. At one point the enemy was driven from his highest and best-defended positions and all of his counter-attacks were met with determined, well organized resistance. The 371st advanced 800 yards and continued to hold some of the high ground in its sector. In the Serchio Valley, all positions lost in December were re-taken.

Evaluation

The most condemnatory "official" report written about the action of 8–11 February, was written on 5 March, 1945 by Lieutenant General Lucian K. Truscott, Jr., Commanding General of the 15th Army Group.[54]

Within only a few days of the battle, the 92nd Division Headquarters was directed to obtain detailed reports from the commanders of all units involved. Most reported by 21 February.

General Truscott's report begins by "The plan was soundly conceived and carefully prepared."

Among the attachments to his report was a chart indicating that the 92nd Division enjoyed a superiority of 2.4 to 1 in infantry, 1.7 to 1 in artillery, and even greater superiority in tanks and air support.

Other major conclusions were:

1. In every case, commanders, down to battalion commanders, exercised close and personal supervision. This is reflected by the percentage of casualties in officers of higher grade.
2. Lack of leadership and control by company grade officers.
3. Infantry units were unable to advance against opposition or to hold ground against determined enemy attack, evidenced by excessive straggling—withdrawals under artillery and mortar concentration.
4. Air support was excellent.
5. Tank and tank destroyer support was adequate.
6. The engineers failed in clearance of minefields for Task Force I and constructing of a bridge over the Cinquale Canal.

He concludes that,

"The failure of this operation is marked by the failure of the infantry and engineers of the 92nd Division. The ——— has clearly demonstrated that, in spite of excellent and long training, excellent physical condition, superior support by artillery and air, the infantry of this division lacks the emotional and mental stability necessary for combat. I do not believe that further training under present conditions will ever make this division into a unit capable of offensive action."

General Truscott noted that conclusions had been studiously avoided by General Almond, making it clear that the report represented his own personal conviction, for which he assumed full responsibility.

His conclusions came as no surprise. He had expressed similar disillusionment in references to the Serchio Valley attack by the Germans in December 1944, and in his autobiography, he coined a phrase which stigmatized not only the black combat soldier in Italy, but everywhere[55]:

> Germans launched ... attacks ... which struck the First Battalion 370th Infantry, and the Second Battalion, 366th Infantry, both of which "melted away"—a term which was to be frequently used in describing action of colored troops.

Such language was seldom if ever, used by responsible military leadership personnel in referring to *any* American fighting units. Even in operations where glaring command errors were committed, or where entire divisions were completely decimated, such as was the case with the 106th Infantry "Golden Lion" Division, any criticism, if any, was couched in such careful words as to almost glorify the happenings.[56]

No such solicitude was exercised in references to black combat soldiers, however. General Mark Clark, himself, expressed a similar opinion about the 92nd Division,[57] and it is quite certain that, even though General Truscott's report was not widely publicized, his views were sanctioned throughout high command echelons in Italy. There is no doubt that even within the 92nd Division, General Almond and his staff concurred; the same was true of most, if not all of the battalion commanders and regimental commanders of the organic divisional regiments that were involved.[58]

There was an important segment in the division, however, who were not questioned and who did not agree with the gloomy assessment of these military commanders.

They were the vast bulk of the infantrymen and engineers and their non-commissioned and commissioned junior officers who fought the battles.

Most felt they had fought well. Many felt that they had been committed to a poorly planned and ineptly directed operation that was doomed to failure from its very inception.

Captain Warman Welliver, put into words the prevailing view about PLAN FOURTH TERM[59]:

> This attack seemed to most junior officers to be poorly planned by the Division commander and staff. It was a simultaneous frontal attack by three regiments (and one separate battalion) on a wide, well-defended front. There was no attempt to concentrate our strength at any point of suspected enemy weakness. There was practically no deception or surprise.

General Truscott's report makes no reference to the successful Diversion in the Serchio Valley, separated by eight miles of impassable mountains, but still under command and control of the 92nd Division.

In a sense it was almost a separate fight miles away from the main effort.

The two other regiments, the 370th and 371st, were assigned two separate mountain masses overlooking the coastal plain where Task Force 1 was to operate. The attacks of each were frontal and each area of advance was toward enemy forces disposed and positioned in anticipation of just such attacks.

Success of the 366th Infantry-led Task Force One, under the plan, was almost completely dependent upon the success of the other two regiments in clearing not one, but both hill masses of enemy infantry and observation posts, and then successfully bridging the Cinquale Canal to facilitate the crossing of armour and supply elements behind the assault units.

The intelligence reports failed to properly estimate the efficiency and stubbornness of the German troops, or the formidability of reducing the fixed fortifications at the many strong points which were a part of the Gothic Line.

They failed to accurately estimate the devastating effect of the Coastal gun batteries from Punta Bianca and La Spezia, instead placing unrealistic reliance on the Air Force to bomb and strafe them into submission and silence.

Inaccurate assessment was made of the variety and volume of enemy artillery and mortar fire.

And, finally, even though the 92nd Division's forces enjoyed the numerical "superiority" in infantry and artillery, as stated, the lessons learned at the Rapido River "Fiasco" in January 1944, should have taught them that a much more overwhelming force would be needed to accomplish the mission.

In that attack by the 36th Infantry (Texas) Division across the formidable Rapido River almost the same situation faced the planners. The crossing was to be executed at points visible to enemy observers from Mount Cassino and other surrounding mountain peaks. The hills, mountains and flat lands approaching the river and extending beyond it towards the foothills were strongly fortified with extensive mine fields, machine gun positions, self-propelled artillery, tanks and mortars, all part of the Gustav Line.

General Truscott himself, at that time Commanding General of the Third Division which was being considered for that mission, was asked by General Clark if he would be willing to undertake the crossing if the heights occupied by the Germans were under attack although actually not in our possession.[60] He stated:

> Yes, but those attacks should be so powerful that *every* German gun would be required to oppose them, for only two or three concealed 88's would be able to destroy our bridges. I doubt our capacity for such attack.

Over 2100 men of two regiments of the 36th Division were killed, wounded or missing in what was termed by many as a "heroic and needless" attack. The same terms could well have been used in referring to the Buffalo Soldiers in this action.

There was no attempt at deception or surprise in the planning, other than to try to screen the troops with smoke. The routes of advance and the objectives of each unit attacking became clear to the enemy as soon as the sun was to rise. German observers had pre-plotted data on all 92nd Division objectives and their approaches and could fire on them at will in darkness and in daylight, even when the entire area was obscured by smoke and dark overcast skies. The targets were easily identifiable to the enemy.

Tank support of the infantry was not satisfactory. This does not mean that the tank units did not perform well or that they did not fight well. Their crews fought magnificently.

They simply were not used as contemplated. The plan was for the tanks to move forward with the infantry riding or advancing under cover of the tanks toward enemy strong points; the tanks would neutralize the strong point by direct fire from one or sometimes two tanks and, at the same time, the infantry would work its way forward under cover of the tank fire to a point in proximity of the enemy position. When infantry reached its position, the tank fire was lifted and the infantry would assault the enemy strongpoint.

On only a few occasions was the scenario enacted. For the most part the tanks were in stationary positions or completely out of action because they had hit mines, been hit by artillery fire, or had fallen into huge craters made by the massive shells from the Coastal guns at Punta Bianca and La Spezia.

Because they could not maneuver in the extensive minefields, they could not provide the close support of the infantry, which was left alone and exposed as they reached for the first Phase Line along the Magro Canal.

The statement that "In every case, commanders, down to battalion commanders, exercised close and personal supervision" is simply not true.

And, the "percentage" of casualties in officers of "higher" grade, with the possible exception of battalion commanders, was actually quite *low*; most were either never in or near the battle zone or were in and out of it too quickly to be exposed to the danger of becoming casualties.

In most instances, the involvement of Division staff officers was confined to activities in the Division Headquarters area in and around Viareggio where they maintained constant vigil over the radios and telephones, and the many maps and charts connecting them to the several units and the distant men fighting desperately against the determined enemy who resisted more ferociously hour by hour.

Those who did venture across the Cinquale Canal in the Task Force One sector, even for a few minutes, were few in number and, in several instances, managed to perform such "heroic" deeds as to be awarded the Silver Star and other decorations. In most cases they were not exercising "close and personal supervision," but were seeking specific information for the Division Headquarters or were delivering messages or plans. Usually when their missions were accomplished or had been deemed impossible, they did not linger in the chaotic front-line areas.

Two officers from the Division Headquarters Staff were killed in action while forward, north of the Cinquale Canal. Major Richard D. Tindall, the Division Signal Officer, was killed by shell fire, while attempting to solve the problem of maintaining the wire communications lines which were repeatedly destroyed by mortar and artillery shelling.

Captain Gilbert S. Holbrook, acting Division G-3 representative, was also killed by shell fire while forward on one of his several forays north of the Canal. He was one of only three men awarded the Distinguished Service Cross from the 92nd Division.

There were few, if any, casualties among higher command officers in the forward areas of the other elements of the attacking forces. No regimental commanders or staff officers were killed in the action, and there is nothing in the records to indicate unusual loss of their numbers due to wounds or other calamities.

Battalion commanders, for the most part, did exercise close and personal supervision over their commands throughout the operation. Two, Major Willis O. Polk, Third Battalion 366th Infantry and Lieutenant Colonel Arthur H. Walker, Third Battalion, 371st Infantry, were killed in action while leading their battalions in assault actions in forward positions. In both critical situations, they were relieved by subordinates in rank, who continued to actively lead their troops with courage and tenacity.

Casualties, however, even among battalion command level officers, were not unusually excessive.

An officer can no longer lead or control soldiers if he is killed or seriously wounded and evacuated from the battlefield. The casualties among company grade officers — captains, first and second lieutenants — were extremely high, and almost without exception, occurred in forward battle zones while they were exercising or attempting to exercise leadership and control under extremely tempestuous and confused circumstances.

The Third Battalion, 366th Infantry, in the first half-day of the battle, lost at least five key officers, among them, the battalion commander and his S-2, who were killed while advancing towards the First Phase Line. The communications officer was seriously wounded and was evacuated; one of his company commanders was wounded in action, and evacuated; he was a leader of one of the assaulting companies at the time, and was well forward. Captain Raymond Diggs assumed command of the battalion and continued to lead it despite the loss of a battalion staff, and key company officers. He remained forward until the battalion was ordered to retire. In the 370th Sector, it appears that at least five officers became casualties on the first day and eight on the second day. In the 371st Sector, at least two officers became casualties on the first day and one on the second day.

According to General Truscott's report the total officer casualties for 8-11 February were forty-seven. A report by 92nd Division Headquarters includes the Serchio Valley Sector and breaks the total down as follows[61]:

Coastal Sector — Officers

Date	KIA	WIA	Total
Feb 8	2	12	14
Feb 9	5	12	17
Feb 10	1	11	12
Feb 11	1	3	4
Total	9	38	47

Serchio Valley Sector — Officers

Date	KIA	WIA	Total
Feb 8	0	1	1
Feb 9	0	0	0
Feb 10	0	7	7
Feb 11	0	1	1
Total	0	9	9
Grand Total	9	47	56

One officer was Missing in Action.

It is significant that of the 56 officer casualties in the organic units of the 92nd Division, over half occurred in the first two days, and the great majority were among company grade officers and were sustained in forward combat areas.

Added to the problems of the commanders of forward units was a correspondingly heavy casualty loss among key non-commissioned officers; it seems conclusive that at least one thousand enlisted men became casualties in the Coastal and the Serchio Valley Sectors. Casualties among enlisted men are shown below:

KIA	WIA	MIA	Total
75	740	260	1075

The majority of casualties among non-commissioned officers also occurred in forward areas.

On occasions during the four-day offensive, air support, particularly "Rover Joe," was excellent in delivery of bombing and strafing attacks on front-line enemy forces. They helped to break up counter-attacks, or to disrupt enemy troop concentrations forming up for local attacks or counter-attacks. They attacked enemy strong points identified by our assault elements, delivering devastating and deadly fire and making it possible for the Buffalo units to advance.

However, when one considers the overall mission of the Air Forces in the operation, it must be concluded that its performance was not "excellent." Presumably, prior to the attack, every known possible enemy position and installation in the zone concerned had been referred to higher headquarters for consideration of the air support.[62]

The air attacks, when rendered, were not effective against the fixed emplacements and fortifications on the mountain ridges and lower hill slopes and summits. Such attacks were sporadic and not coordinated sufficiently to deliver a heavy and continuous systematic volume of fire to reduce them. Time after time, after such attacks, the German cannon and machine gun fire resumed within minutes, even during the bombing and strafing.

Air attacks against artillery and mortar installations were equally ineffective, partially because most enemy positions were not known until the day the battle was joined, when 21 "previously inactive" enemy positions were discovered to be firing on our troops in the Coastal Zone. By the 11th of February, 49 such "previously inactive" enemy artillery positions had been discovered.

Similarly, repeated attempts to destroy the coastal batteries at Punta Bianca and La Spezia with light dive bombing and strafing attacks failed completely. In a special report, 23 March 1945, Lieutenant Colonel Donald Mac Willie confirms this conclusion.[63]

> Many dive-bomber missions failed to impair the effectiveness of these guns.

In the same report, General Almond writes:

> They have been attacked repeatedly by light bombers without any apparent effect.... In the recent operations of 8-11 February these guns caused heavy casualties among our troops in the sector just North of the Cinquale Canal.

Another report for the Army Ground Forces Board, MTOUSA, by Colonel W.F. Millice, Field Artillery, further confirms the inadequacy of the Air Forces effort[64]:

> Previous trials (referring to 8-11 February) with "Rover Joe" and dive bombers had caused losses by our air corps due to the German Heavy AAA (Anti-Aircraft Artillery) on PUNTA BIANCA. On previous occasions the six (6) heavy AAA guns in PUNTA BIANCA had caused our air corps the most concern.

The heavy coastal batteries, completely out of range of friendly artillery of sufficiently heavy calibre to be effective, and well protected from attacks by light dive bombers, continued to fire at will on installations and troop formations, particularly in the Coastal Sector, throughout the four days of the operation, day and night, without cessation.

On the 8th, the weather was good and many sorties over the front lines were flown by "Rover Joe" planes. Many were successful, it is true. However, on the first day of the battle, troops of the 371st Infantry, struggling, but moving forward with élan and courage against enemy strong points along the heavily defended ridges, were dive-bombed and strafed by Air Force planes by mistake. Two officers became casualties, one the company commander, and the troops' attack was blunted and momentum was lost at the high water mark of the assault.

On the second day, there was *no air support*, due to bad weather. On the third day, "Rover Joe" was active but only on order of IV Corps, miles and miles away from the battle area now covered with the smoke from artillery and chemical mortars, which limited observation from air Observation Posts and even ground Observation Posts.

So, due partially to the inadequacy and ineffectiveness of the Air Force effort, fixed fortifications that had dug in and protected enemy strong points before the advancing troops were not neutralized or destroyed.

Very few enemy artillery positions were destroyed. Although such positions were classified as prime bombing and strafing targets, the air attacks were not sufficiently effective to prevent enemy artillery and mortars from firing heavily and accurately, and seemingly at will throughout the operation.

No significant damage, sufficient to interrupt the schedule of firing and instant response to their observers on the peaks, was done to any of the concrete emplaced guns at Punta Bianca and La Spezia.

Engineers of the 317th Engineer Combat Battalion performed as well as any other Engineer unit could have under similar circumstances.

Their companies were assigned to assaulting companies of all infantry battalions in the coastal sector, including the 371st and 370th Regiments fighting in the mountains. In those two sectors they effectively performed mine-clearing functions, destroyed enemy obstructions and installations, laid minefields when necessary, and fought as infantrymen in opposing enemy counter-attacks. In the mountains they were unable to completely clear all minefields because there were simply too many, and they were too extensively spread throughout the mountain slopes and ridges, as well as along all draws, and valleys and trails leading to the enemy. Like the infantry in the daytime, any movement brought instant machine gun and mortar fire cascading down on them, augmented often by heavy and accurate artillery and sniper fire. At night, the ever-revealing flares exposed engineer mine clearing details and work parties to the same fire.

On the coast, in the zone of Task Force One, similar problems faced the engineers except that they were magnified tenfold by many factors not operative in the hills and mountains.

The flat terrain in the narrow zone of action north of the Cinquale Canal, criss-crossed by canals and streams, was mined in great depth along the beach and almost everywhere along the routes of advance. The area along the beach and the ground south of the leading to the Canal was similarly mine infested.

The audacious engineers successfully cleared a path for tanks along the beach to the Canal in two successive night time, skillful clearing operations, two days before the attack, but they were *not* ordered to clear mines beyond the Canal. As a result, the tanks carrying engineers and assaulting infantrymen during the assault on the 8th, hit mines north of the Canal and halted. When they dismounted and attempted to clear minefields ahead of the tanks—in clear daylight—heavy enemy small arms, machine gun, sniper fire, and mortar fire devastated and decimated their ranks and those of the infantry trying to advance and to protect the tanks and engineers at the same time. Added to the bedlam and confusion and fear, was the accurate and heavy volume of enemy artillery fire coming from "previously inactive" positions (so described in Intelligence reports), and the terrifying, active and destructive shelling from the coastal batteries at Punta Bianca.

Despite the devastating enemy fire attendant to their every effort, the valiant engineers continued, day and night throughout the four days, to attempt to clear minefields for the tanks; their gallant, determined efforts were interrupted many, many times, not only by the heavy enemy fire, but by enemy counter-attacks, and they had to fight as infantry along with their Buffalo comrades.

They made numerous attempts to bridge the Cinquale Canal, day and night, but it was impossible to conceal any such endeavors from the ever searching, never ceasing enemy long range guns and enemy artillery, mortars and small arms and machine guns firing at the men working at the bridge sites.

Even the vaunted 337th (IV Corps) Engineer Battalion, ordered to build a treadway bridge, abandoned their plans after only a few hours at the site, reporting that construction of a bridge under "existing" conditions was impossible. The truth was, also, that even had they been able to construct it, it would have been impossible to maintain it and keep it in operation.

One can find a great similarity between the "failure" of the 317th Engineers to effectively clear minefields and to bridge the stream impeding the advance of their main forces, and the "failure" of the 36th Division engineers to accomplish the same mission for their assaulting forces at the Rapido River.

The only difference was that the 36th Division engineers were labelled as "brave," "determined," "intrepid," etc., by their immediate as well as their Division officers corps, and right on up to that of IV Corps and Fifth Army. Even though they too, fled in panic and terror from the overwhelming and deadly hail of enemy fire—even though there were many so-called "stragglers" among them on the confused battlefield, very few, if any, references were made to any lack of courage and resourcefulness, and certainly none is intended here.

Such was not the case in references by similar echelons of reviewers of the 317th Engineers of the 92nd "Buffalo" Division in the 8-11 February operation.

They were maligned unfairly, and dishonestly.

They were truly magnificent, and among the bravest of the brave, as were the engineers of the 36th "Texas" Division.

It has been said: Infantry is the Queen of Battle.

This has been doctrine in every war—large or small—in which the United States Army has been engaged.

All echelons—cavalry, artillery, engineers, service and supply forces, medical facilities, and in more recent conflagrations, air forces, special forces, inter-continental ballistics units, space forces—all become involved, sometimes utilizing thousands and thousands of men and machines. However, the final resolution falls to the Queen of Battle—the Infantry—who must close with the enemy and wrest from him the disputed ground and destroy him in the process, using hand-held weapons, sometimes rifles, sometimes automatic weapons, sometimes bayonets or knives, and sometimes even bare hands. Sometimes hundreds, sometimes thousands or even hundreds of thousands out of the total forces involved, reach this point of face to face conflict with the enemy.

In Italy and in other places, more often than not, this force often consisted of a small group of infantrymen, a single squad or platoon, fighting to the death at a single position of significance, critical to the success of the entire operation.

And so it was with the 92nd Division in the four days of battle in the Coastal Zone and the six days in the Serchio Valley. On the first day in both sectors the battalions advanced and secured objectives despite a poorly conceived plan of attack, some incompetency in leadership in higher echelons, miscalculations as to the strength and disposition of enemy weapons, particularly artillery and mortars and uninterrupted enemy observation from high elevations. As the action continued, enemy resistance stiffened, and remarkably well coordinated artillery, mortar and machine gun fire continued to exact a heavy toll; uncharted and extensive minefields, much deeper than anticipated, continuous counter-attacks launched against every position taken by the asaulting troops, and monstrous supply problems in the mountains and on the flat, open coastal sector — all contributed to the gradual attrition of the attacking forces; added to all the difficulties, was the weather and terrain, sometimes a more formidable enemy than the German troops.

Some of the troops, literally gave up in the end; however, when the order was given to withdraw, platoons and squads of infantrymen were still in positions at *all* front line sectors, and such heavy casualties had been inflicted on the enemy that they did not have sufficient strength to pursue.

There is some question whether the Division and IV Corps maps, far in the rear of the fighting, accurately reflected the actual locations of the Buffalo Soldiers throughout the battle.

This would not be a strange phenomenon, as this was not an uncommon occurrence in other Divisions in the Fifth Army.

During one of the four battles for Cassino, New Zealand troops relieved the U.S. 34th Infantry Division in what was called the Snakeshead area, February 12, 1944. A New Zealand Division commander questioned the American Commanders closely prior to the relief as to the condition of their troops and came away convinced that "none of them had been forward or was at all in touch with their men."[65] Later, when the New Zealand troops took over, it was discovered that the 135th Infantry was not on Point 573, as II Corps (U.S.) had stated; nor were the U.S. troops in control of the Point 450-455 ridge, but actually were in the gullies 200 yards below it. The Germans actually controlled the ridge. They also found that only four U.S. battalions, each only *100* strong, from three different regiments of two different divisions, held the entire sector.[66]

In the Rapido River "Fiasco," so-named by many reviewing sources, 36th Infantry Division had suffered nearly a thousand casualties by the second day of battle with two of its regiments completely decimated, one of them virtually destroyed. Major General Geoffrey Keyes, Commander of the U.S. II Corps was not yet convinced of the hopelessness of the situation, and wanted another attack to be made using the remaining regiment, then held in Corps reserve. He apparently believed "the enemy morale was low and that they might even be preparing to withdraw."[67]

In explaining his reason for wanting to continue the attack, he pointed out that at one time on the 22nd, the maps and reports at the Divisional Command Post, and as transmitted to his headquarters, showed nearly six battalions on the far side of the river (in fact there were never more than the remnants of four battalions across the river).[68]

General Truscott himself provided a revealing description of the difficulties facing troops in the Italian campaign, while he was Division Commander of the U.S. Third Division[69]:

> Conditions on the mountain tops were appalling. All supply was by man and mules. Casualties had to be carried out on litters, which required

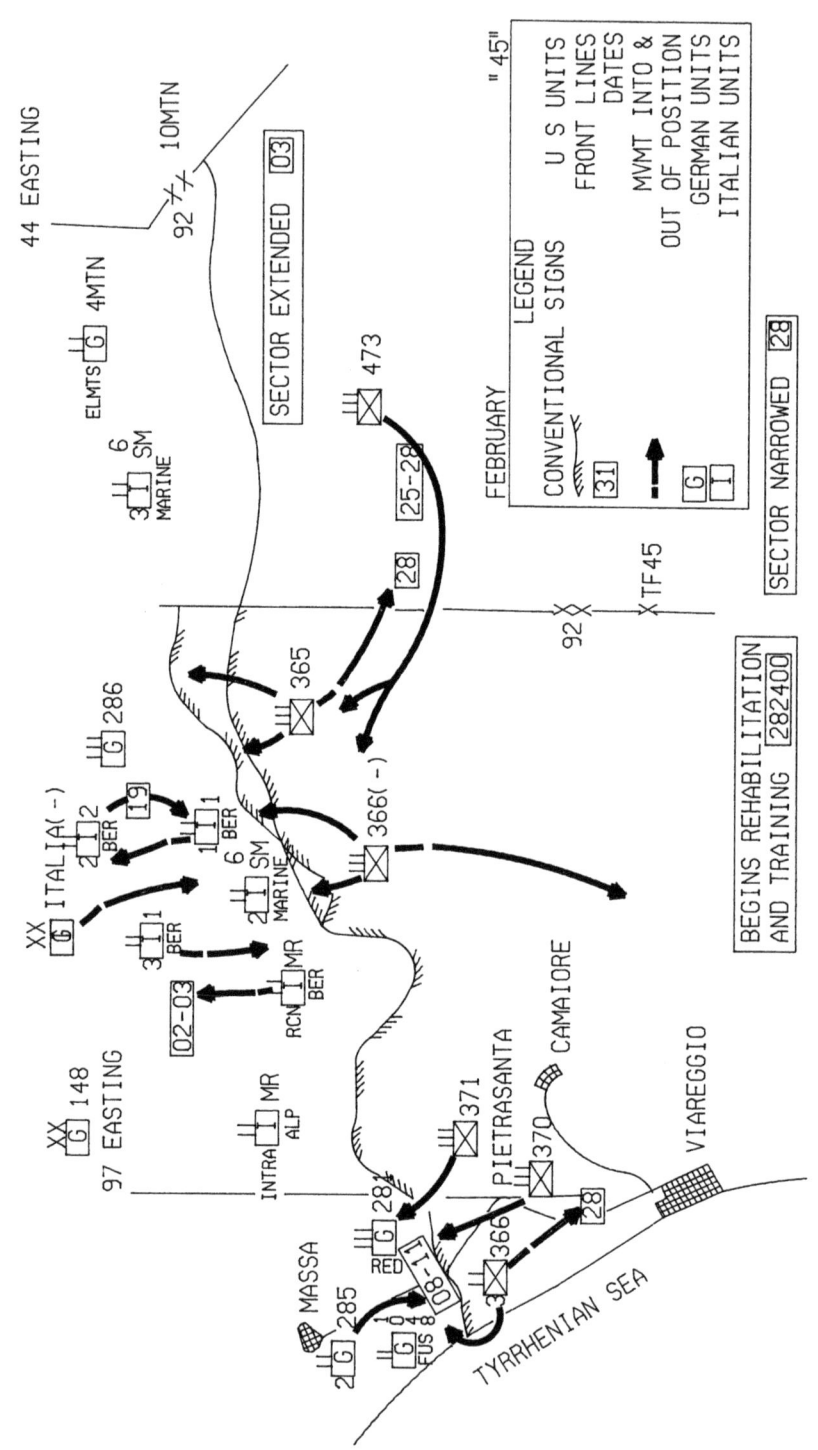

Allied and Enemy Dispositions February 1945

hours in many cases. Hot food was out of the question. Incessant cold rain not only added to discomfort, it reduced visibility almost to nothing, interfered with the scheduled air support, and vastly increased the difficulties of the attacking troops. Companies were becoming seriously reduced in strength by casualties and sickness. Morale suffers under long-continued exposure to battle and the exertion of campaign.

He could not concede, in making his evaluation of the 92nd Division, that the black troops of the 92nd Division and the battalions of the 366th Infantry were facing the exact conditions and attendant problems as his beloved Third Division, and that the morale and efficiency could be as seriously affected as theirs.

Most U.S. and British Divisions' front-line battalions, companies and platoons did not *always* accomplish their missions, for various reasons. The Battles for the Anzio Beachhead, Cassino and Salerno provide overwhelming evidence of that fact. There were many, many failures; however there is here no intent to disparage the conduct of the many, many thousands of infantrymen who fought with limitless courage and determination in all the battles.

The point is that General Truscott, General Clark and General Almond were unable to bring themselves to extend the same compassion and objectivity in evaluating the black Buffalo Soldiers, as they did when analyzing white soldiers. General Truscott said[70]:

> Every other Division in the line, both British and American, was in a condition comparable to that of mine. The British had been unable to clear the Germans from Mt. Cassino — and were compelled to check some of the gains made. Nor had the 34th and 45th Divisions been able to do more than gain a good foothold on the mountains north and west of Venafro."[71]

General Clark was similarly careful, generous, and compassionate in his references to the infantry soldiers of the 36th Division during the Rapido River "Fiasco." Note his reference to the colossal casualties among them, which included 875 listed as "missing."

> The missing comprised largely the men who had become separated from their units and who later turned up for duty.[72]

There is no doubt in the mind of every soldier of the 92nd Division that had General Clark been referring to 875 "missing" in their black Division, he would have called them "stragglers" as did General Truscott in his report, and General Almond in *his* orders to establish and maintain a "Straggler Line." He would not have softened his statement and acknowledged that many black soldiers became separated from their units, and would have — and, in fact did — "turn up for duty," just as the soldiers of the 36th Division had done.

General Truscott, in his report did not even list any men as "missing" and went so far as to break the report down by organization.[73]

Stragglers by Organization

Unit	8 Feb	9 Feb	10 Feb	11 Feb	Total
Third Battalion 366th Infantry	110	75	260	72	507
370th Infantry	11	27	165	41	244
371st Infantry	0	0	0	0	0
Total	121	92	425	113	751

He presents the table above as further proof of the "unreliability," etc., of the troops of the 92nd Division. He does not confirm that most of those listed as "stragglers" did become separated from their units during night operations—counter-attacks, movement of battalions, companies, platoons, squads, to other sectors, or reliefs of front-line units—and rejoined their units *during* the fighting or were assigned to other units as required.

He made no comment about the 365th Infantry, which had *no* "stragglers," or the 371st except to show "*zero*" for each day in his table.

The truth is that every American Division in the Fifth Army and those fighting in the European Theatre had "Stragglers" and had so-called "Straggler Lines" manned by Military Police and assigned officers. "Straggling" occurred at Cassino, Anzio, Salerno, and all the other places where American troops were involved in large scale operations. In the battle of Schmidt, Germany in November, 1944, "straggling" at one point, reached epidemic proportions in one regiment of the 28th Infantry Division.[74]

The 92nd Division was the only Division in the U.S. Forces about which published reports in magazines, newspapers, and books, such as those by Generals Clark and Truscott, referred to "Straggling" as a major problem and strongly condemned it as proof of the lack of courage and capability for combat readiness of black soldiers.

It is interesting to note some comments in Colonel Armstrong's report of 21 February, 1945 (Commander, 365th Infantry Regiment):[75]

Q. How did Negro enlisted men conduct themselves in combat?
A. In general, very well. The attack on Lama di Sotto by Companies I and L was well executed, as was the attack by Second Battalion on Hill 608.
Q. Combat performance of Negro officers?
A. Those who demonstrated their fitness during the recent action now have the confidence and respect of their men.
Q. Any companies led by Negro officers?
A. Companies A, B, D, E, G, H, and K committed with good results.
Q. What percentage of Negro officers committed to combat measured up well in all respects?

February Attack in Coastal Sector 141

A. About 90 percent.
Q. Your evaluation of the colored non-commissioned officers?
A. Except for about 20 percent of the personnel, his general proficiency is good. Reports from battalion commanders are that Negro commanding officers functioned well.
Q. What disciplinary offenses were most common among colored officers?
A. No disciplinary action has been taken against any officer.

In view of this generally favorable assessment by a regimental commander it is worth noting that of *all* the black officers in his regiment not one did he regard as having Field Grade potential. When asked for recommendations as to use of Negro soldiers in a "future emergency," he wrote[76]:

> Regimental commander and staff should consist of white officers; battalion commanders and battalion executive officer, the S-1, and S-2, should be white officers. About 50 percent of the company commanders should be white, preferably *all* of them. While this Regiment apparently has done well, I am not convinced that it has good potential *despite the favorable comments of the battalion commander* as to the fighting ability of their troops. A possible use of Negro troops, in a future emergency, in addition to being used as labor troops, would be their employment in anti-aircraft organizations. I do not recommend their use as combat troops.

There were many examples of outstanding leadership and courage by officers and enlisted men in the February operation, as demonstrated in the following Bronze and Silver Star award winners, some white, some black:

> Ulysses B. Glover, First Lieutenant, 365th Infantry, Oak Leaf Cluster/ Bronze Star. On 6 Feb 1945, Lieutenant Glover being given the mission of seizing and holding his objective, without regard to personal safety, proceeded to and beyond his objective, encountering bitter enemy resistance and drawing an abundance of enemy fire, thus enabling his battalion to accomplish its mission.
>
> On 10 Feb, 1945, being given the mission of spearheading a battalion attack, Lieutenant Glover, stopping his platoon, proceeded alone with one scout, encountering an enemy patrol and although having his stock shot from his tommy gun and being wounded, succeeded in killing four of the enemy and wounding three, thus enabling his battalion to advance and carry out its mission.
>
> James A. Martin, Captain, Infantry, Silver Star. On 10 February 1945, when his battalion commander was killed in an attack on enemy fortified positions, Captain Martin, the battalion S-3, voluntarily assisted in the continuation of the attack. Under heavy enemy artillery and small fire, he took command of two platoons of an attacking company and led them

forward to reinforce the lines. Without regard for personal safety, he returned through the enemy fire and brought up a heavy machine gun section to cover the battalion's exposed right front. On one occasion, Captain Martin purposely exposed himself to enemy fire to locate the enemy position. When approximately 30 of the enemy, armed with far-sited weapons, counter-attacked, he directed such effective artillery and weapons platoon fire, that the enemy fled after sustaining numerous casualties.

Richard Tatum, Jr., Private First Class, Infantry, Silver Star. On 11 February, 1945, Private First Class Tatum, a rifleman, was acting, in an exposed condition, as a forward observer for a mortar squad. Spotting a group of enemy in a house to his front, he directed mortar fire on the target, despite the fact that he came under enemy machine gun fire. He remained in this position securing two hits that routed the enemy. He then killed six of the escaping enemy with a Browning Automatic Rifle. When the enemy counter-attacked he held his ground, using his weapon with maximum effect until the attack was repulsed.

Johnnie L. Toliver, Sergeant, Infantry, Silver Star. On 10 February 1945, Sergeant Toliver's company had gained its objective in the vicinity of Lama Di Sotto when the enemy counter-attacked vigorously. One man of a light machine gun crew was hit and seriously wounded. Sergeant Toliver administered first aid and had him evacuated in plain view of the foe, then manned the machine gun himself. For ten hours, he remained in the position without relief, through continuous hostile counter-attack. Once a group of enemy soldiers called out that they were friendly troops. Sergeant Toliver held his fire to verify this fact and the hostile group advanced to within hand-grenade range of his position when he opened fire, killing them all. Thirty minutes later they counter-attacked his position again. Holding fire until they were 30 yards away, he opened fire suddenly, killing all but three. Six times thereafter, the same actions were repeated until Sergeant Toliver had killed 22 and wounded two of the enemy.

William S. Meadows, First Lieutenant, Corps of Engineers, Silver Star. On February 1945, Lieutenant Meadows' mine party were being led up a hill under cover of darkness by his company guides for the purpose of breaching an enemy minefield. The guides lost their way and led the party into an unknown anti-personnel minefield, where an explosion killed the two guides instantly, wounded a member of the party, and caused the enemy to fire a heavy concentration of mortar and machine gun fire on the area. Knowing that the original minefield had to be reached that night to allow a scheduled infantry attack in the morning, Lieutenant Meadows left the party and went up alone, regardless of the intense enemy fire, to attempt to discover an exit from the present minefield.

Walter H. Merritt, Private First Class, Infantry. (Posthumous), Silver Star. On 11 February 1945, Private First Class Merritt, an automatic-rifleman, advanced with his company in an attack on enemy fortified positions. Upon reaching his objective, the company was ordered to withdraw because of heavy concentration of artillery, mortar, and machine gun fire. During the withdrawal an enemy machine gunner and sniper began to fire on the friendly troops. Private First Class Merritt volunteered to silence the enemy weapons that delayed the withdrawal. He advanced upon the enemy machine gun positions, but before he reached the hostile position he was hit several times by enemy sniper fire. Turning in the direction of the enemy sniper and firing several rounds from his BAR, he killed the sniper instantly. Although seriously wounded, Private First Class Merritt then resumed his advance upon the enemy positions and continued his fire until the crew was either killed or had abandoned the positions, and he himself was struck by an enemy mortar shell.

Kenneth Watkins, Private First Class, Infantry. (Posthumous), Silver Star. On 8 February 1945, Private First Class Watkins' squad had been pinned down by one of the snipers. Observing three snipers in a gun emplacement to his front, Private First Class Watkins, without regard for personal safety, and under heavy hostile artillery fire, moved out alone and threw three hand grenades into the enemy position which killed a German soldier. As his squad resumed its advance, he noted an enemy machine gun crew covering the side of a house. Quickly exposing himself, Private First Class Watkins shot the two enemy soldiers before they could fire their weapons. He then captured three enemy soldiers as they emerged from a dug-out and turned them over to his platoon sergeant. Following this, he began establishing a defensive position with his squad, and while thus engaged, was mortally wounded by an enemy sniper.

Rudolph E. Raiford, Second Lieutenant, Infantry, Silver Star. On 4 February 1945, plans for an attack on an enemy fortified position necessitated safe routes of advance through mine-infested terrain and knowledge of the exact location of hostile strong points which had defied aerial observation. Lieutenant Raiford volunteered to lead a daylight patrol to secure this vital information. With utter disregard for his own safety he led the patrol under intense small arms and mortar fire to its objective. Without communication, he accomplished his mission and exposed himself to enemy fire, which severely wounded him. He refused to leave because of his wounds until he had secured all information necessary and then led every member of the patrol back without casualty.

Mansfield Mason, Technical Sergeant, Infantry, Silver Star. 15 Jan 45, as a member of a patrol sent out to capture a known hostile position, Sergeant Mason was the first to reach the house in which the enemy was located. When one of the enemy stuck an automatic weapon out of the window to cover the patrol's approach, Sergeant Mason quickly maneuvered to a favorable position and threw a hand grenade in the window. He then led two other men to positions where hand grenades could be used most effectively against the house. The rest of the patrol was then able to charge the house under fire and without casualty to itself and capture all of the enemy force which consisted of one officer, 10 enlisted men and one Italian Fascist, all heavily armed with rifles, automatic weapons and hand grenades.

Jesse E. Jarman, Captain, Infantry. (Posthumous), Silver Star. On 2-8-45, Captain Jarman personally led his company over difficult mountain terrain in an attack on an enemy hill. Under the pressure of intense enemy mortar, artillery and small arms counter-fire, he encouraged and exhorted his men to continue their aggressive advance by personal example. After each desperate burst of withering small arms fire, he positioned his men more advantageously and pushed forward with zeal and fortitude. With total disregard for snipers, Captain Jarman continually exposed himself to strengthen his position, undaunted in the face of the enemy. His capture of the hill yielded 15 prisoners and two machine guns. The company held their position against many vicious and determined enemy counter-attacks and inflicted numerous casualties on the enemy. His courageous initiative in extreme combat hazard exemplifies the American soldier's highest standard of fidelity to duty.

William S.M. Banks, Jr., Captain, Infantry. 2-6 to 2-14, 1945, Silver Star. Captain Banks' company attacked and seized a heavily mined hill. During the following 8 day period the enemy launched 8 separate determined counter-attacks against the position. Captain Banks personally deployed his company each time constantly supervising and encouraging his men and directing counter-mortar and artillery fire time and time again. On one occasion he personally commanded a group that repulsed a hostile attacking force, killing one enemy soldier and nine enlisted men. Captain Banks' extremely effective personal leadership of his company under hazardous combat conditions was in keeping with the gallant traditions of the United States Army.

Oak Leaf Cluster to Silver Star: Oscar Simpson, Staff Sergeant, Infantry. On 8 February, Staff Sergeant Simpson, a squad leader, was assigned the mission of protecting his company's left flank. During the assault, two other platoons of the Company became pinned down by enemy machine gun fire from well emplaced enemy dugouts. Sergeant Simpson, moving his squad on the right flank, was unaware of the platoon's being held-up and continued up the slope. Half-way up, he received enemy fire from an enemy bunker. Quickly he, single-handed and armed only with two hand grenades, assaulted the enemy bunker. He threw in a hand grenade and one enemy soldier surrendered; he prepared to throw the other when eight others piled out of the dugout, all surrendering to Staff Sergeant Simpson. In the dugout, he found American equipment and ammunition, and captured three enemy machine guns and five enemy rifles.

Six

Dismemberment of the Buffalo Division

High Level Discussions

In February, plans were in process by the American Fifth Army and the British Eighth Army to resume the general offensive in April.

At that time, General Mark Clark had been elevated to command of the 15th Army Group, and General Truscott had replaced him as Commander of the Fifth Army.

Command and staff from higher headquarters apparently concurred with General Truscott's damning report and negative conclusions about the 92nd Division. They also recognized that the Fifth Army must be able to maintain "an offensive attitude" on the west coast and be powerful enough to capture La Spezia, Carrara and other key objectives, when called upon to do so. There was doubt that the 92nd Division could attain these goals. Yet, in considering the constant reductions of forces available, and the high combat and attrition losses during the winter, it was decided that the division was too much needed to justify removing it entirely.

From the multiplicity of investigations going on concerning the division's operations, came many recommendations. These came from company commanders, battalion commanders, regimental commands, the division commander and some members of his staff—and General Truscott.

Significantly, there appears to be no evidence that any opinions or proposals were solicited from or forwarded by any of the very few black company commanders from the organic regimental combat teams; and none was solicited from any of the officers of the all black 366th Infantry, which included in its ranks many fine officers who were destined to become career officers in future wars of the United States.[1]

Had their opinions or recommendations been sought, it is certain that the consensus would have been that General Almond and his staff should be held fully responsible for the alleged "poor performance" of his command, and therefore relieved of it and replaced by another commander. It is equally certain that such a recommendation, had it been submitted as suggested above, would have been ignored.

It is doubtful had the 92nd Infantry division been composed of white American soldiers that the command would have remained unchanged under similar circumstances.

In his book, *Command Missions*, General Truscott said "no officer should expect to retain rank or assignment unless he fulfilled his responsibilities; or if another could fill them better, and "throughout my service, I have heard you young officers blamed for everything that went wrong. I believed that the blame was wrongly placed."[2]

One proposal seriously discussed was that certain of the division's battalions, including one from the 370th Infantry, and two of the 366th's three battalions, not be used again for offensive action unless urgent military necessity required it.[3]

In considering such action, it was determined that "without regard to efficiency, the 92nd Division could only be considered a defensive unit because of the scarcity of replacements for them."[4]

A critical problem, never previously mentioned publicly, had been the matter of trained, black officer and enlisted infantry replacements for the 92nd Division and the 366th Infantry since the fighting began. Part of the problems in command and control in combat situations was due: (1) to lack of replacements when casualties occurred, and, (2) when they were furnished, their lack of proper training and physical condition as infantrymen. It was an extremely serious problem.

There was no problem in stocks of replacements — officer or enlisted — for white infantry units. However, it was determined that replacement stocks of black troops would not be enough to maintain the 92nd Division in any sustained offensive. It now seems, that, in the 8-11 February attack, there may have been some doubt that enough black replacements were available to maintain the units involved had the attack not been planned as a "limited operation," but one in which they were supposed to advance beyond the limited objectives.

Note the comments regarding this conclusion[5]:

> Neither on 1 March or 1 April would sufficient Negro replacements be available to keep both the 92nd Division and the 366th Infantry up to ... levels for more than a few days in an offensive, although there should be enough replacements to maintain these units through limited operations of the type engaged in before February. If current shortages in the 366th Infantry were filled, not more than three to four hundred Negro infantry replacements all together, would be on hand 1 March.

As it worked out on 1 April, there were 2,000 Negro replacements for the entire 92nd Division in contrast to 1,200 available for the 442nd (Japanese-American) Regiment.[6]

The replacement problem was never discussed publicly as having any relation to the alleged "poor offensive performance" of the 92nd Division.

As in previous "crisis" situations, "high level" discussions continued, to decide what disposition to make of the 92nd Division. This time General George C. Marshall himself was on hand in Italy and participated along with General Truscott, Clark, Crittenberger and Almond. It is reported that General Marshall proposed that the most reliable officers and men from the three organic regiments of the division be used to form one regiment, and that the other two regiments then be replaced by a white regiment, the 473rd Infantry, and the Japanese-American 442nd Infantry.[7]

And so it was agreed.

Who would dare to question *any* suggestions by the most powerful soldier in the entire American military establishment?

General Almond's proposal was far reaching and called for virtual dismemberment of the 92nd Division as a so-called "black" infantry division; it also reflected his deep-seated hostility toward the 366th Infantry.

The 366th Infantry was to be removed entirely from the front lines, and he expressed no concern for its eventual disposition.[8] The 365th Infantry was to move south of Viareggio as a training replacement center for the division. The 371st Infantry was to take over from the 366th and the 365th in the Serchio Valley. The 473rd was to be attached to the division promptly and assigned to the Coastal Sector, and when this was done, the 370th was to be removed from front line responsibilities and re-organized in a rear area. Transfer of officers and men from the other two organic division regiments would begin immediately. The 442nd Infantry would be attached and assigned a training area near Viareggio, with organizational equipment turned in by the 366th assigned to it.

In General Almond's plan, no mention of transfers would be made. Units attached would not wear 92nd Division insignia until a "later date"; when both attached units had been thoroughly assimilated, they were then to be *assigned* to the 92nd Division.

General Truscott made some changes and his plan detailed as follows, was approved by 15th Army Group.[9]

The 473rd would be attached to the division in its present Cutigliano Sector on the right. The 365th Infantry would then gradually relieve the 473rd and the 366th (in the Serchio Valley). He felt such a use of the 365th was more profitable than its use as a replacement source for the division. The 371st would be removed from the lines and referred for control and used by Fifth Army as soon as practicable. Currently, the 371st and attached troops would hold the division's left flank to conceal the identity of the 473rd and the 442nd when any attack was commenced. The "new" 370th, as well as supporting troops, was to be utilized in any such attack. The 366th was then to be detached from 92nd Division control, and, he recommended, could be converted into a general service engineer unit "without occasioning any comment whatever." Further, the possibility of further return to the division of 366th personnel would be nullified. He too, shared General Almond's animosity toward the all-black regiment.

> Possibly, the designation "366th Infantry" might be preserved. By organizing two general service regiments all personnel of the 366th could be used, thereby avoiding returning any to replacement depots from which they might be routed individually back to the 92nd Division.

Letters, memos and reports travelled to and from the various command levels between 92nd Division and the 15th Army Group (and undoubtedly, even higher levels) about the reorganization.

There was concern expressed by General Guenther, Chief of Staff of 15th Army Group about the negative effect on the combat efficiency of the 365th and 371st regiments in the reorganization of the 370th; however, General Almond felt that it would not be serious as many experienced officers and non-commissioned officers would remain in the two affected regiments as all could not be used in the "new" 370th.[10] He stated quite frankly that he did not feel "that the combat reliability of the newly vitalized 370th Infantry will be greatly raised." He also felt that the divisional potential would be greatly increased by the use of the two attached regiments.

Both General Almond and General Truscott expressed concern about "political publicity aspects" (General Almond) and "occasional comment and unfavorable publicity, at least in the Negro Press" (General Truscott).

By 1 March the plan was almost completely implemented. By 17 March, 62 officers were transferred out of the 370th Infantry and 70 transferred in; 1264 enlisted men and 1 warrant officer, almost half of the regiment, were transferred out, and 1358 enlisted men and 1 warrant officer was transferred *in*. The total strength was then 139 officers, 3 warrant officers and 2800 enlisted men.

The exchanges between the 365th Infantry and the 473rd Infantry were completed and the 366th Infantry was withdrawn.

When the time for the spring offensive arrived the 92nd Division, formerly with all black enlisted men, presented a truly "Rainbow Division" as it prepared to join in what was destined to be the final offensive in the Italian campaign. It included:

> 1 white regiment, the 473rd Infantry;
> 1 Japanese-American regiment, the 442nd Infantry;
> 1 "new" black regiment, the 370th Infantry; with racially mixed officers (all company commanders were white),
> Organic artillery and service units of the 92nd Division which were black.
> Attached units, racially mixed, in a manner similar to the 92nd Division, included:
>
> 1 black (758th) and
> 1 white (the 760th) tank battalions;
> 1 black (the 679th) and
> 1 white (the 894th) tank destroyer battalions.

The 371st and the 365th Infantry were scheduled to operate in the Serchio and Cutigliana Sectors under *IV Corps* control. The newly constituted 92nd Division was to operate under Fifth Army control for the attack.

Seven

The Spring Offensive — 5 April–2 May 1945

The Allied Plan

The American Fifth and the British Eighth Armies' strategy was developed, as in earlier offensives, to[1]:

1. Hold steadfast against any enemy offensive gestures,
2. Force the maximum of enemy forces to remain in Italy; and
3. Seek, find, and completely destroy the enemy on the ground.

The Eighth, attacking from positions along the Adriatic Coast, and the Fifth moving forward along Highway #64, were to converge on and capture Bologna.

Barring their way were the formidable fortifications of the Gothic Line, aided and abetted by rugged terrain features, and some of the best trained and most experienced German units, who had been ordered by Hitler to defend the front at all costs.

If the majority of German forces south of the Po River could be destroyed and Bologna taken, the door would be opened to northern Italy and its great industrial and communication centers. The resulting capture of Verona would then cut off the German escape route through the Brenner Pass in northeast Italy.

The German Command worried about possible 92nd Division successes in the Serchio Valley and the Coastal Sector. They feared most an amphibious landing near La Spezia, which, with the now thoroughly and well-organized Partisan Forces debouching from mountain strongholds could open the way to Genoa and the Po River.

They watched to learn if sizeable reserves were being built-up in the Buffalo Division rear areas. As time passed, the Germans, seeing no evidence of such a build-up of strong reserves, concluded that no amphibious landing or even a major offensive in the Serchio Valley, would be forthcoming. Nevertheless they continued to improve their Gothic Line defenses.

Allied planners now realized that the Coastal Plain was the most heavily defended area within the U.S. IV Corps boundaries. The February operation convinced them of the futility of advancing along the coast directly into the face of these formidable enemy defenses without using massive and powerful forces to neutralize enemy artillery (including La Spezia and the Coastal guns at Punta Bianca), and to clear the enemy from the mountain masses east of Highway #1. Massa and Carrara must, too, be taken.

If successful, the offensive could lead to the collapse of all German forces in Italy.

The date for the drive was 9 April 1945, with initial moves for the main effort to be made by the Eighth Army.

On the Ligurian Coast, the 92nd Division was to launch a diversionary attack four days prior to the Allied offensive. It was hoped that it would at least *contain* all German forces in that sector, and also force the enemy to commit its local reserves as well as many from other German fronts.

Early Moves — Troop Dispositions

D-Day on the 92nd Division front was 5 April 1945.

In the pre-dawn hours, units of the "new" 92nd Division moved silently towards assembly areas in front of their initial objectives.

In the 370th Infantry, the First and Third Battalions were poised to assault the familiar high ground east of Highway #1. The Second Battalion, moving up behind the First Battalion, planned to cut sharply to the west onto the Coastal Plain after reaching Porta, with the object of seizing the flat lands north of the Cinquale Canal, then clearing out the enemy south of the Frigido River. The Third Battalion was to drive on Strettoia an hour after "jump off," then advance to the high ground overlooking Montignoso.

The First Battalion of the 371st Infantry was in the Serchio Valley. The Second Battalion was loosely dispensed along the Coastal Plain in front of the Cinquale Canal, destined only to make a "demonstration" towards the Canal once the attack commenced. Its Third Battalion was still in positions and holding the Mt. Cauala–Florida Ridge Line, where it was relieved by the 100th Battalion of the 442nd Infantry on the eve of the attack.

During the night of 3–4 April, the Third Battalion of the 442nd Infantry entered Azzano after a five-hour climb up steep, rocky trails and in drizzling rain. This little town, located on a peak in the Mt. Cavallo hills, was separated from the battalion objective, 2500 foot high Mt. Folgorito, by a narrow valley, and was under direct observation of the enemy. All day, on the 4th, the Nisei lay hidden in houses, unseen by the enemy. The next night the 100th Battalion relieved the Third Battalion, 371st Infantry on FLORIDA, just south of enemy-held GEORGIA. Simultaneously, the 442nd Cannon Company moved to Vallechia and tied into the Fire Direction Center of the 92nd Division's 599th Field Artillery Battalion.

At 2200 on 4 April, the Third Battalion moved two companies and a machine gun platoon between Mt. Folgorito and Mt. Carchio, from where an assault was to be launched against Mt. Folgorito from the rear; at the same time the 100th Battalion was set to attack GEORGIA frontally.

The Second Battalion, 442nd Infantry was held in mobile reserve.

The First and Third Battalions of the 473rd Infantry were in defensive

The Spring Offensive—5 April–2 May 1945

positions in the Serchio Valley, having relieved the Buffaloes' 365th Infantry, which had been sent to the Cutigliano Sector. The Second Battalion was held as Division Reserve in the Coastal Sector on 5 April.

Although two of the organic black regiments were detached from the 92nd Division they did continue to fight as infantry under IV Corps control.

The Buffalo Division was now composed of the white 473rd Infantry, the Japanese-American 442nd Infantry, and only *one* black (370th) Infantry. However, all of its organic units in which all enlisted men, and some junior officers, were black, continued to function in this final offensive. These units included the Division Artillery, the Combat Engineer Battalion, the Medical Battalion, the Cannon Companies, the air observation planes and all the other elements utilized throughout the combat experience of the 92nd Division. Thus, over one-half of the "new" 92nd Division was still black, and their performance was to be of vital importance to the eventual victory.

Attached and added to these black components in the "new" 92nd Division were several combat elements—previously mentioned—with all-black enlisted men and some black junior officers. The sum total then, of all black soldiers involved in the 92nd Division's offensive, could well be sufficient to justify the continuing label of "black" Division.

At 0500 on 5 April, the 92nd Division attack began.

In the center the 370th Infantry moved forward with the 597th and 598th Field Artillery Battalions, and three companies of Tank Destroyers, in support.

On the right, 442nd units attacked Mt. Folgorito from the north, and Mt. Carchio from the south, while its 100th Battalion struck GEORGIA behind a heavy preparatory barrage by the 599th Field Artillery Battalion, the Cannon Company, a company of tank destroyers, a chemical battalion (4.2 mortars), and the assault guns of the black 758th Tank Battalion.

The "new" 370th Infantry now had all white company commanders, and only one or two black junior officers in each company. They were strangers, for the most part, to one another, and many non-commissioned officers were in similar positions with enlisted men.

This situation created many problems in the battles to follow.

Nevertheless, the 370th attack moved well initially. The enemy, however, reacted quickly, and, as they had done in February, discovered that the 92nd Division plan of attack was along the same terrain and routes as before, and they covered the hills with pre-sited mortar and artillery fire and raked the ranks with machine gun and small arms fire in heavy volume throughout the day.

At dawn, shortly after Company A had frontally attacked HILL X, the company commander, Captain Doiranoff could not be found and the Artillery Forward Observer had been somehow separated from his radio.[2] It was soon discovered that Captain Dorianoff had been killed. By 0730, Company A was on HILL X, but was under heavy fire.

Despite the heavy mortar and artillery fire, Company B reinforced Company A on HILL X and moved to assault HILL Y. Heavy machine gun fire from enemy positions on HILL Y and the continual mortar and artillery fire caused many casualties, among them the company commander, Lieutenant Bailey, who was killed just short of the top of HILL Y.

In the meantime, C Company moved towards the west slope of HILL X before dawn surprising the enemy. They were halted temporarily, however, while a detail of infantrymen cleared a path through a minefield. When they resumed the attack, the enemy had become aroused and bombarded the company with mortar and machine gun fire and as they continued forward the fire increased and anti-personnel miles caused some casualties. Elements of two platoons and the mortar section were cut off and the radio operator became separated from the company commander, Captain John F. Runyon. Nevertheless, he ordered the company forward. He and three officers and twenty-five enlisted men set out along the Porta Ridge to within 250 yards of Castle Aghinolfi.

One of the officers with Captain Runyon was Lieutenant Walker, the Artillery Forward Observer. As fast as possible as they advanced, he called for artillery fires to their front. They moved at a run and had advanced so far and so quickly that their calls for artillery fire were often delayed for several precious minutes while the coordinates cited were re-checked. Once the artillery became convinced, however, they dropped shells on call as close as 75–100 yards in advance of the assault units.

As the company sped towards Castle Aghinolfi, the men stopped only to cut enemy wire communications lines and to catch their breath. More than a dozen communications wires were cut, and this saved many lives later. Their attack was so swift that it caught the enemy in the vicinity of the Castle by surprise; some were destroyed and their occupants killed, but as they drew nearer to the objective, the now thoroughly aroused enemy came out of dugouts and positions and resisted strongly. Enemy mortar fire increased and heavy enemy machine gun fire was concentrated on the exposed right flank. The enemy fire and small counter-attacks left them in a precarious position.

Captain Runyon, feeling that the position could be held, called for reinforcements. At first the Regimental S-3 refused to accept the forward observer's word for the company's position, and once again, Company C had to convince the regiment that it had moved as far forward as it had.[3] Captain Runyon was told that no reinforcements were available, since other elements of the 370th Infantry were having massive difficulty in moving and holding in positions.

Captain Runyon, noting that of his group of 25 enlisted men and 4 officers, 18 enlisted men and 2 officers were either killed or wounded, decided to withdraw five hundred yards to prepare a defensive position. Lieutenant Botwinik, who was severely wounded by mortar fire and temporarily blinded for about thirty minutes, protested the decision to withdraw. Lieutenant Baker, the only black officer in the Company, wanted desperately to remain in position and fight on, and he, too, protested the decision.

Captain Runyon and Lieutenant Baker made one last effort to place their men in a strong defensive position, but by this time the enemy mortar, artillery and machine gun fire was so intense that it was impossible to move, even for a short distance, without casualties resulting. Several key non-

The Spring Offensive—5 April–2 May 1945

commissioned officers had already become casualties, adding to the difficulty of control.

The withdrawal was organized into two groups. Lieutenant Baker volunteered to cover the withdrawal of the first group which consisted of most of the walking wounded, and to remain to help remove the more severely wounded. Eight enlisted men and the wounded artillery officer stayed with him. During the withdrawal, the first group destroyed four different machine gun nests without loss to itself.[4] Lieutenant Baker's party followed, immediately behind. A sniper killed one of his men and mortar fire wounded another, just as they started out. Private James Thomas, his Browning Automatic Rifleman, located the sniper and killed him. Shortly thereafter, the party ran into two machine gun nests by-passed earlier in the attack. Covered by the Browning Automatic Rifle fire of Private Thomas, Lieutenant Baker crawled carefully and patiently to the positions and destroyed both with hand grenades, clearing the way for the safe evacuation of the wounded to the battalion aid station. For his actions on this day and for leading a battalion advance the following night, Lieutenant Baker was awarded the Distinguished Service Cross. Here are the words of his citation:

> Vernon J. Baker, Second Lieutenant, Infantry, U.S. Army. For extraordinary heroism in action on 5 and 6 April 1945, near Viareggio, Italy. Second Lieutenant Baker demonstrated outstanding courage and leadership in destroying enemy installations, personnel and equipment during his Company's attack against a strongly entrenched enemy in mountainous terrain. When his company was stopped by the concentrated fire from several machine gun emplacements, he crawled to one position and destroyed it, killing three Germans. Continuing forward, he attacked an enemy observation post and killed its two occupants. With the aid of one of his men, Second Lieutenant Baker attacked two more machine gun nests, killing or wounding the four enemy soldiers occupying these positions. He then covered the evacuation of the wounded personnel of his company by occupying an exposed position and drawing the enemy's fire. On the following night, Lieutenant Baker voluntarily led a battalion advance through enemy minefields and heavy fire towards the Division objective. Second Lieutenant Baker's fighting spirit and daring leadership were an inspiration to his men and exemplified the highest traditions of the Armed Forces. Second Lieutenant Baker had previously been awarded a Bronze Star and the Purple Heart medals. He now became the only black officer in the 92nd Infantry Division and in the Mediterranean Theatre of Operations to win the Distinguished Service Cross, the nation's second highest military award.

Many felt he should have received the Congressional Medal of Honor.

Captain Runyon, who received the Silver Star for this action, and his intrepid group of 29 men from C Company, accounted for at least twenty-six German enlisted men and two German officers killed, and ten strongpoints (observation posts, bunkers, dugouts, and machine gun positions) destroyed.

There seems no doubt that their assault, with the results indicated, created much disorganization among the forces of the 281st German Infantry Regiment, which was not completely resolved within the next two days.

By 1030, C Company had completed its withdrawal and immediately began to reorganize near the base of HILL X.

Company A, dug in desperately on HILL X, fighting back with their own supporting artillery, mortars and all available infantry weapons. Although heavy casualties were inflicted on the enemy, the companies of the First Battalion were unable to advance any further on the first day.

Just as in the 8–11 February attack, the men found themselves moving into the face of heavy and accurate enemy artillery and mortar fire and mutually supporting machine gun fire from surrounding hills. They were forced into the same avenues of approach to HILLS X, Y, and Z that they had found covered with wire obstacles and minefields in February.

All that day, the troops of the First Battalion were pounded by enemy fire, and subjected to several counter-attacks, but by 2200 were still doggedly holding on to HILL Y.

At 1040 the Second Battalion, then in reserve, moved up to pass through the First Battalion, which covered the advance by the base of fire from small arms and automatic weapons. An artillery preparation preceded them and smoke was laid to cover their movement across the open flats to the base of HILL X. Despite the smoke covering the advance, enemy mortar and artillery, previously sited on the route of advance, struck the troops of the Second Battalion as they moved forward towards and up HILL X, causing many casualties and some disorganization. There was some confusion as the two battalions moved around HILL X, but by 1410 Company E of the Second Battalion was digging in on HILL Y.

The night of 5–6 April found two companies of the Second Battalion firmly atop HILL Y and one of its companies, along with elements of the First Battalion on HILL X.

The Third Battalion on the right, moved out against Strettoia and HILL Z, located just beyond a jagged ridge line above the west of the heavily defended town.

At 0600 just as K Company began its advance, it was bombarded by a massive concentration of enemy mortar fire which caused seven casualties. Simultaneously, the company received heavy and accurate machine gun fire from HILL Z, and were temporarily stopped. While K Company was reorganizing, I Company moved through it and launched the assault against HILL Z. L Company, meanwhile, had begun their attack on Strettoia, but were hit by heavy automatic weapons and mortar fire from HILL Z and German troops in strong points near the edge of town. Supported by fire from a platoon of tanks, they continued to forge ahead until slowed down because three of the tanks were neutralized by mines. With the tanks, a small group of infantrymen from the company remained in position the rest of the day unable to advance but returning the fire from the town and HILL Z.

By 1135, elements of Company I had fought to a point near the crest of HILL Z.

During the first day of the attack the enemy resistance was light at first, but increased in intensity as the day wore on. He was very strongly entrenched in well prepared defensive positions in the Strettoia Hill mass, which he had worked diligently to improve since the 8-11 February attack by the 92nd Division.

Although the 442nd Infantry, maneuvering brilliantly, was achieving spectacular success in its envelopment of the German forces on the high ground to the right, no visible depreciation of German resistance from their pill boxes, dugouts, bunkers and sniper posts, was yet discernable in the 370th sector. Artillery fire from light artillery pieces in the sector, and mortar fire continued to rain down with unerring accuracy on the battalions of the 370th Infantry moving up in the bright sunlight along routes pre-decided by the enemy and from the break of dawn, the deadly coastal guns fired uninterruptedly.

During the first day, four officers and ten enlisted men were killed; five officers and 109 enlisted men, and 15 enlisted men were missing.[5] Almost all of the casualties occurred in forward positions.

When darkness fell, elements of the First and Second Battalions were digging in on HILLS X and Y, and elements of a platoon from Company I of the Third Battalion were clinging to positions near the crest of HILL Z.

The 442nd Moves on the Mountains

This Japanese-American regiment, returning to the Italian Theatre after six months of fighting in France, was one of the finest regiments in the United States Army. It had fought in all the major allied offensives in Italy, beginning on the beaches at Salerno, in September, 1943. It was among the most decorated regiments in the war, and was led by outstanding officers and non-commissioned officers.

Its Regimental Staff, given free rein, apparently, to accomplish their mission, devised the brilliant maneuver to envelope the right flank, attack the enemy from the rear of his high mountain positions, simultaneously with a powerful frontal attack on the lower ridge line strong points.

This plan was in direct contrast to the frontal attacks ordered for the 92nd Division, in the 8-11 February attack, and currently still followed in this operation.

The 442nd staff had studied the patrol reports of the 92nd Division troops that had been gathered throughout their operations in the winter, and learned much about enemy dispositions and defenses as well as trails and approaches along the Mt. Cerretta-Mt. Folgorito Ridge.

At 0600, the Third Battalion attacked, with one platoon striking north on Mt. Carchio, and one company, south towards Mt. Folgorito. The enemy was completely surprised and initial objectives were taken quickly, but at considerable cost. Realizing the threat from the rear, the reaction was quick and violent, but the element of surprise and the fury of their assault led to the victory of the 442nd.

Two companies were caught in a heavy enemy mortar concentration, but despite 42 casualties, they pressed on and with the rest of the Third Battalion, they dug in on Mt. Folgorito, and held fast.

They decided to forego seizing Mt. Carchio at that time, so the small enemy force was driven into the recesses of the peak and contained with artillery fire (which destroyed two observation posts), and small arms fire.[6]

During the night of 5 April, the Second Battalion of the 442nd Infantry, in reserve, was sent over the same route of the Third Battalion the previous night, to pass northwest through the Third Battalion and attack Mt. Belvedere, the last massive mountain overlooking the city of Massa, the Division Objective.

At 0500, after a ponderous concentration of fire from all supporting weapons, the 100th Battalion attacked, advancing through dense minefields. They stormed the crest of GEORGIA, driving the dazed and demoralized Germans down the reverse slopes towards the OHIO peaks in a fire-fight that lasted throughout the day.

The 442nd suffered 20 killed and 123 wounded in the first day of fighting.[7]

On 6 April, the 370th Infantry resumed the attack.

During the night, considerable enemy artillery fire had been directed against HILL X and approaches to other enemy positions.

The Second Battalion, with troops on HILLS X and Y, again prepared to attack and seize the high ground around Castle Aghinolfi. The First Battalion, with its companies A, B, and C completely its reorganization on HILL X, was poised to pass through the Second Battalion on order. The Third Battalion was alerted for movement on call across the Porta Ridge, then to attack north of Porta to seize the area along the Magro Canal. During the night, the 317th Engineers were able to build a bridge across the Cinquale Canal, opening Highway #1 to Porta.

At 0610, after a ten-minute preparation by the 598th Field Artillery Battalion, the Second Battalion moved forward. No sooner had their attack begun, however, when a heavy concentration of enemy artillery and mortar fire blanketed the entire hill, causing heavy casualties and slowing the advance. It seems the enemy had monitored radio messages from the Headquarters of the attacking forces giving the time and place of the attack.

Despite heavy casualties, the Second Battalion prepared to attack again at 0800 after another artillery preparation fired on enemy positions. But the enemy was again prepared, and again pounded the front lines with heavy mortar and artillery fire. Monitoring of enemy radio messages revealed they had the necessary information to justify their calling for reinforcements to repel the attack. In addition to the accurate artillery and mortar concentration, enemy small arms and automatic weapons fire added to the toll.

The Second Battalion continued to struggle forward, while trying to reorganize under the fire which continued in spite of almost continuous defensive fires by the 598th and 597th Field Artillery Battalions.

At 0930 the First Battalion attempted to pass through the struggling Second Battalion, but could not move due to the heavy curtain of mortar and

The Spring Offensive—5 April–2 May 1945

artillery fire directed on the narrow corridor through which they all had to pass. They continued, however, with determination, to try to clear the hills. At 1330, from positions on HILL X, the First Battalion reached out to assault an enemy position on the Porta Ridge. Company C, low in spirits after their ordeal on the previous day, began to work their way into their attack formation. In the midst of this critical maneuver, the company commander, Captain Runyon, was taken out of the line for special duty with the 473rd Infantry, and the Company preceeded with another *new* commander. While running across a flat, open, area, newly assigned Captain Donald M. Counts, was seriously wounded by automatic weapons fire. He died later that day.[8] The First Battalion had now lost all of its three commanders who began the battle on 5 April, as well as a replacement company commander. Despite their demoralizing experience, the battalion proceeded as ordered, to organize a defensive line on HILL Y.

On the right, the Third Battalion was in a line from Mt. Castiglione to Strettoia shortly after midnight, with three officers and some 60 enlisted men as casualties.

The Buffalo Soldiers continued to fight with great courage and determination and inflicted heavy casualties on the enemy during the day's fighting. The Germans, despite their heavy losses, zealously carried out their orders to hold at all costs. Division supporting artillery and mortars continued to bombard enemy positions on the crests of the hills and all routes of approach were harassed by searching fires. Enemy installations and supply routes in the rear areas were pounded by the artillery and planes bombed and strafed everything that moved within their view.

The problems and difficulties faced by the black enlisted men were not all of their own making. The Third Battalion Commander had this to say[9]:

> One company commander was "discouraged," and *asked* to be relieved. The company commander of I Company was evacuated for shell shock, and the executive officer was wounded, leaving a second lieutenant in command. The zone assigned to the battalion initially was such that it made one of the attacking companies subject to fire from both flanks as well as the front.

On 6 April, after a full day of fierce fighting, the 442nd Infantry, using its Second and Third Battalions, completed the task of reducing Mt. Carchio to the northwest and Mt. Folgorito and Mt. Cerretta to the south, preparatory to moving on Mt. Belvedere.

The 100th Battalion fought desperately against the well-entrenched enemy on the OHIO peaks, for two hours without making any gains. Then, after pin-point bombing and strafing air attacks, followed by a ten-minute artillery concentration, they moved forward beyond the OHIO's to Mt. Cerretta. All opposition there had been eliminated after two hours of bitter fighting and by Third Battalion elements coming from the north.

Before the day ended, an assault against Mt. Belvedere was made by the Second Battalion.

During the day, the 442nd Infantry casualties were 13 killed, 60 wounded.

On 7 April, the First Battalion, 370th Infantry withdrew before dawn and moved to the Serchio Valley.

The Second Battalion, 370th Infantry, still in its positions after its First Battalion withdrew, now again lay patiently while the Second Battalion, 473rd Infantry, passed through them on their way up to the Porta Ridge line.

The movements were made without artillery preparation and under complete pre-dawn darkness. During the day, the Second Battalion, 370th Infantry continued to fight against the enemy, in their emplacements on HILLS Y and Z.

By 0800, they had taken HILL Y and were reaching out to HILL Z. By 1730 Hills Y and Z were in the hands of the Second Battalion, after a day of bitter, hard fighting, and elements of the battalion had moved into the village of Strinato.

The Third Battalion, with a tank force consisting of elements of the 894th Tank Destroyer Battalion, the 370th Tank Battalion and the 758th Tank Battalion, was alerted to move down Highway #1 and to seize the area south of the Magro Canal.

With the Second Battalion, 473rd Infantry, and the Second Battalion, 370th Infantry gradually wearing down the German defenders along Porta Ridge up to the near-summit of Castle Aghinolfi, and on Hills X, Y, and Z, it was expected that the Third Battalion Tank Force would be able to forge right through to the objective. The tanks, however, were held up by minefields, and increased fire from artillery and mortars and machine guns to their immediate front. The battalion ordered a reinforced platoon to occupy Porta and later, the rest of the company moved forward to reinforce the platoon. South of the village the company was halted by the heavy enemy fire from the Porta Ridge and efforts to outflank the enemy force failed. By 2315, Company K drew to within 400 yards of Porta.

On 7 April, the Second Battalion, 473rd Infantry was guided through the First Battalion, 370th Infantry by Captain Runyon, Lieutenant Baker and some of their men who had fought their way along the same fearful route 24 hours earlier.

The enemy forces defending the slopes and hill tops of the Strettoia Hill mass had been badly mauled and battered by the intense pressure by the three battalions of the 370th Infantry. Although they had been able to hold their ground near and on the summits of Hills Y, Z, and Aghinolfi, their troops were taxed to the utmost because of the repeated assaults by the Buffalo Soldiers. Minefields had been breached, with no opportunity for them to re-sow them; many of their "impregnable" pill boxes and bunkers had been destroyed; several strong-points of resistance had been overwhelmed, or severely reduced in strength; many prisoners had been taken and many weapons and material captured.

Their positions had been pounded continuously by all supporting elements of the attack by the 370th Infantry. These included: Air Force bombing and strafing of great accuracy and precision; and uninterrupted

The Spring Offensive—5 April–2 May 1945

flow of accurate and devastating fire from the 598th and 597th Field Artillery Battalions, which led Buffalo infantrymen by as little as 75–100 yards in their advances, helping to break up several counter-attacks, and whose defensive fire plans placed a curtain of steel before the enemy during critical phases of the action; the terrifying, flat-trajectory fires from supporting tank destroyers, tanks, depressed anti-aircraft guns, which, though not always able to destroy concrete pill boxes and dug-outs and bunkers, continually drove the defenders into these emplacements for shelter and protection, thus limiting their mobility; and all of the supporting infantry weapons—mortars, 50 and 30 calibre heavy machine guns, and 60 and 81 mm mortars—of the assaulting battalions. Added to the fire on these enemy positions for the two days, was the supporting fire from all the infantry weapons of the Second Battalion, 371st Infantry, along the Cinquale Canal near the coast.

Even as the Second Battalion, 473rd Infantry advanced through minefields and under heavy enemy fire, the gallant 442nd Infantry had swept clean the enemy installations along the Mt. Cauala–Mt. Cerretta–Mt. Folgorito–Mt. Carchio ridge line and had begun its reduction of enemy forces atop 2800 foot-high Mt. Belvedere, paving the way for the imminent seizure of Carrara and Massa from the north. And, even as the battalions of the 473rd and 370th Infantry moved to clear the Strettoria Hills of the enemy, a general German withdrawal was beginning up Highway #1.

Nevertheless, the enemy troops facing them continued to fight ferociously, determined to hold their line at all costs.

The 473rd, by-passing Strettoia and Porta Ridge, had its three companies deployed along a line running east from Porta, to the left-front portion of HILL Y, by 0900.

By 1800 they had fought their way almost to Castle Aghinolfi, where C Company, 370th Infantry had been.

At that point they paused to reorganize and consolidate positions, preparatory to resuming the attack the next morning.

On the 7th, while engaged in reorganization, the 442nd Infantry continued to contend with opposition from the German forces. The Third Battalion in a furious two-hour battle wiped out an enemy force which was trying to infiltrate its positions on Mt. Folgorito.

The 100th Battalion cleared its sector of enemy forces and improved their defensive positions along the ridge from Mt. Cauala to Mt. Cerretta. A patrol from Company B moved into the town of Strettoia, below ROCKY RIDGE, and occupied it without opposition.

Meanwhile, the Second Battalion battled on against troops of the Machine Gun Battalion "Kesselring," fighting as infantry. These German soldiers were veterans of fighting in the Italian Campaign, and were supported by heavy concentrations of mortar, artillery and fire from the deadly coastal guns on Punta Bianca. They also made expert use of their machine guns, and other infantry weapons, giving ground reluctantly.

By 1800, the Second Battalion had overcome enemy resistance on Mt. Belvedere and on the night of 7–8 April, a strong enemy counter-attack was repulsed with heavy enemy losses.

The 442nd Infantry was now on the summit of Mt. Belvedere, with the Second Battalion preparing to clear out remaining enemy positions and drive down the reserve slopes toward the Frigido River. The Third Battalion prepared to attack German strong points along the Colle Piano spur and seize Montignoso. The 100th Battalion was in control of Strettoia, and the Mt. Cauala-Mt. Cerreta Ridge.[10]

In the center, the Second Battalion 473rd Infantry and the Second Battalion, 370th Infantry had driven the enemy from the Strettoia Hills— X, Y and Z and around Castle Aghinolfi; on the flat ground below Porta Ridge, and Third Battalion, 370th Infantry was preparing to advance up Highway #1 with a Tank Force; and on the coast, the 371st Infantry stood watch over the Cinquale Canal.

The German defenses had suffered a severe pummeling from troops of the 92nd Division—white, black and Japanese-American—and evidences of a beginning deterioration began to appear the next morning.

By daybreak of 8 April, the pre-planned shifting of elements of the original 92nd Division Regiments continued.

The Second Battalion, 370th Infantry relieved the Second Battalion, 371st Infantry along the Cinquale Canal, leaving its Company E to hold the high ground between Highway #1 and Strettoia. The Second Battalion, 371st Infantry joined the rest of its regiment, now under control of IV Corps, east of the zone of advance of the 92nd Division. The Third Battalion, 370th Infantry was attached to the 473rd Infantry, while the First Battalion, 473rd Infantry was moving into an assembly area near Pietrasanta. The Third Battalion, 473rd Infantry, was still in the Serchio Valley, attached to the 370th Infantry.

Two hours past midnight, as elements of K Company, 370th Infantry approached Porta, they received heavy bazooka and machine gun fire, and withdrew to reorganize. Despite not being able to assemble all the company in the darkness, Company K moved out at 0600 along the base of Porta Ridge, while Companies I and L made contact with 473rd Infantry and coordinated the attack with them.

Patrols, finding no enemy in Porta and the hills immediately east, moved up Highway #1 and by 1120, Company K had reached the road junction of Highway #1 and the Montignoso Road beyond the Castle. The Third Battalion then advanced to the south back of the Magro Canal and the Montignoso draw. A patrol to Montignoso determined there were only a few wounded enemy in the town; however, a patrol to the outskirts of Massa drew heavy enemy and artillery fire. That night the companies deployed to sectors between the highway and the sea and set up security positions.

During the day, the 473rd Infantry was given responsibility for the Coastal Sector and the 370th Infantry, less the Third Battalion, took over the Serchio Valley. The Third Battalion remained attached to the 473rd.

On the morning of 8 April, troops of the Second Battalion, 473rd Infantry, like those of the Third Battalion, 370th Infantry, were a bit slow in moving out.[11] There was little or no fire, however, as it became quickly evident that the enemy had pulled out of Porta during the night.

The Spring Offensive—5 April–2 May 1945

When they did get organized, they moved rapidly down to the flats and advanced to the Montignoso draw and occupied Montignoso and other small towns, sending patrols to contact elements of the 442nd Infantry on the right.

That night, the First Battalion accompanied by tanks of the 760th Tank Battalion, attacked up Highway #1 towards Massa. Tank traps, mines, heavy artillery and mortar fire, coupled with strong rearguard enemy installations, temporarily impeded their progress. The heavy fighting continued throughout the night of 8–9 April.

The Third Battalion, 442nd Infantry, cleared Colle Piano of the enemy, after hard fighting, by 1430, and two hours later they entered Montignoso, capturing fifty prisoners and making contact with elements of the 473rd Infantry.

On the right of the 442nd Combat Team sector, its Second Battalion, in a dawn attack, overran remaining enemy positions on Mt. Belvedere and clearing the mountain top, killing 20 enemy and capturing 30. Then, overcoming heavy artillery and mortar fire, concentrated and coordinated heavy machine gun fire, the Second Battalion, in a three-hour battle, destroyed several heavily defended enemy strongpoints, and finally seized the Colle Tecchione spur, a 2000 yard long ridge overlooking Massa from the east. They then withstood heavy mortar fire and barrages from enemy self-propelled guns on the coastal plain, and repelled several strong enemy counter-attacks, two of which penetrated their positions.[12]

Meanwhile, other elements of the Second Battalion advanced down the slopes of Mt. Belvedere to attack the towns of Altagnana and Pariana. By nightfall, they were on the out-skirts of both towns.

During the night of 9 April, the coastal gun batteries at Punta Bianca fired all along Highway #1 and on inland targets.

The enemy's main defensive positions now appeared to be behind the Frigido River Line.[13]

After having advanced some 3–5 kilometers on 8 April, the Third Battalion, 370th Infantry resumed the attack at 0600. By 0900, L Company on the left, had advanced to within 200 yards of the Frigido River, while Companies I and K advanced more slowly in the center and on the right.

The enemy put up savage resistance, and it became obvious that there was no intention of abandoning their positions. Tanks assisting K Company ran into mines and the troops received heavy machine gun fire from the *south* bank of the river, as well as a heavy volume of artillery fire.

Company I, in the center, was held up by three machine guns about 800 yards south of the river and enemy riflemen fired rifle grenades into their left flank, now open because of the more forward position of L Company on its left. Elements of the company attacked the machine gun positions, silencing them, but suffering eleven wounded, including the acting company commander. They captured 4 prisoners in this action, and continued to advance slowly under continued heavy fire from all available enemy weapons.

In order to improve the positions of Companies I and L several tanks were sent through Company L's position to neutralize some machine guns in several buildings to the immediate front. According to the plan, once the tanks accomplished that mission, they were to turn east and move toward Massa, with infantry of I and K to move *forward* at the same time. Heavy minefields and accurate artillery and mortar fire caused diversion from the plan by the leading tank and the tanks' mission was not carried out.

The two companies continued to make slow progress.

That night, after fighting the stubborn, reluctantly yielding enemy for five days and having maintained a forward position all day, the Third Battalion moved to the east side of the Serchio River. It joined the First Battalion and its parent 370th Infantry Regimental Command now in action in the Serchio Valley Sector.

Officers and men of the Third Battalion felt cheated because they were being withdrawn from the sector at a time when maximum pressure from three sides was beginning to cause serious perceptible weakening in the alignments of enemy forces. It was felt that the fall of Massa was imminent and somehow they felt they should have been given the honor of being a part of the conquest.

The Second Battalion now was the only element of the 370th Infantry remaining in action in the Coastal Sector. After clearing Strettoia on 8 April, they moved through Montignoso and took over the security of the right flank of the Coastal area.

The Third Battalion positions west of Highway #1 and south of Frigido River were taken over by E Company and a machine gun platoon of the Second Battalion on the morning of 10 April.

The First Battalion of the 473rd Infantry fought all night on 8-9 April, supported by tanks of the 760th Tank Battalion; during the day they advanced slowly through tank traps, extensive minefields and heavy enemy artillery and mortar fire, and strong rearguard enemy strongpoints. By dusk they had reached the outskirts of Massa, and during the night of 9-10 April, its elements were engaged about a quarter of a mile from the center of the city. Tanks of the 758th and 760th Tank Battalion reached the center of the city but were forced to withdraw. The coastal guns at Punta Bianca continued to fire on the entire coastal sector front line units, despite aerial and naval attacks. Approximately ten vehicles were lost to them during the operation.[14]

The Second Battalion, 473rd Infantry, meanwhile, was fighting its way against resolute enemy resistance towards Rocca, east of Massa, drawing even with the First Battalion.

Both battalions now stood poised to enter Massa.

The Second Battalion, 442nd Infantry, resumed the attack against Altagnana and Pariana clearing both strongholds. A vicious all-day battle at Pariana resulted in the destruction of the remnants of the Machine Gun Battalion Kesselring.

At the same time, the Third Battalion intercepted a large force of Germans infiltrating back to the Colle Tecchione Ridge Line and threatening the Second Battalion. Caught in an indefensible position, this force was destroyed by the Third Battalion mortar, machine gun and rocket fire.

The Spring Offensive—5 April–2 May 1945

The enemy was now in headlong retreat towards his second defensive line.

The 100th Battalion on Mt. Folgorito, Mt. Carchio, and Mt. Belvedere, was relieved by the Second Battalion, 370th Infantry (less E Company), and moved to the vicinity of Altagnana and Regimental Reserve.

The enemy defending Massa suffered heavy casualties among its men and material and, during the night of 9-10 April, began to pull out toward its second defense lines north of the Frigido River Line.

Although the guns at Punta Bianca continued to fire, elements of the First Battalion, 473rd Infantry, moved into Massa unopposed, and the Second Battalion moved forward to the south bank of the Frigido River.

From the hills surrounding Massa, large units of well-organized and vengeance-seeking Italian partisans, struck at 0800.

Towering Mt. Brugiano, a few rugged miles north of Massa, fell to troops of the 442nd Infantry, eliminating vital escape routes for the hard-pressed enemy.

Massa was taken, fully occupied on 10 April 1945, and became the first major objective taken by the Allied Forces in the spring offensive, yet to begin.

Although "Plan Second Wind" specified the main effort to be made in the Coastal Sector, full consideration was given to the strategic and tactical importance of the Serchio Valley; it was fully realized that the Serchio Valley represented a possible route of approach by strong enemy forces situation along the dominating Llama di Sotto Ridge Line which included Gothic Line installations and fortifications.

It was recognized, too, that a victory in the Coastal Sector would cause the forces in the Serchio Valley to risk being outflanked, and thus it was necessary to maintain a strong, actively patrolling contact force there, prepared to engage in strong pursuit of the enemy; or to provide a force to exploit any successes or to reinforce any positions undergoing difficulty in the Coastal Sector.

The First and Third Battalions, 473rd Infantry were firmly holding positions in the Serchio Valley, with orders to engage in constant, aggressive patrolling. Its Second Battalion was in Division Reserve. Eventually, all elements of the Regiment were united in the offensive in the Coastal Sector, and the First and Third Battalions of the 370th Infantry took over in the Serchio Valley. The Second Battalion, 370th Infantry made a two day forced march over very precipitous terrain to rejoin the Regiment at Gragnola on 23 April.

Destruction and Pursuit—11 April-2 May

After the fall of Massa, it was clearly evident that the enemy was acutely disorganized and beginning to disintegrate. Resistance, though confused, was fanatical, however.

The attack continued north and east, on 11 April, with the 473rd

Infantry aiming for La Spezia and the 442nd Infantry moving in the direction of Aulla.

Task Force Curtis was given the mission of clearing the coast area west of Massa to the sea. This tank-infantry force consisted of elements of the 760th and the 758th Tank Battalions, and the 894th Tank Battalion; the infantry force consisted of E Company, 370th Infantry with the Anti-Tank Company, 473rd Infantry, attached. The Third Battalion was in the Serchio Valley Sector with the mission of maintaining its present positions at all costs, aggressive patrolling and to be prepared to quickly follow up any enemy withdrawal.

The 473rd Infantry attacked north across the Frigido River; the First Battalion, with tank support, crossed west of Massa, while the Second Battalion began to cross east of the city. Their advance was slow and strongly resisted by the enemy. Enemy artillery fire was heavy and the coastal guns at Punta Bianca continued to fire with devastating effect. By 17 April, troops of the 473rd had occupied Ortonova, Lama, and Casano and Castelnuovo.

On 20 April, the Third Battalion moved from the Serchio Valley, joining the Regiment at Avenza. Strong enemy resistance delayed the occupation of Sarzana by the First and Third Battalions on 22 April while the Second Battalion assembled near Carrara.

On 20 April it was learned that La Spezia was now occupied by Partisan forces. That night a forward observer from the black 600th Field Artillery Battalion, led by Partisan guides and accompanied by an officer and two enlisted men from the 473rd Infantry, crossed the Magro River. He set up an observation post from where he could observe the coastal gun batteries which had been pounding Allied forces for several months. During the next 24 hours several of these guns were silenced—at last—by the 600th Field Artillery and attached units, as soon as they came within range.

All thirty-six of the 76 mm guns of the 679th Tank Destroyer Battalion were adjusted to fire on them, whenever the coastal guns fired. In six days, firing from 60 to 180 rounds simultaneously, they fired 11,066 rounds on the guns.

An 8 inch howitzer from the 530th Field Artillery Battalion joined in from 14 April to 23 April.

On the 24th a task force of tanks and infantry, led by the executive officer of the black 758th Tank Battalion, Major Roy L. Chatham, entered La Spezia without opposition. Elements of the 92nd Division's 317th Engineer Combat Battalion were a part of that Task Force.

Meanwhile, Task Force Steinman, built around the 92nd Reconnaissance Troop, with a platoon of Anti-Tank Company, 473rd Infantry, moved into La Spezia also. This task force had been engaged in patrol and reconnaissance activities between the 442nd Infantry and the 370th Infantry to the east.

At this time, the 473rd Combat Team was designated, and it included the following organic elements from the 92nd Division: 598th Field Artillery Battalion, B Company, 317th Engineer Battalion, and the 317th Medical Battalion.

The Spring Offensive—5 April–2 May 1945

The next objective of the 473rd Combat Team was Genoa.

The 442nd Infantry, having seized the commanding ground overlooking the entire coastal plain, now prepared to press on towards Aulla, key transportation, trade, and communications hub, which controlled the only avenues of escape to the Po Valley for German forces in this sector.

By destroying the enemy garrisons on Mt. Folgorito, Mt. Carchio, Mt. Brugiano and Mt. Belvedere, they forced the enemy to withdraw from Punta Bianca, La Spezia, and Massa. Because of their lightning-like strikes against these key mountain fortifications, they found themselves impatiently waiting to plunge forward because of the 473rd Infantry's slower progress on the coast against strong, but essentially rear-guard actions by the rapidly disintegrating German defenses.

While the 100th Battalion moved north to protect the regiment's eastern flank, elements of the 370th Infantry took over the garrison of Mt. Belvedere and Mt. Carchio.

On 11 April Carrara was occupied, in coordination with a well-organized partisan group. The 100th Battalion was then held in Carrara to protect the regimental left and rear until the 473rd Infantry should advance that far.[15]

Once La Spezia and Carrara were secured, the way was opened for the final drive to Genoa along the coast, and towards Aulla.

On 14 April the regiment moved out swiftly and, after a two-and-a-half hour firefight with crack German troops from the sparse reserves shifted in desperation from the hard-pressed Bologna front, they moved on to assault formidable Mt. Pizzacato.

By noon of 24 April, a tank-infantry task force of the 442nd Infantry had occupied Mt. Grosso, south of Aulla.

The 370th Infantry, now the only organic regiment of the 92nd Infantry Division to be operating in the offensive, was not idle.

The enemy occupied strong positions on both sides of the Serchio River and commanded all of the high ground. Terrain features provided the same advantages to the enemy as had existed throughout the preceding winter months.

The 370th Infantry exerted heavy pressure on the enemy. Strong combat patrols went forward at night and in the daytime to contact the enemy, destroy his installations, capture prisoners, and to try to locate unmined trails for future use.

Direct artillery support was provided by the 597th Field Artillery Battalion, augmented by tanks and tank destroyers.

Between 8 April and 15 April, it became clear the enemy was beginning to withdraw. On 8 and 9 April, enemy patrols were very active, but some were driven off. Long range machine gun and heavy mortar fire fell into positions on Hill 437 above Gallicano, leaving the initial impression of an impending attack. When nothing further developed, and with reports of enemy withdrawals to the west and north, Buffalo patrols accelerated their aggressive probing.

The enemy reacted with mortar and artillery fires as well as machine gun fire, and kept the skies filled with flares. On 11 April, 100 rounds of mortar fire and 15 rounds of artillery fell on troops in Calomini and Sommocolonia. On 13 April, 60 rounds of mortar fire, and a few rounds of artillery struck Calomini. On Hill 608 in the right sector, on 14 April enemy troops fired rifle grenades and automatic weapons at 370th Infantry troops and patrols. Heavy mortar fire continued as on previous nights and days. The enemy was pounded by artillery and mortar fire, and the combat patrols consistently pressed forward.

On 15 April heavy casualties were inflicted on the enemy by mortar fire, with only 29 rounds of mortar and 20 rounds of artillery being received. On 16 April enemy mortar and artillery fire again increased significantly; 147 rounds of mortar, 276 rounds of light artillery and 62 rounds of medium artillery pounded the advancing Buffalo troops.

Civilians and partisans reported movements of enemy garrisons from several towns and villages to the front, and that artillery of the Italia Division was pulling back towards Aulla.

Coordinating its movements with the 473rd Infantry and the 442nd Infantry, strong daylight combat patrols moved boldly into Fiattone and other patrols fanned out through the valley, encountering machine gun, automatic weapons and small arms fire from strong rear-guard detachments, which were quickly neutralized and overrun. The towns of Campo and C. Bechelli were taken on the 17th.

Withdrawal of the enemy on the night of the 18th, was closely followed by a general advance, and on 19 April, strong combat patrols pushed forward, again over-powering rear guard installations.

General Almond then ordered the Regiment to capture Castelnuovo di Garfagnana.

On 19 April, the First Battalion advanced along the left of the Serchio River while the Third Battalion attacked along the right, seeking to block any attempt by the enemy to escape to the east or the west. By 0700 a platoon of Company I entered the city, and by 0930, the First Battalion, pressing on, was in full pursuit of the enemy northwest along the main road to Aulla.

The ultimate mission now was to join up with the 442nd Infantry at Aulla, necessitating an extremely wide envelopment maneuver, eventually involving utilization of all three battalions of the regiment.

The enemy's extensive road demolitions, blown bridges and mined roads continued to delay the advance. The mines and obstacles on the roads particularly impeded the movement of tanks, tank destroyers, artillery, and the support vehicles.

The destruction was so complete that the attached 317th Engineer unit was unable to effect road clearing of mines and other obstacles rapidly enough to enable vehicles to keep up with the infantry.

Notwithstanding these difficulties and handicaps, the Buffalo Soldiers slogged forward. More enemy rearguard forces were met and neutralized or destroyed at Poggio, Piazza al Serchio, and Camporgiano, several miles north of Castelnuovo di Garfagnana.

At this time, Company F was in position as flank security for the

442nd Infantry on Mt. Altissimo. The company was ordered to move out and to contact the regiment at Poggio and Piazza al Serchio. As the company moved northeast, the remainder of the Second Battalion moved into Montignoso (near Castle Aghinolfi) and from there it made a two day forced march over very precipitous terrain to make contact with the Regiment at Gragnola on 23 April.

Back at Gallicano and Fornaci, the supporting guns for the 370th Infantry were dive-bombed and strafed by three planes, resulting in destruction of two vehicles and many casualties. "The planes were of friendly manufacture, but identity of pilots was never determined."[16]

The First Battalion pressed forward beyond Castelnuovo and as Company B resumed the advance it ran into an ambush by a strong force, identified by partisans as 50 Russians and 50 Germans, who had taken over after Italian Fascist troops had deserted the night before. Several mules were killed and others dispersed, but the company suffered no personnel casualties and the four enemy machine gun posts and the riflemen were quickly overcome and the battalion pressed onward.

During the night of 22–23 April the Third Battalion assembled all its units and moved by motor to Vagli di Sopra and from there made a forced foot march for 20 miles, securing an important road junction and surprising the strong German garrison at Casola. All this was without artillery support and with enemy on both flanks *and* to the front. They surrounded the town and after a brief, but vicious firefight, they captured 2 officers and 24 enlisted men, two automobiles, two motorcycles and much miscellaneous equipment. This constituted completion of a continued advance of over 30 hours duration over mountainous terrain on trails impassable much of the time, even to mules. The Third Battalion supply line now was extended over the steep and winding trails, and food and ammunition were running short.

A captured enemy document revealed the enemy's outpost and delaying intentions in the vicinity of Fivizzano, Cerreta Pass, and Cisa Pass, imminent objectives of the 370th Infantry. Two regiments of mixed German and Mongolian troops were reported moving south through Cisa Pass.

At 1850, a patrol had a 15 minute firefight at Orzaglia, then moved on.

Demolished bridges and road craters made vehicular movement extremely difficult and all advances were now by foot. It was impossible to maintain wire lines, so radios and runners were relied on completely to maintain open communications.

The First Battalion, reaching S. Michele, swept through the town. A determined rearguard, in positions a few kilometers ahead, resisted the advance. Pausing only long enough for a brief skirmish, the battalion deployed, and out-flanking the strongpoint, continued onward to vicinity of Gragnola, not far from Aulla, as the enemy withdrew.

With the First Battalion progressing beyond S. Michele, the Third Battalion changed its direction to attack towards Gragnola.

The First Battalion then forged onward towards Fivizzano. Heavy mortar fire was received at Gragnola, and a furious firefight resulted in several enemy being killed and 15 captured.

On 24 April, the Third Battalion silently moved up shortly after midnight, to seize the high ground commanding Aulla, to contact the 442nd Infantry, already entering Aulla. The recently arrived Second Battalion, far in front of its line of supply, but still fit, ready and eager for the fray after its long tortuous march from Mt. Altissimo, followed the Third Battalion. Two of its companies were dropped off to protect the lines of supply and to be prepared to engage any by-passed enemy coming from the south; the other company followed the Third Battalion.

The First Battalion continued forward to Fivizzano, dropping one company there with the remainder advancing to Licciano.

Several rounds of artillery and mortar fire fell west of Gragnola during the early morning hours and a stubborn rearguard hampered the advance of the Third and Second Battalions. One man was killed, six wounded and some vehicles damaged by artillery fire, and heavy enemy artillery, mortar and small arms fire was received from Aulla. An enemy column attempting to escape from Aulla northeastwards along Highway 62 was taken under fire by the Cannon Company of the 442nd Infantry, and supporting guns of the 599th Field Artillery Battalion. The 679th Tank Destroyer Battalion, attached to the 370th Infantry, fired 7220 rounds into Aulla during this engagement.

The 442nd Infantry was contacted in Aulla, and, as organized Partisan bands descended from the mountains and poured into the city, the hard-driving Third Battalion by-passed it and again changed direction. Terrarosa, 30 miles away to the north, was its next objective.

Considerable resistance was encountered. In addition to delays due to abandoned and destroyed material, large numbers of dead animals and scores of dead enemy soldiers, blown bridges and demolished roads, the 370th Infantry was overwhelmed with surrendering prisoners. In one case, 560 surrendered to the Buffalo Soldiers through the Partisans. Evacuation of prisoners was by foot, which created many problems.

On 25 April, Division orders were received changing the direction and mission. The Third Battalion was to advance up Highway 62 and block Cisa Pass; the First Battalion was to move forward to Highway 63 and block in vicinity of Cerreta; and the Second Battalion was to press on to block a secondary road net between Highway 62 and 63.[17]

No enemy resistance was encountered on 25 April, except for some mines and booby traps, and demolished roads and bridges, which caused delays. It was necessary to construct by-passes and remove mines and obstacles before vehicular traffic could follow the infantry.

On 26 April, the Third Battalion continued to press forward to Terrarosa, overcoming several rearguard pockets of resistance. Reaching the objective, they forged on beyond Villa Franca where they were halted temporarily by artillery, mortar and small arms fire coming from hills above the village of Filatteria. Civilians reported that 800 Germans were in the foothills surrounding the city of Pontremoli, and Partisans, again descending from the mountains, reported that the German and Fascist forces were desperately attempting to escape through Cisa Pass.

The Third Battalion drove the enemy back, as hundreds of Partisans participated in the fight. The enemy resisted with emplaced machine guns, self-propelled guns and tanks, but the heavy pressure forced him out of Pontremoli. Three hundred prisoners were captured.[18]

Partisans then reported that 17 artillery pieces and a large number of enemy troops had abandoned Pontremoli in the early morning hours and that already elements of the 148th and Italia Divisions were reported in the vicinity of Cisa Pass.

A First Battalion patrol, moving swiftly over Highway 63 on 26 April, met no enemy resistance, and boldly advanced all the way to Reggio on Highway 9. They surprised IV Corps by establishing contact with elements of its blocking force on its left flanks, from the Brazilian Expeditionary Force.

The Second Battalion patrolled their assigned road net, encountering no enemy resistance.

On 27 April, the Second Battalion was ordered to move to Chiavari, on the coast, to assume occupation duties. The First Battalion was alerted for a similar move, leaving in position the Cannon Company and a platoon of the Anti-Tank Company.

Prize for the Brazilians

No enemy contacts were made on 28 April. Efforts were being made by the 428th Field Artillery Group to put some heavy artillery units into position near Aulla, to support the Third Battalion in its pursuit of the retreating enemy forces. Elements of the 758th Tank Battalion and a Tank Destroyer Battalion were available for direct support fire.

The nearly impassable roads were made worse by several hours of heavy rains flooding the streams and washing out by-passes.

On 29 April, with the Third Battalion scarcely a few hours behind them, remnants of the two enemy divisions, desperately trying to avoid capture by the 92nd Division troops, reached the end of Cisa Pass. The Brazilian Expeditionary Force, in position as a blocking force, without having to fire a shot, accepted the surrender of the enemy, numbering 6000 officers and men, 1000 vehicles and 4000 horses.[19] This was the first major surrender of enemy troops in Italy.

Although the 370th Infantry was denied the honor of capturing the Divisions that had fought them for several months, they had the satisfaction of knowing they had driven them into the desperate position that led to their capitulation.

Official reports had rare and welcome praise for the Regiment in this difficult operation:

> The close pursuit of the enemy by the 370th Infantry was effective through its long marches and flanking movements over difficult terrain. The pursuit caused the enemy to withdraw in a confused manner and to abandon much of his equipment."[20]

During the operation, the Third Battalion alone had advanced 65 miles inflicting heavy casualties on the enemy in dozens of violent actions involving strong rearguard detachments, and capturing over 400 prisoners and large amounts of equipment.

Tedesco è Finito (The German Is Finished)

As the German and Italian Forces reeled back from the increasing rapid and destructive blows of the 370th Infantry, in the Center, the 473rd Infantry Combat Team on the coast, the 442nd Infantry Combat Team, moving on an island route, converged towards the final objective of the 92nd Division—the City of Genoa.

The 92nd Division Reconnaissance Troop, having performed flank reconnaissance duties in the advance up the Serchio Valley, was shifted to the coastal sector. On the 24th they moved into La Spezia to secure the city[21] and the 473rd Combat Team started movement towards Genoa on the next day, with the 92nd Reconnaissance Troop screening the advance.

Progress was slow due to difficult terrain and demolitions in the road. Infantryment and Partisans assisted the 317th Engineers in clearing the routes of mines and obstacles and building by-passes to enable the supporting tanks, tank destroyers, artillery and other support elements to advance.

Strong rearguard forces put up frenzied resistance and, in some instances, engaged in fierce firefights using all types of weapons, before retiring to their next line of defense. Heavy enemy resistance was met before Chiavari, and after a five-hour battle, the enemy was driven back. Initially, only two tanks had advanced forward far enough to fire in support of the troops, but later in the day, the Division's 598th Field Artillery Battalion, and tanks and tank destroyers caught up and finished off the remnants of the enemy forces.

In the action before Chiavari, the enemy inflicted heavy casualties, which included Major Robert Crandall, Second Battalion Commander, who was mortally wounded. Killed in action, too, on that day was Captain Murray Steinman, Commanding Officer of the 92nd Reconnaissance Troop. He was very popular with the black officers and enlisted men in the troop, and they eagerly followed him into every fray.

Heavy fire was received from the coastal defense guns at Portofino near Chiavari, causing the destruction of many jeeps and trucks and other equipment.

The final resistance came from a defiant German anti-tank crew at Santa Margherita Ligure. It was destroyed, and the troops set out for Genoa, which was entered without opposition on 27 April.

Organized Partisans had effected the surrender of the German garrison of 4000 men on the 26th the previous day. The Partisans, in a series of lightning line moves, had divided the German garrison into several groups, and surrounded them, within the city boundaries.

The 442nd Infantry moved its units across country and flanked enemy

The Spring Offensive—5 April–2 May 1945

forces north and east of Genoa, and entered the city on 28 April, joining the 473rd Infantry and other 92nd Division elements.

The 92nd Division Artillery played a dominant and effective role in delivering support to all infantry elements in the final offensive. The 598th Field Artillery Battalion followed the Second Battalion, 473rd Infantry, which was motorized and moving fast. The Artillery Battalion displaced forward by echelon so that at least one battery of 105 mm howitzers (four guns) was always able to give fire support to forward units. At Chiavari, at least three active enemy batteries of artillery were silenced by the 598th.

The artillery of the 92nd Division also played a dramatic role in the surrender of a German garrison of 175 men manning a fortress on Mt. Moro, towering above Genoa. This fortress contained two 381 mm coastal guns, three 152 mm guns, and four 99 mm guns; inside were elevators, reinforced concrete and steel emplacements, ammunition stores, food supplies, and access to the entire area was protected by extensive minefields and man-made obstacles. An ultimatum to surrender was given to the garrison commander, on 28 April, which was complied with, yielding 175 prisoners and the entire arsenal of guns and supplies.

At the time of surrender all guns of the division's 598th Field Artillery Battalion were prepared for direct fire of its 12 guns 1200 yards away, and all 12 guns of its 600 Field Artillery Battalion (155 mm) were 3000 yards away, aimed at the fortress.

The 599th Field Artillery Battalion provided direct support fire to the 442nd Infantry and the 597th Field Artillery Battalion supported the 370th Infantry in this final offensive.

Official reports praised the 92nd Division Artillery:

> The artillery gave excellent support under difficult conditions throughout the operation.

Results of the Offensive

With the fall of Genoa, all organized enemy resistance in the area had collapsed by 2 May, although some isolated groups had not yet surrendered. Partisans were everywhere; as elements of the division fanned out to the key cities and towns in northern Italy, they found many of them, such as Torino, already occupied and in control of Partisan formations.

The German 148th Infantry Division and the Italia Division opposed the 92nd Division throughout the operation. Prisoners numbering 3117 from these two units were captured by the division and the remnants, 6000 officers and men, had been driven into the hands of the Brazilians by the hard-driving troops of the Third Battalion, 370th Infantry. Near the end of the period, wholesale surrenders of naval, coastal defense and rear echelon troops increased the number tremendously.[22]

Prisoners of War

Enemy Unit	15 April–2 May	2 May–15 May	Total
148th Div.	1,677	2	1,679
Italia Div.	1,432	6	1,438
Other Units	10,410	6,016	16,426
Grand Total	13,519	6,024	19,543

Ground Gained

The 92nd Division advanced some 100 miles conquering a 3000 square-mile area.

Casualties

Unit	Battle	Non-Battle	Total
370th Inf.	149	351	770
442nd Inf.	614	532	1,146
473rd Inf.	172	299	1,120
Other Units	150	232	382
Grand Total	1,904	1,514	3,418

Replacements

Unit	Officers	Enlisted Men	Total
370th Inf.	18	454	472
442nd Inf.	1	752	753
473rd Inf.	24	956	980
Other Units	13	64	77
Grand Total	56	2,226	2,282

No accurate estimate of the number of enemy casualties was possible, but captured enemy soldiers confirmed complete units wiped out, and some reorganized, only to be destroyed again. They also attributed large numbers of casualties to devastating artillery, naval and air bombardment.

Equipment Captured

Artillery	308 pieces
Artillery Ammunition	8,627 tons
Small Arms	6,627 pieces
1. Rifle and Machine Gun	1,628,000 rounds
2. 20 mm	110,000 rounds
3. Mortar	4,000 rounds
Miscellaneous	
1. Motor Vehicles	87
2. Tanks	3
3. Wagons	158
4. Kitches	14
5. Power Plants	7
6. Radar Sets	6
7. Range Finders	16
8. Mines	4,000
9. Grenades	4,000
10. Explosives	150 tons
11. Miscellaneous Supplies	200 tons

The nature of the combat action in this operation was such that elements of most of the organic units of the 92nd Division were in operation either directly on the front lines or following closely on the heels of the three assaulting regiments. These units included:

    597th, 598th, 599th and 600th Field Artillery Battalions
    92nd Division Reconnaissance Troop
    Division Headquarters Units
    317th Engineer Combat Battalion
    317th Medical Battalion
    317th Signal Company
    792nd Ordnance (LM) Company
    92nd Military Policy Platoon
    92nd Division Mule Pack Battalion

The success of the 92nd Division operation, began as a "diversion," quickly had developed into a full-scale offensive that rolled up all enemy forces in the area of action. It undoubtedly contributed immensely to the victory by the American Fifth and British Eighth Armies in their main effort on the right of the 92nd Division.

The 365th and 371st Infantry Regiments of the 92nd Division, operating under IV Corps, performed well, engaging in close contact combat operations against rearguard enemy elements retreating in that area.

And, so, when the Italian Partisans proclaimed "Tedesco è Finito," the Buffalo Soldiers of the 92nd Division, it is significant to note, were present, and very much involved in the finish.

Postwar activities for the division included occupation duties and prisoner of war processing.

365th and 371st Detached from Main Effort

The 365th Infantry, on 27 February, was relieved in the Serchio Valley by the 473rd Infantry, detached from the 92nd Infantry, and attached to IV Corps, then moved to the San Marcello Valley, where it assumed command of the Task Force 45 Sector. A 15 mile-wide area was assigned it, in mountainous and in some cases, impassable terrain. One battalion was in the area north of Bagni di Lucca, and one was in the Cutigliana area. The other battalion remained in reserve in vicinity of San Marcello.

On 16 March, Task Force 45 was dissolved, leaving the 365th in command of the sector, with all units formerly attached to Task Force 45, and with the same mission and responsibilities.

Thereafter, there were several attachments of its battalions, all in and under control of IV Corps. On 27 March, the First Battalion moved to the Mt. Belvedere Sector, attached to the 10th Mountain Division (American). On 17 April the Third Battalion was detached from the 365th Infantry and attached to the 371st Infantry leaving their sector in control of Partisan forces. The Second Battalion remained in the Cutigliano Sector. On 20 April, the Second Battalion advanced up Highway 12, taking several towns with little resistance in the next few days.

While in the San Marcello sector the regiment was opposed by the Third Battalion, 5th San Marco Regiment (Italian) and the Fourth Mountain Battalion (German). They captured 220 prisoners of war from those units, and also captured 12 enemy agents.

The 371st Infantry continued its supporting mission until 8 April, when it was detached from the 92nd Division, and attached to IV Corps. The commanding officer was in Lizzano in Belvedere, and the regiment began taking over part of the sector of the Brazilian Expeditionary Force.

On 10 April, the First Battalion of the 365th Infantry was attached.

In the next two weeks, the 371st conducted active, aggressive patrolling, engaging in some lively fire fights. Company strength patrols were not unusual and were usually productive.

Attachments with the 365th Infantry began 18 April and elements of both regiments conducted joint actions against the enemy.

On 25 April, the regiment was detached from IV Corps and attached to Fifth Army. Its duties thereafter consisted primarily of processing prisoners of war.

It is difficult to justify the decision of the Fifth Army and 92nd Division Commands to exclude the 365th and 371st Infantry Regiments from joining in the main effort, in view of their generally favorable performance in the 8-11 February attack.

The implication is left that these units were considered untrustworthy and unreliable. It would have been more honest to attribute the relegation to a "follow-up" role in the IV Corps area, to the action taken to "dismember" the 92nd Division, and to the unresolved problem of training black infantry replacements.

In the diversion attack in the Serchio Valley from 5 February-11 February, the 365th Infantry, in its first Regimental combat action as an entity of the 92nd Infantry Division, performed very well. They attacked aggressively, took and held ground, repelling over 30 enemy counter-attacks, and inflicted heavy losses on the enemy, in personnel and material. They captured 288 prisoners and neutralized the Second Battalion, First Bersiagleri Regiment (Italian), and inflicted heavy casualties on the two battalions of the 286th Regiment, 148th Division (German). The Regiment suffered 52 enlisted men and 1 officer killed and 241 enlisted men and 8 officers wounded in that battle, which continued beyond the 11th of February.

The 371st Infantry also acquitted itself quite well in the 8-11 February operation. Their objective was to take the high ground along the steep, rocky Mt. Cauala-Mt. Folgorito Ridge Line which included strongly defended enemy positions on several peaks ROCKY RIDGE, MAINE, FLORIDA, GEORGIA, and OHIO 1, 2, and 3. In the 5-10 April offensive, the 100th Battalion of the 442nd Infantry successfully attacked GEORGIA and OHIO peaks *after* other elements of their regiment had taken the higher mountains to the rear of their enemy in a classic envelopment maneuver, and had begun to close the pincers on the enemy troops on GEORGIA and the three OHIO peaks.

Too, the 371st Infantry, at the close of the February Operation, had remained in position on ROCKY RIDGE, MAINE and FLORIDA, continuing to deny these strategic strongpoints to the Germans even after the other 92nd Division units had withdrawn. In their attack they did not enjoy the advantage of surprise, or the fact of disaster to the rear of the enemy, or the accuracy of intelligence data about strength and dispositions of enemy installations on the objectives. It would appear that the 371st could have taken GEORGIA and the OHIO peaks under the circumstances, in April.

Both the 365th and the 371st performed well in their assigned missions. The commanding officer of the 371st Infantry wrote:

> We were given the mission of sending three combat patrols (of Reinforced Company each) to (1) kill Germans, (2) capture PW's and (3) uncover enemy positions. We ... accomplished the mission. All three companies reached ... the Boche MLR north of the Leo River. They broke through the outpost all through the line. L Company moved fast enough to overrun a platoon combat patrol, capturing one NCO in his underwear.
>
> For the first time our troops maneuvered on *level* ground, in *superior* numbers and with *superior* supporting fires.[23]

Both regiments moved steadily forward. On 25 and 26 April, they began guarding prisoners of war. After the war was over, they were returned to division control.

The Partisans

No story about the Fifth Army or any of its divisions would be complete without including the important part played by the partisan resistance movement.

Official reports by American and British commanders, during and after hostilities in the Italian Campaign, were lavish in their praise of the Allied units which gained the final victory. In the fall of 1944, the German resistance stiffened at the forward points of the Gothic Line defenses, and the Allies, with reduced forces at their disposal, were temporarily halted. By spring, however, sufficient strength had been gathered to mount the final offensive which destroyed the German and Italian Fascist armies opposing them.

There was one significant ingredient in the military machine which American and British commanders, then and subsequent to the conflict, make little if any mention of, in their accounts of operations. It was an ingredient which produced great concern and consternation to German military staffs and forcing them to make alterations in tactical and strategic plans, in order to contend with it.

That ingredient was the Italian Resistance movement which, by autumn 1944, had developed into a powerful force, organized along military lines, operating mainly behind the German lines, and creating chaos and confusion for the German military forces.

To the Germans, this force, named "Partigiani" or "Partisans," became an additional *military* force to be reckoned with and against which desperately urgent measures were required. A state of virtual civil war was created in the territories occupied by the Germans because of the Partisans.

Organization

In small villages, towns, and cities, Partisans began operating singly or in small groups initially, not organized or connected—and generated considerable isolated disruption to local German units and installations. Shortly after the Italian surrender in September, 1943, Mussolini, who had been driven into exile, set up another Italian government in northern Italy and began to marshal and coordinate Fascist support. The Partisans, then began to organize small, isolated bands in the Apennines and the Alps. To their ranks flocked hundreds of dissident and willing fighters; former loyal Italian soldiers, escaped prisoners of war, young men slated by the Germans for forced labor or military duty in Germany or on the several German fronts in Europe, and many men and women who had lost loved ones in the many reprisals by German military forces.

As they grew in numbers, their organization began to assume structure and form. They developed a strong corps of leadership; they diversified their efforts so as to deal with strong Fascist opposition and the German Army. As they continued to increase in numbers, it became apparent to the Allies that

The Spring Offensive—5 April–2 May 1945

they represented an additional potentially powerful threat to the common enemy. Lines of communication were established with Partisan leaders and plans were agreed upon to help organize the Partisans among military lines — brigades, and smaller groupings down to companies, platoons, squads, etc. — and to train and supply them with arms, ammunition, special equipment, food, and even special uniforms.

The Office of Strategic Services (OSS) took on this task for the Fifth Army.

As the Partisan movement flourished in its early days, German repressive measures — mild at first — became savage and violent. The Partisans progressed from local sabotage, intelligence and demolition of bridges, tunnels, and similar activities to bold, well-organized attacks against German formations. The Germans then resorted to violent reprisals which reached massive proportions, including massacres of hostages.

One such mass bloodletting was the Massacre in the Ardeatin Caves along the ancient Appian Way. On March 23, 1944, a small, but well-organized and heavily armed Partisan band attacked a German strategic services formation which was marching along a Roman street. They killed and wounded many German soldiers, and then escaped unscathed, vanishing into their hiding places in the city. The next day hundreds of Italians were herded into sealed trucks, driven to the caves, where they were brutally and sadistically murdered, one by one. The entrances of the Caves were then blown up and sealed beneath tons of earth and stone. It is believed that ten hostages perished for each German soldier killed — a total of some 300–320.

The Massacre of the Ardeatine Caves was followed by similar atrocities, which continued throughout the duration of the Italian Campaign.

After the war, many German commanders were prosecuted as war criminals for those atrocities, among them Field Marshall Albert Kesselring. He was found guilty of responsibility for the murder of hostages and sentenced to death, but the death sentence was later commuted to a life sentence.

By mid-spring, 1944, the Partisan armies numbered about 60,000 and were causing heavy casualties to the German forces. In addition, by dominating the roads crossing the Apennines and the Alpine passes they posed a serious threat to those narrow, vital supply routes; the enemy positions to the south, in turn were becoming difficult to hold.

Of the four Italian (Fascist) Divisions training in Germany, two — the Monte Rosa and the San Marco — were then committed. They became part of the Army Liguria; the Army Liguria had responsibility of protecting northwest Italy against either Allied coastal landings or attacks through the Alpine passes; actually, because of the constant pressures and military successes by Partisan formations against German installations, the Army Liguria spent most of its efforts in an anti-Partisan role.

Thus, with the Allied forces opening the assault against the Gothic Line, the Army Liguria which had three German Divisions in addition to the two Italian divisions, was forced to divert a large part of its potential reserves to fight battles with the Partisans.

Special anti-Partisan "Black Brigades," made up of armed Fascist Party members were formed. Because of their savage, maniacal brutality, they became the most hated military unit in Italy and this probably did more to solidify the strength of the Partisans than any other single occurrence.

Field Marshall Kesselring, writing after the war, stated that from June–August, 1944, his losses were "5,000 killed, and 7,000–8,000 killed or kidnapped, to which should be added a maximum total of the same number of wounded."[24]

Other studies confirm that German casualties during that period were higher than those of the Partisans.

Repressive measures by the Germans became increasingly barbarous and brutal, with many authenticated examples of hostages taken and tortured, shot or hanged, and villages burned and destroyed.

And yet, the resistance continued to grow steadily more powerful.

By September, 1944, with excellent communication, supply and special troop reinforcement systems from OSS Mission Teams, Partisan raiding parties roamed almost at will among German forces behind the front lines. At this point their strength rose to a hundred thousand or so, and their effectiveness led the Germans to consider the Partisans an actual menace to their military establishment. Thus, to the Germans, it became urgent to deal with them as such.

In the fall of 1944, many factors caused the Allied offensive to grind to a halt before the very gates of Bologna. The bitter Italian winter made its onset, freezing the roads and trails and mountain passes; the enemy, exhorted by Hitler to hold their lines at all costs, made any advances by Allied forces extremely slow and costly in men and machines. The terrain itself constituted a formidable obstacle. In addition, troop demands for the fighting on the mainland siphoned off vital combat divisions from both Fifth and Eighth Armies. Critical ammunition shortages occurred in basic, essential supplies. On 13 November it was estimated that for only a fifteen day offensive in December, Eighth Army would have only enough shells for fifteen days of fighting; and Fifth Army only enough for ten days.

When the planned Allied offensive was cancelled, notice to the Partisan forces to also abandon their planned participation was broadcast by radio and it was *also* heard by the Germans. As Allied help diminished and ammunition, weapons, and critical supplies dwindled away, the Partisan formations too, dwindled away. Those Partisans who managed to remain in action found themselves alone, facing a full-scale German-Fascist campaign against them now undeterred by Allied forces.

Much distrust and disillusionment was felt by Partisans, many of whom questioned the motives of the Allies.

Enough survived the rough winter, to provide the base for a reorganization for the spring offensives in 1945. Indeed, by April 1945, it was estimated that 200,000–300,000 were involved in operations.

Some of the strongest Partisan formations were established in the area of operations of the Buffalo Division, from the time they first took their place in the lines in August 1944.

The Spring Offensive—5 April-2 May 1945

Personnel from Office of Strategic Services (OSS), attached to 92nd Division Headquarters helped to organize Partisans for Intelligence operations along the lengthy front and behind the enemy lines. Contact was made with organized Partisan units in enemy rear areas.

As the Buffalo Soldiers advanced across the Arno River, over and through Mt. Pisano and the many towns and villages towards their first major objective, the city of Lucca, Partisan personnel accompanied them. They were used to screen the many Italian civilians moving back and forth across the lines, and were helpful in identifying enemy agents, Fascists, civilian spies; they assisted by performing acts of sabotage to enemy military installations, dumps, railways, roads, bridges and telephone lines.

When the Buffalo Division became involved in operations against Gothic Line positions in the late fall of 1944, the Partisan formations had been organized along semi-military lines. Brigades numbering 300-5000 operated, with headquarters behind the Germans, and these brigades were organized into groups, companies, platoons, and squads, with various duties and missions assigned.

In addition to intelligence functions, these Partisan groups operated with frontline Buffalo units. They helped to set up observation posts for artillery and mortar forward observers, helping to locate and identify targets; they led patrols over trails and passes to and from enemy front lines; they identified minefields, sometimes helping to clear them or lead the Buffalo Soldiers around them; they pin-pointed hidden obstacles, enemy strongpoints, bunkers, pillboxes and bridges.

In many instances they took places in the lines. Members of the 366th Infantry speak with admiration and respect of the Partisan band which fought with them at ill-fated Sommocolonia in December 1944. Even though, in at least one instance during the battle the Americans, holding their fire until almost too late, mistaking Fascist troops (dressed like the Partisans) for the Partisans, and suffering some casualties as a result, the admiration and respect for them was never diminished. Partisan elements were present in almost every major operation of the Division after that.

They provided supply and medical evacuation personnel—under enemy fire, assisted engineers in removing mines, road blocks, and in building by-passes and bridges, during the advance to Genoa in April 1945.

Although official reports tend to give major credit to the Combat Teams—473rd, 442nd, and 370th—for capturing major towns and cities, the records establish that much of the credit should be given to the Partisans.

When the 370th Infantry entered Lucca in October, Partisans were there.

During the German counter-offensive in the Serchio River Valley in December 1944, the Partisans were dug-in in defensive positions all along the line.

When the February 1945 offensive began, contact had been established and plans coordinated with Partisan formations numbering in the thousands to have them assist in the assault on enemy held towns and cities as the Americans advanced.

During the final April offensive the assault forces of the 92nd Division found Partisans already inside most of their major objectives when they arrived. When La Spezia was entered by elements of the 92nd Division Reconnaissance Troop and the 473rd Infantry, they found the Germans gone and the city under control of the Partisans. When Massa was entered by elements of the 473rd, the 442nd and the 370th Regiments, although some hard fighting was necessary, Partisan formations were very much in evidence and remained in control of the city as the Division moved on. At Aulla and Pontremoli, although, again, some fighting was necessary, Partisans had descended into these two enemy strongholds by the hundreds and thousands and were already inside the city limits when elements of the 442nd and 370th Regiments entered.

Close to 14,000 Partisans took part in the capture of Genoa and other smaller communities around it. They fought German troops in the city for 48 hours and induced the German garrison, numbering more than 6,000 to surrender, and when elements of the 92nd Division entered Genoa, German resistance had already collapsed.

After Genoa had been freed, the Partisans helped to locate and take charge of some 12,500 prisoners and help the 92nd Division collect 3000 more prisoners in the surrounding areas.

There is no doubt that the many battles participated in by the 92nd Division would have involved much more time and resulted in tremendously heavier losses had it not been for help of the "Partigiani."

Chapter Notes

Chapter One

1. H.R. 17541, 63rd Congress, 2nd Session, July 27, 1914. A bill to prevent appointments of Negroes as commissioned or non-commissioned officers in the army or navy (never passed, the same bill introduced in 1915 and 1916). H.R. 17183, 80th Congress, 1st Session, July 27, 1916. A bill to prevent the enlistment or reenlistment of Negroes in the military service.
2. Ulysses Lee, *The Employment of Negro Troops* (Washington, D.C.: Officer of Chief, Military History, U.S. Army, 1966), p. 142. Hereafter cited as Lee, *Negro Troops*.
3. Paul Goodman, *A Fragment of Victory: A Special Study of the 92nd Infantry Division*, prepared at the Army War College, Carlisle Barracks, Pa., 1952), p. 1. Hereafter cited as Goodman, *Fragment*.
4. *Ibid.*, p. 4.
5. *Ibid.*
6. *Book of Facts, 92nd Infantry Division* (General Almond designated a special committee to compile this document). January 3, 1949. p. 4. Included in General Personal Papers of General Almond at the Army War College Library.
7. Lee, *Negro Troops*. pp. 333–34.
8. *Ibid.*, p. 334.
9. *Ibid.*
10. Goodman, *Fragment*. p. 6.
11. *Ibid.*
12. Lee, *Negro Troops*. p. 339.
13. Goodman, *Fragment*. p. 13.

Chapter Two

1. Lee, *Negro Troops*. p. 536 (4).
2. Goodman, *Fragment*. p. 22.
3. Roman numerals are used to designate the U.S. II and IV Corps, and Arabic numerals for British Corps.

Chapter Three

1. *New York Times*, August 31, 1944.
2. In WW II, a unique 24-hour time system was used; e.g., one minute after midnight is 0001; one minute before midnight is 2359. Noon is 1200.
3. Goodman, *Fragment*. p. 28.

4. "Eighth Army Drives for Po, Pisa Falls," *New York Times*, September 2, 1944, sec. 1, p. 10, col. 1, 2, 3, 4.
5. Goodman, *Fragment*. p. 29.
6. Lee, *Negro Troops*. p. 541.
7. Goodman, *Fragment*. p. 30. (On 5 September, the 100th Battalion rejoined its parent 442nd Infantry Regiment [Japanese-American]. It was replaced by an antiaircraft unit converted to infantry.)
8. Goodman, *Fragment*. p. 32. (IV Corps Commander, on visit to combat team headquarters, gave high praise to 370th Combat Team for excellent patrol activities, particularly the Third Battalion).
9. *Ibid.*, p. 36.
10. Lee, *Negro Troops*, p. 544.
11. Goodman, *Fragment*. p. 38.
12. Lee, *Negro Troops*, p. 544. (Lee reports 248 sick, wounded or injured, and 22 missing or captured.)
13. Douglas Orgill, *The Gothic Line: The Italian Campaign, Autumn, 1944* (New York, W.W. Norton, 1967), pp. 35-36.
14. Goodman, *Fragment*. p. 53.
15. *Operations Report*, 370th Combat Team, Aug.-Dec., 1944.
16. *Ibid.*
17. *Ibid.*
18. Goodman, *Fragment*. p. 57.
19. *History*, 371st Infantry, Nov., 1944.
20. *Ibid.*
21. *Ibid.*
22. *Ibid.*
23. Personal letter from Second Lieutenant Albert E. Seay, dated 26 June 1946, to Hargrove.
24. *History*, 371st Infantry, Nov., 1944.
25. *Operations Report*, 365th Infantry, 10 Oct. 1944-15 Aug. 1945.
26. *Operations Report*, 371st Infantry, Nov., 1944.
27. Lee, *Negro Troops*. p. 556.
28. *Operations Report*, 371st Infantry., Nov., 1944.
29. *Operations*, 370th Combat Team, Aug.-Dec., 1944.
30. *History*, 92nd Cavalry Reconnaissance Troop, Aug., 1944-July, 1945.
31. *Operations, 370th Combat Team*, Aug.-Dec., 1944. November, 1944.
32. Lee, *Negro Troops*. p. 559.
33. Second Lieutenant Sidney Thompson, *Questionnaire*. 25 June, 1981.
34. First Lieutenant John T. Letts, *Questionnaire*. 26 June, 1980.
35. First Lieutenant Robert A. Brown, *Questionnaire*. 19 Oct. 1980.
36. Lee, *Negro Troops*. p. 559.
37. *Ibid.*, pp. 558-559.

Chapter Four

1. General E.M. Almond, *Letter to Commanding General, Fifth Army: Air Bombardment, Coastal Guns*. 31 March, 1945. Hereafter cited as Almond, *Air Bombardment*.
2. In "TOT," all available artillery and heavy weapons are fired simultaneously at set times on designated targets.
3. *History, The Legionnaires*, 371st Infantry, December, 1944.
4. *History, 370th Infantry*, December, 1944.
5. *Ibid.*

6. *Field Order No. 4.*, Headquarters 92nd Infantry Division 17 1200. December, 1944.
7. *Operation Instructions No. 1 to F.O. No. 4.* 23 1400. December, 1944. Almond, Major General.
8. *Intelligence Annex No. 2 to F.O. No. 4*, 23 1400. December, 1944. Donald M. MacWillie, Lieutenant Colonel., A C of S, G-2.
9. Second Lieutenant Sidney Thompson, *2nd Questionnaire*. 29 February, 1980.
10. *Journal, G-2*, Headquarters 92nd Infantry Division, 20–31 December, 1944.
11. Captain Samuel Tucker, S-2, Second Battalion, 366th Infantry, *Letter to Hargrove*. 14 July, 1980. Hereafter cited as Tucker, *Letter-Hargrove*.
12. *Intelligence Annex to F.O. No. 5*, Headquarters 92nd Infantry Division 25 1600A. December, 1944.
13. Tucker, *Letter-Hargrove*.
14. Major E.A. Raymond, "Black Buffalo." *Field Artillery Journal*. January, 1946. p. 15.
15. First Lieutenant Lewis Flagg III, *Interview*, 9 September, 1980.
16. *Transmittal of Resume of Events, 26–27 December, 1944, Serchio Valley Sector.* To Commanding General, 92nd Infantry Division Captain John J. Kelly, Adjutant, 370th Infantry, 4 March, 1945. Hereafter cited as Kelly, *Resume*.
17. *Ibid.*
18. Raymond, *Black Buffalo*. (Author's note: Goodman does not include the battery in his account; neither does Lee. However, official reports of 598th Field Artillery Battalion confirm it was used.)
19. Kelly, *Resume*.
20. *Ibid.*
21. Tucker, *Letter-Hargrove*.
22. Goodman, *Fragment*. p. 80.
23. *History*, "The Legionnaires," 371st Infantry, December, 1944.
24. General Mark W. Clark, *Calculated Risk* (New York: Harper & Brothers, 1950), p. 413. Hereafter cited as Clark, *Calculated Risk*.
25. Lieutenant General L.K. Truscott, Jr., *Command Missions: A Personal Story* (New York, E.P. Dutton, 1954), p. 455. Hereafter cited as Truscott, *Command Missions*.
26. Kelly, *Resume*.
27. Tucker, *Letter-Hargrove*.
28. Goodman, *Fragment*. p. 199.

Chapter Five

1. *Plan Fourth Term: The Enemy Situation*, Headquarters, 92nd Infantry Division. 15 January, 1945. Hereafter cited as *Plan Fourth Term*.
2. Goodman, *Fragment*. p. 94.
3. In "Rover Joe," fighter-bombers attacked ground targets on front lines, with fire control by radio from ground units to planes above. In "Horsefly," fighter-bombers were led to targets by 92nd Division Artillery light liaison planes.
4. *Plan Fourth Term*.
5. Note: Except where otherwise indicated, information about operations of 365th Infantry is taken from *Operations Reports, 365th Infantry Jan.–July 1945* and *Operation Highlights, Oct., 1944–Aug., 1945. 5 Sep., 1945*.
6. *S-1 Journal* 365th Infantry, 4–19 February, 1945.
7. Goodman, *Fragment*. p. 100.

8. *G-2 Summary of Intelligence Activities, Operation of Feb. 8–11, '45;* Section III, *Results of the Attack.* 8–12 February, 1945.
9. *Intelligence Annex to F. O. No. 7.* 92nd Infantry Division, 6 February, 1945.
10. *Narrative of Action.* Headquarters, Second Battalion, 370th Infantry, 8–11 February, 1945.
11. *Ibid.*
12. *Report of Raider Company*, S-3, 370th Infantry, February 20, 1945.
13. Lieutenant General L.K. Truscott, Jr., Commanding Headquarters, Fifth Army: *Report on Operations of 92nd Infantry Division, 8–11 February, 1945. March 5, 1945.* Hereafter cited as Truscott, *Operations 8–11 February.*
14. Almond, *Air Bombardment.*
15. First Lieutenant Dennette Harrod, *Questionnaire,* 6 May, 1980.
16. Colonel W.F. Millice, F.A., *Report to Army Ground Forces: Reduction of Concrete Emplaced Coast Defense Guns.* 1945.
17. Goodman, *Fragment.* p. 105.
18. *Ibid.*
19. *Ibid.*, p. 106.
20. *Ibid.*
21. First Lieutenant Dennette Harrod, *Interview,* 18 May, 1980.
22. Major Alvin D. Wilder, Jr., *Operations of the 317th Engineer Combat Battalion, during 4th Term Operation 8–11 Feb., inclusive.* 21 February, 1945.
23. *G-2 Periodic Report,* Headquarters, 92nd Infantry Division, 9 February, 1945.
24. Truscott, *Operations 8–11 February.*
25. *Regimental History*, 370th Infantry, January–August, 1945.
26. *Narrative of Operations,* Third Battalion, 370th Infantry, 8–12, 1945.
27. Truscott, *Operations 8–11 February.*
28. *Ibid.*
29. Major Sanford P. Sussell, S-3, *Report on 371st Infantry Attack During Period 080600 February to 111800 February, 1945. 21 Feb., 1945.*
30. Lieutenant Colonel E.J. Rowny, CE, *Operations of Task Force #1, Annex #2.* 11 February, 1945. Hereafter cited as Rowny, *Task Force.*
31. Captain Raymond A. Diggs, *Report of Operations,* Third Battalion, 366th Infantry, 20 February, 1945.
32. Rowny, *Task Force.*
33. *Operations in Italy,* Headquarters, 760th Tank Battalion, February, 1945.
34. *Operations, 8–11 February 1945,* Headquarters, First Battalion, 370th Infantry, 19 February, 1945.
35. *Ibid.*
36. *Ibid.*
37. *G-2 Periodic Report,* Headquarters, 92nd Division, 9 February, 1945.
38. Rowny, *Task Force.*
39. *Narrative of Attack Phase, Feb 8–11, 1945.* Headquarters, Third Battalion, 371st Infantry, 20 February, 1945.
40. *Ibid.*
41. *History, The Legionnaires,* 371st Infantry, February, 1945.
42. *Report on 371st Infantry Attack 080600 Feb. to 111800 Feb. 1945.* 21 February, 1945.
43. *Ibid.*
44. *Operations in Italy,* Headquarters, 760th Tank Battalion, February, 1945.
45. *Operations 8–11 Feb 1945,* First Battalion, 370th Infantry, 19 February, 1945.
46. *History, The Legionnaires,* 371st Infantry, February, 1945.

47. *Report on 371st Infantry Attack 8-11 Feb., '45.*
48. Goodman, *Fragment.* p. 99.
49. *Ibid.*, p. 196.
50. *Ibid.*, p. 195.
51. Truscott, *Operations 8-11 February.*
52. *Summary of Intelligence Activities, Operation of Feb. 8-11 1945*, 11 February, 1945.
53. Goodman, *Fragment.* p. 113.
54. Truscott, *Operations 8-11 February.*
55. Truscott, *Command Missions.* p. 455.
56. Frank, S. "Glorious Collapse of the 106th," *Saturday Evening Post.* 219 (9 November 1946): 32-3 +.
57. Clark, *Calculated Risk.* p. 414.
58. Colonel J.D. Armstrong, *Report of Combat Efficiency of 365th Infantry*, Headquarters, 365th Infantry, 21 February, 1945.
59. Captain Warman Welliver, "Report on the Negro Soldier," *Negro Digest*, June, 1967.
60. Truscott, *Command Mission.* p. 295.
61. *Consolidated Casualty Report Ending 2400 Each Night for Period 8-11 Feb., '45, Inclusive.* (Totals include 9 casualties from "Other Units"; does NOT include casualties in Serchio Valley for February 5-8.)
62. Truscott, *Operations 8-11 February.*
63. Almond, *Air Bombardment.* (Special Report attached by Lieutenant Colonel D. MacWillie), 23 March, 1945.
64. Colonel W.F. Millice, *Reduction of Concrete Emplaced Guns—Hard Way*, 28 May, 1945.
65. Dominick Graham, *Cassino* (New York, Ballantine Books, 1970), p. 70.
66. *Ibid.*, pp. 70-71.
67. E.D. Smith, *The Battles for Cassino* (New York, Charles Scribner's Sons, 1975), p. 285.
68. *Ibid.*, p. 285.
69. Truscott, *Command Missions.*
70. *Ibid.*, p. 285.
71. *Ibid.*
72. Clark, *Calculated Risk*, p. 277.
73. Truscott, *Operations, 8-11 February.*
74. Charles B. MacDonald, *Three Battles: Arnaville, Altuzzo, and Schmidt* (Washington, OCMH, Department of the Army, 1952), pp. 352-355.
75. Colonel J.D. Armstrong, Commanding Officers, 365th Infantry, *Combat Efficiency of 365th Infantry.* 21 February, 1945.
76. *Ibid.*

Chapter Six

1. Lieutenant Colonel John T. Martin, *Memorandum: The Negro Officer in the Armed Forces of the United States of America* (Washington, Officer of Secretary of Defense, 1960), pp. 5-18.
2. Truscott, *Command Missions*, pp. 176-77.
3. Lee, *Negro Troops*, p. 572.
4. *Ibid.* (Same conclusions for BEF and the Italian Legnano Group.)
5. *Ibid.*, p. 573.
6. *Ibid.*
7. Goodman, *Fragment.* p. 115.

8. Lee, *Negro Troops*, p. 573.
9. *Ibid.*, p. 574.
10. *Ibid.*

Chapter Seven

1. Headquarters IV Corps, *Annex #1, G-2 Estimate of the Enemy Situation to Accompany Plan "Second Wind,"* 25 February, 1945.
2. Lieutenant Colonel Ernest V. Murphy, *Narrative of Action*, First Battalion, 370th Infantry, 5 April, 1945.
3. Lee, *Negro Troops*, p. 582.
4. *Ibid.*, p. 583.
5. Goodman, *Fragment.* p. 134.
6. Headquarters, 92nd Infantry Division, *Citation of Unit* 7 October, 1945. Hereafter cited as 442nd, *Citation.*
7. *Ibid.*
8. Lee, *Negro Troops.* p. 584.
9. Lieutenant Colonel C.H. Daughette, Jr., Commanding Officer, Third Battalion, 370th Infantry, *Summary of Third Battalion During Period 1210 3 April 1945 to 2400.* 11 April, 1945.
10. 442nd, *Citation.*
11. *Regimental History*, 370th Infantry, 92nd Infantry Division, January-August, 1945.
12. 442nd, *Citation.*
13. *Report of Operations, 92nd Infantry Div., between 05 April-02 May 1945*, Headquarters, 92nd Infantry Division, 15 June, 1945. Hereafter cited as *Operations, 05 April-02 May 1945.*
14. Lee, *Negro Troops.* p. 584.
15. 442nd, *Citation.*
16. *Regimental History*, 370th Infantry, January-August, 1945.
17. *Ibid.*
18. Goodman, *Fragment.* p. 173.
19. *Ibid.*, p. 175.
20. *Operations, 05 April-02 May, 1945.*
21. *With the 92nd Infantry Division October, 1942-June, 1945.* Information-Education Section, MTOUSA. 1945.
22. *Operations, 05 April-02 May, 1945.* (All tables in this grouping are from this report.)
23. *Personal letter* from Lieutenant Colonel Notestein to General Almond. 15 April, 1945.
24. Field Marshall Albert Kesselring, *A Soldier's Record.* Greenwood Press, 1953. p. 272.

Bibliography

Books

Barbeau, Arthur E., and Henri, Florette. *The Unknown Soldiers: Black American Troops in World War I*. Philadelphia: Temple University Press, 1974.
Burchard, Peter. *One Gallant Rush*. New York: St. Martin's Press, 1945.
Blumenson, Martin. *Bloody River: The Real Tragedy of the Rapido*. Boston: Houghton Mifflin, 1970.
Carroll, John M. *The Black Military Experience in the American West*. New York: Liveright, 1971.
Clark, Mark W. *Calculated Risk*. New York: Harper & Brothers, 1950.
Congdon, Don. *Combat: European Theatre World War II*. New York: Dell, 1958.
Dalfiume, Richard M. *Desegregation of the U.S. Armed Forces*. Columbia: University of Missouri Press, 1969.
Faulk, Odie B. *The Geronimo Campaign*. New York: Oxford University Press, 1969.
Fletcher, Marvin. *The Black Soldier and Officer in the U.S. Army 1891–1917*. Columbia: University of Missouri Press, 1974.
Foner, Jack D. *Blacks and the Military in American History*. New York: Praeger Publishers, 1974.
Fowler, Arlen L. *The Black Infantry in the West 1869–1891*. Westport, Conn: Greenwood, 1971.
Graham, Dominick. *Cassino*. New York: Ballantine, 1970.
Higgins, Trumbull. *Soft Underbelly: The Anglo-American Controversy Over the Italian Campaign 1939–1945*. New York: Macmillan, 1968.
Higginson, Thomas Wentworth. *Army Life in a Black Regiment*. Boston: Beacon Press, 1962.
Kahn, E.J., and McLemore, Henry. *Fighting Divisions*. Washington: Zenger, 1945.
Karon, Bertram P. *The Negro Personality*. New York: Springer, 1958.
Kesselring, Albert, Field Marshal. *A Soldier's Record*. Westport, Conn.: Greenwood Press, 1953.
Leckie, William H. *The Buffalo Soldiers: A Narrative of the Negro Cavalry in the West*. Norman: University of Oklahoma Press, 1967.
McCarthy, Agnes, and Reddick, Lawrence. *Worth Fighting For*. Garden City: Doubleday, 1965.
Macksey, Kenneth. *Kesselring: The Making of the Luftwaffe*. New York: David McKay, 1978.
Mosti, Emidio. *La Resistenza Apuana—luglio 1943–aprile 1945*. [The Apuan Resistance—July 1943–April 1945]. Milan: Longanesi, 1973.
Motley, Mary P. *The Invisible Soldier*. Detroit: Wayne State University Press, 1975.
Muller, William G., Captain. *The Twenty-Fourth Infantry—Past and Present*. Fort Collins, Colo.: Old Army Press, 1972.

Nankivell, John H., Captain. *History of the Twenty-Fifth Regiment, U.S. Infantry, 1869-1926.* Fort Collins, Colo.: Old Army Press, 1972.
Nye, W.S., Lieutenant Colonel. *Carbine & Lance: The Story of Old Fort Sill.* Norman: University of Oklahoma Press, 1943.
Olsen, Jack. *Silence on Monte Sole.* New York: G.F. Putnam's Sons, 1968.
Orgill, Douglas. *The Gothic Line: The Italian Campaign, 1944.* New York: W.W. Norton, 1967.
Palla, Emilio. *Popolo e partigiani sulla linea gotica: Storia politica della communità massesse (1943-1945)* [The People and the Partisans on the Gothic Line: The Political History of the Massa Community 1943-1945]. Legnano: Edizioni Landoni, 1974.
Quarles, Benjamin. *The Negro in the American Revolution.* New York: W.W. Norton, 1961.
———. *The Negro in the Civil War.* Boston: Little, Brown and Company, 1953.
Ridgeway, Matthew B., General, U.S. Army, Retired. *The Korean War.* Garden City: Doubleday, 1967.
Roth, Noble Paul. *Brave Men All.* New York: Kensington, 1981.
Schwartz, Barry N., and Disch, Robert. *White Racism.* New York: Dell, 1970.
Shirey, Orville C. *Americans: Story of the 442nd Combat Team.* Washington: Infantry Journal Press, 1946.
Sterling, Dorothy. *Captain of the Planter: The Story of Robert Smalls.* New York: Washington Square Press, 1958.
Truscott, L.K., Jr., Lt. General. *Command Missions: A Personal Story.* New York: E.P. Dutton, 1954.
Wallace, Robert, and the Editors of Time-Life Books. *The Italian Campaign.* Alexandria, Va.: Time-Life Books, 1978.
Webster's American Military Biographies. Springfield, Mass.: G. & C. Merriam, 1978.
Westmoreland, William C., General. *A Soldier Reports.* Garden City: Doubleday, 1976.
Whiting, Charles. *Death of a Division.* New York: Stein & Day, 1980.

Special Studies

These volumes are from the series "United States Army in World War II." All are closely related and present a comprehensive account of the activities of the Military Establishment in World War II.

Blumenson, Martin. *Salerno to Cassino.* Washington: Office of Chief of Military History, U.S. Army, 1969. (Reprinted 1970.)
Cole, Hugh M. *The Ardennes: Battle of the Bulge.* Washington: Office of Chief of Military History, 1965.
Fisher, Ernest F., Jr. *Cassino to the Alps.* Washington: Center of Military History, U.S. Army, 1977. (Reprinted 1979.)
Goodman, Paul, Major. *A Fragment of Victory: In Italy During World War II, 1942-45.* Carlisle Barracks, Pa.: Army War College, 1952.
Lee, Ulysses. *The Employment of Negro Troops in World War II.* Washington: Office of Chief of Military History, 1966.
MacDonald, Charles B., and Mathews, Sidney T. *Three Battles: Arnaville, Altuzzo, and Schmidt.* Washington: Office of the Chief of Military History, Department of the Army, 1952.

A Special Study concerned with the 92nd Infantry Division and its principal attachments, including the 473rd, the 442nd, and the 366th Infantry Regiments. It was prepared by Major Goodman and other staff at the Army War College.

Magazines

"Almond, Edward—Portrait." *Time.* **56** (25 Sept., 1950): 31.
"A Behavior Pattern." *Newsweek.* **XXV** (26 Mar., 1945): 37.
"Experiment Proved?" *Time.* **42** (20 Sept. 1943): 66+.
Feder, Sid. "They'll Never Forget Mark Clark." *Saturday Evening Post.* **218** (18 May, 1946): 20-1+.
Frank, S. "Glorious Collapse of the 106th." *Saturday Evening Post.* **219** (9 Nov. 1946): 32-34.
Hargrove, Hondon B. "Il Corsaro—A Story of War and Friendship." *Michigan History* **64** (Jan./Feb., 1980): 14-20.
Heller, Charles E. "The 54th Massachusetts: Between Two Fires." *Civil War Times Illustrated.* **XI-1** (Apr. 1972): 32-41.
"The Luckless 92nd." *Newsweek.* **XXV** (26 Feb., 1945): 34.
Milner, L.B. "Jim Crow in the Army." *New Republic.* **110** (13 Mar., 1944): 339-42.
"Negro Division Prepares to Go Overseas." *Life.* **15** (9 Aug., 1943): 37-40.
"Negro Soldiers Blame War Department." *Christian Century.* **61** (8 Nov., 1944): 1278.
"Negroes in the Army: Race Discrimination in the South. *New Republic.* **111** (25 Dec., 1944): 871-2.
"Report on the Negro Soldier: 92nd's Battle Performance." *Time.* **45** (26 Mar., 1945): 22.
Sherman, J.H., "Our Negro Soldiers." *New Republic.* **113** (19 Nov., 1945): 667-8.
Welliver, Warman. "Report on the Negro Soldier." *Harper's.* **192** (9 Apr., 1946): 332-9.

Newspapers

"Major General Almond Commands Task Force Entering Genoa." *New York Times.* 28 Apr., 1945. 1:4.
Bracker, Milton. "Americans Lose Ground in Italy." *New York Times.* 14 Feb., 1945.
———. "Negro Courage Upheld." *New York Times.* 15 Mar., 1945.
———. "When the Fight Means Kill or Be Killed—On the Italian Front." *New York Times.* 28 May, 1944. Mag. p 10+.
"The Gibson Report." *Pittsburgh Courier.* 24 Mar., 1945.
Schuyler, George S. "Views and Reviews." *Pittsburgh Courier.* 31 Mar., 1945.

Official Records of the 92nd Infantry Division

Extensive use has been made of the official records of the 92nd Infantry Division, the units attached to it, as well as the higher commands to which it was subjected.

There are great numbers of records, which include: Operational Reports, Journals, and Histories—by all command levels, some kept on a day-to-day basis, some monthly; complete Plans for each operation—at all levels—and the Field Orders to carry out the Plans, along with Annexes and Changes dictated by the changing tide of battle. Also included are the voluminous records of Administrative and Supporting Services attendant to maintaining the combat effectiveness of a voluminous Division of 13,000-14,000 soldiers.

Specific references to the official records have been cited throughout the book and are listed in the Notes of Chapters.

The records of the Division are on 44 index cards (5" × 8"). Copies of the cards as well as the records listed are available from the National Archives and Records Service, Washington National Records Center, Washington, D.C. 20409.

The Personal Papers of General Almond are kept at the U.S. Army Military History Institute at Carlisle Barracks, Pa. They include: speeches, letters, media news clippings, statistical data, photographs, rosters, citations, maps, etc.

Statistical Data, Tables

Intelligence Statistics

▶A total of 102 enemy espionage, sabotage and propaganda agents were seized.
▶Twenty-eight roadblocks were set up and serviced 24 hours a day using 250 Italian Carabinieri and the Division Military Police.
▶A total of 5561 propaganda leaflet shells (105 mm) were fired into enemy territory daily.
▶An average of 12 combat patrols went out to enemy territory daily.
▶Direct liaison and contact was made with Partisan sources to a depth of 20 miles behind enemy lines.
▶A company of 180 Partisans and another of 250 Partisans were organized and operated with front-line units in the 92nd Division.

Prisoners of War

From 1 September to 6 October, 1944, 45 Prisoners of War were captured by the 370th Infantry Combat Team.

Prisoners of War for Entire Division

Month	Number	Month	Number
October, 1944	124	February, 1945	1,001
November, 1944	702	March, 1945	516
December, 1944	636	April, 1945	7,981
January, 1945	166	May, 1945	12,351
		To June 8, 1945	368

TOTAL: 23,890

Strength on Departure for Overseas (Grand Total 14,516)

Officers	Warrant Officers	Enlisted Men
852	44	13,620

Strength on Entry into Action (Grand Total 12,846)

Officers	Warrant Officers	Enlisted Men
749	38	12,059

Units of 92nd Division

365 Infantry Regiment
370 Infantry Regiment
371 Infantry Regiment
Hq. & Hq. Co., 92nd Infantry Division
Hq. & Hq. Battery, 92nd Division Artillery
597 Field Artillery Battalion
598 Field Artillery Battalion
599 Field Artillery Battalion
600 Field Artillery Battalion

317 Engineer Combat Battalion
317 Medical Battalion
Hq. Special Troops
92nd Military Police Platoon
92nd Quartermaster Company
92nd Signal Company
792nd Ordnance (LM) Company
92nd Cavalry Reconnaissance Troop

Enemy Units Opposing 92nd Infantry Division

German
148 Infantry Division
42nd Jaeger Division
232 Infantry Division
90th Panzer Grenadier Division
5th High Mountain Division
Kesselring Machine Gun Battalion
4th High Mountain Battalion
Mittenwald (LEHR) High Mountain Battalion
Task Force Kannitz

Italian
Monte Rosa Division
Italia Division
San Marco (Marine) Division
Brigato Nero (Black Brigades)
X Flotilla Mas

Casualties

Tables 1, 2, and 3 below are from Operations Report, Adjutant General's Section, Hq., 92nd Infantry Division. 3 August, 1942 to 15 August, 1945. p. 17-18.

From commitment to combat until 2 May, 1945:

1. Total Casualty Breakdown†

Rank	KIA	WIA	POW	DOW	MIA
Col.	1	*	*	*	*
Lt. C.	2	4	*	*	*
Maj.	4	4	*	*	*
Capt.	7	20	*	2	*
1st Lt.	16	41	*	*	1
2nd Lt.	17	47	1	1	2
W. O.	*	1	*	*	*
Total, Officers:	47§	117	1	3	3§
Total for all Enlisted Grade:	471	2163	22	64	51
Grand Total:	518	2280	23	67	54

*None serving in these grades.
†KIA—Killed in Action. WIA—Wounded in Action. POW—Prisoner of War.
  DOW—Died of Wounds. MIA—Missing in Action. NBC—Non-Battle Casualties.
§No explanation for difference in Tables 1 and 3.

2. Casualties — White Officers

Rank	KIA	WIA	POW	DOW	MIA	NBC
Col.	1	*	*	*	*	1
Lt. C.	2	4	*	*	*	1
Maj.	4	4	*	*	*	1
Capt.	5	11	*	1	*	12
1st Lt.	1	3	*	*	*	9
2nd Lt.	2	11	*	1	*	7
W. O.	0	0	*	0	*	0
Totals:	15	33	*	2	*	31

3. Casualties — Black Officers

Rank	KIA	WIA	POW	DOW	MIA	NBC
Col.	*	*	*	*	*	*
Lt. C.	*	*	*	*	*	*
Maj.	*	*	*	*	*	*
Capt.	2	9	*	1	*	8
1st Lt.	15	38	*	*	1	36
2nd Lt.	14	36	1	*	3	40
W. O.	*	1	*	*	*	5
Totals:	31	84	1	3	4	89
Grand Totals (Officers)	46§	117	1	3	4§	120

Casualty report from Goodman, *Fragment of Victory*, p. 217, differs from above reports.

4. From August 1944 to May 1945

	KIA	WIA	MIA	DOW	Died, NB	POW
Totals:	515	2242	620	67	62	21

5. For Units Attached During Combat

Unit	KIA	WIA	MIA	Totals
442nd Inf.	96	513	5	614
473rd Inf.	128	571	22	721
Other Units	20	128	2	150
Totals:	244	1212	29	1485

Does not include the 366th Infantry, attached from 26 November, 1944 to 28 March, 1945. Unable to obtain accurate casualty figures.

6. The Official Program for the 92nd Division Armistice Day Program, in Italy, November 11, 1944, also differs:

	KIA	WIA	DOW	MIA
Totals:	555	2293	68	18

Awards

3 Distinguished Service Crosses
1 Distinguished Service Medal
16 Legion of Merits
145 Silver Stars and
47 Oak Leaf Clusters
6 Soldier's Medals
723 Bronze Stars and
30 Oak Leaf Clusters
31 Air Medals and
36 Oak Leaf Clusters
1891 Purple Hearts and
19 Oak Leaf Clusters
410 Medical Badges
7996 Combat Infantryman Badges

33 Expert Infantryman Badges
670 Driver's Badges
126 Mechanic's Badges
205 Division Commendations
4 Meritorious Service Unit Plaques
8 Orders of the Crown of Italy
17 Military Crosses for Military Valor (Italian)
22 Military Crosses for Merit in War (Italian)
1 Military Cross for Merit in War (Italian) 92nd Division Colors
1 War Medal (Brazil)

From Official Program, 92nd Division Armistice Day Program, 11 November, 1945, in Italy. All other data in this section from 92nd Infantry Division *Book of Facts*, 3 January, 1949.

Index

Military units in this index are those of the United States unless otherwise identified.

ALASKA 53-54, 60
Albano Mountain 16, 75
Allen, Moses, Lieut. 39
Almond, Edward M., Major Gen. 4-10, 30-31, 47-48, 54-55, 60, 62, 79, 88, 98-99, 128-129, 134, 139, 145-148, 166
Apennines 13, 18, 26, 32
Apuan 26-27
Arezzo Line (German) 13
Armstrong, John D., Col. 140-141
Army (American): *Fifth* 12-14, 16-17, 20-21, 23, 26-27, 37, 47, 55, 59-61, 136, 140, 145, 149-150, 173-174, 176, 178
Army (British): *Eighth* 12-14, 27, 61, 145, 149, 173
Army Group, 15th 14, 127, 145, 147-148
Army Units *see* Army; Army Group; Brigades; Corps; Divisions; Regiments (American)
Arno Line (German) 13
Arno River 12-13, 16-18, 20, 25
Artillery Battalions (American): *597th* 5, 36, 46, 151, 156, 159, 165, 171, 173; *598th* 5, 11-12, 15-18, 23-26, 28, 54, 58, 64, 66-68, 92, 108, 110-111, 117, 125-126, 151, 156, 159, 164, 170-171, 173; *599th* 5, 31, 37, 54, 94, 119, 150-151, 168, 171, 173; *600th* 5, 31, 54, 164, 171, 173; *27th Armored* 100-101; *530th* 164
Aulla 165-169
Azzano 32-33, 35, 37, 48, 150

Baker, Newton D. 10
Baker, Vernon J., 2nd Lt. 152-153, 158

Banks, William S.M., Jr., Capt. 85-87, 144
Barbara Line (German) 13
Barber, Frank E., Col. 5
Barga 30-31, 39-40, 48, 54, 57-58, 61-75, 85-86
Borgo a Mozzano 23, 40, 58
Basati 30, 32-33
Battalions (German): *4th Mountain* 174; *Kesselring Machine Gun* 157, 162, 172; *Mittenwald (LEHR) High Mountain* 13
Bebbio 35, 40-42, 44, 61-75
Belvedere Mountain 30, 154-163, 174
Bernhard Line (German) 13
Biggs, Aubrey A., Maj. 16, 19
Birdsong, John, 2nd Lt. 25
Bolling, Royal L., 2nd Lt. 38
Bologna 14, 26, 46, 53, 59, 77, 79, 149, 165, 178
Bombiana 47
Brazilian Expeditionary Force (BEF) 23-24, 30-31, 41, 44, 59, 149, 169, 171, 174
Brigades (British): *19th* 71, 73-74, 77, 79-80, 83; *21st* 72-73, 77, 79-80, 83
Brigades, Black (Italian) 178
Brown, Robert A., 1st Lt. 48
Brucciano 41-42, 58-59
Buffalo Bill (Mascot) 6, 9
Buffalo Soldiers: In the West 1-3; In World War I 2-4, 9-10
Bundara, Wejay S., Capt. 103
Buti 17

Caesar Line (German) 13

Calcinaia 16
CALIFORNIA 54
Calomini 40, 46, 57, 59, 62, 69–70, 166
Camps: Atterbury 5; Breckinridge 5; Robinson 5
Canale Reggio 19
Capennori 19
Carasoma 19
Carrara 27, 99, 145, 159, 165
Cascina 17
Cassino 139, 140
Castelnuovo di Garfagnana 41, 61, 83, 166
Castiglione Mountain 157
Castle Aghinolfi 17, 84, 89–90, 152, 156, 158, 160, 167
Casualties 13, 16–19, 21, 23–24, 28, 30–31, 33–36, 38–41, 43–46, 54–57, 84–87, 92–93, 95–98, 101–122, 124–126, 130–137, 157, 167, 170, 172
Casual Camp 6–7, 10
Cauala Mountain 28–39, 50–54, 58–61, 83, 150, 159–160, 175
Cavallo Mountain 27, 30, 32
Cavalry, 9th and 10th 1–2
Cavalry Reconnaissance Troop (92nd) 41–45, 54, 61–67, 69–77, 71–76, 164, 170, 173
Chandler, Jake, 1st Lt. 16, 25
Chatham, Roy L., Major 164
Chemical Mortar Battalion, 984th 100
Churchill, Winston S. 15, 26
Cinquale Canal 36, 46, 83, 98–107, 121–123, 131–132, 135–136, 150
Cisa Pass 164, 167–169
Clark, Mark W., Lt. Gen. 11, 15, 78, 129–130, 139, 140, 145–147
Coastal Gun Batteries 54–55, 91, 98–107, 115–116, 121–123, 133–135, 150, 164–165
Coastal Sector 20–27, 32, 36, 46, 48, 54, 60, 77–78, 82–144
Combat Command B. 17, 19, 23, 29–30, 41
Combat Engineers: *317th* 17, 25, 54, 58, 89, 91–93, 100–102, 104–106, 113, 122, 134–135, 151, 156, 164, 166, 173; *337th* (IV Corps) 105, 135–136
Combat Teams: *365th* 32, 36, 46–47, 53, 77, 83–88, 140–144, 147–148, 151, 173–175; *370th* 11–49, 54, 56–57, 62–81, 89–93, 107–110, 116–118, 121, 125–126, 129, 132, 150–151, 156–165; *371st* 30–49, 53–56, 59–60, 77–78, 83, 94–97, 110–112, 116–121, 123–126, 140, 147–148, 173–175; *442nd* 20, 146–148, 150–151, 155–170, 172; *337th* (85th Division) 61; *339th* (85th Division) 61
Cooke, William E., 1st Lt. 39–40
Corps (American): *II* 14–15, 20, 23, 25–26; *IV* 14–16, 20, 23–26, 47, 59–62, 71, 105, 134–137, 148–149, 151, 173–175
Corps (British): *13th* 14
Counts, Donald M., Capt. 157
Crittenberger, Willis D., Major Gen. 15, 71, 146
Cutigliano 24, 28, 147–148, 151, 174

Dabney, Walter E., Capt. 53–54
d'Anima Mountain 41, 43, 45
Davidson, Frederick E., Major Gen. 49
Davis, Benjamin O., Brig. Gen. 9–10, 15, 26
Davis, Jerry B., 1st Sgt. 16
Del Giglio 20
Dell Elto Mountain 21–22, 25
Dickerson, Irving F., 2nd Lt. 70
Diggs, Raymond A., Capt. 104–105
Distinguished Service Cross 64–66, 131, 152–153
Division (American): *1st Armored* 15, 17, 21, 25, 39; *3rd Infantry* 130, 137–138; *10th Mountain* 174; *28th Infantry* 138; *45th Infantry* 138; *85th Infantry* 61; *88th Infantry* 46–47, 77; *106th Infantry* 128
Division (British): *8th Indian* 61, 71, 74, 77, 79–80, 83
Division (German): *148th Infantry* 89, 111, 169, 171–172, 175
Divisions (Fascist): *Italia* 82, 169, 171–172; *Monte Rosa* 82, 177; *San Marco* (Marine) 82, 174, 177

Esprit de Corps 9–10
Essholm, Edmund, Capt. 95
Everman, Harold R., Lt. Col. 109, 114, 122–123

February Attack: Coastal Sector 82–144; Serchio Valley 82–88
Ferguson, Alonzo, Lt. Col. 49

Index

Field Artillery Group, 428th 169
Field Artillery Journal 64-65, 67-68
Fivizzano 167-168
Flagg III, Lewis, 1st Lt. 65-66
Florence 14, 27
FLORIDA 94-96, 118, 120, 124, 150, 175
Fogg, Trueheart, PFC 68
Folgorito Mountain 150-165, 175
Fornaci 31, 40, 57-58, 66-68, 71-75, 80, 86, 167
Forte dei Marmi 24, 36, 54, 85, 107, 114, 123
Fort Huachuca 4-10, 25
Fort McClellan 4-5, 9
Fox, Arlene 65
Fox, John R., 1st Lt. 152-153
Fraser, Roland F., 1st Lt. 56

Gallicano 30-31, 35, 40, 54, 57-58, 60, 62, 71, 75-77, 84
Gandy, Charles F., Capt. 15-16
Gibson, St. Clair, PFC 50
Giustagnana 28-32
Glover, Ulysses B., 1st Lt. 141
Gothic Line 12-14, 18, 20-21, 25-27, 42, 54, 89, 94, 129, 163, 176-177, 179
Graham, Eugene A., Sgt. 50
Grice, Ernest T., Sgt. 50
Grottorotondo 41-42
Gruenther, Alfred M., Major Gen. 148
Gustav Line (German) 13

Haines, Norris E., 1st Lt. 36
Hall, Milton, PFC 78
Hamlett, James F., Major Gen. 65
Harris, David, Technical Sgt. 43
Harrod, Dennette A., 1st Lt. 99, 103
Hill 906 84-87
Hilliard, Jefferson H., Technician 5th Grade 45-46
HILLS "X," "Y," "Z" 32-35, 89-94, 108-110, 116-118, 125-126
Hobbs, Wallace H., Tech. 5th Grade 52
Holbrook, Gilbert S., Capt. 131
Horner, Reuben L., 1st Lt. 28-29
Horsefly 83

Ivey, Curtis J., Capt. 34

Jarman, Jesse E., Capt. 144
Jenkins, Graham H., 1st Lt. 63, 66
Johnson, Allen L., Capt. 18-19

Kelly, John J., Capt. 70, 79-80
Kesselring, Albert, Gen. Field Marshal 177-178
Keyes, Geoffrey, Major Gen. 137

Lama di Sotto 62-63, 84-87, 163
Lancaster, Charles H., 1st Lt. 38
La Spezia 121, 129, 131, 133, 145, 149-150, 164-165
Letts, John T., 1st Lt. 47, 103
Lucca 18-20, 24, 179

McInnis, Jake, Private 25
McNair, Leslie, Lt. Gen. 26
Madison, John M., 1st Lt. 92-93, 116-117, 125-126
MAINE 27-29, 35, 37, 39, 53, 55, 94-96, 118-120, 175
Mars, Magellan C., 1st Lt. 33, 39, 42-43
Marshall, George C., Gen. 26, 146-147
Martin, James A., Capt. 141-142
Mason, Mansfield, Tech. Sgt. 143-144
Massa 27, 77, 82, 150, 159-163, 165
Meadows, William S., 1st Lt. 142
Medical Battalion, 317th 46, 151, 164, 173
Merritt, Walter H., PFC 142
Miles, Aurelius A., 1st Lt. 93, 109
Mitchell, John Q., Private 106
Molazzana 58-59, 62-63, 68-70, 75, 77, 96-97
Morale, Troop 7-10, 138
Moro Mountain 171
Morris, William, Staff Sgt. 63

Nebelwerfer rockets 21, 24-25
New Zealand Troops 137
Notestein, James, Col. 31

Office of Strategic Services (OSS) 177, 179

Index

OHIO 94–97, 110–112, 117–120, 123–124, 175
Oldham, Major 45

Parish, James W., 1st Lt. 39, 52
Partisans 21, 45, 63–64, 149, 163, 169–170, 173, 176–180
Patterson, Robert 36
Pedona 67, 73–74, 80
Peeks, Edward, 1st Lt. 80
Phelan, John J., Lt. Col. 73, 80
Pietrasanta 24, 28, 34, 37
Pinard, George E., Major 53
Pisa 13, 17, 20, 24
Plan "Fourth Term" 82–83, 129
Po River 14, 149
Polk, Willis D., Major 100, 103–104
Pontedera 14, 16–17
Ponte Maggiore 19
Ponte Nuovo 17–18
Pontremoli 168–169, 180
Porta 93, 150, 156–160
Porter, William E., 1st Lt. 81
Powell, Sherman F., Sgt. 56–57
Pritchard, Vernon E., Major Gen. 15
Promiana 58, 69
Prunetta 23–24
Punta Bianco 98, 121, 123, 131, 133, 135, 150, 159, 161–163, 165

Queen, Howard D., Col. 48
Querceta 93, 108–109, 114

Raiders 89–90, 93–94, 105
Raiford, Rudolph E., 2nd Lt. 143
Rapido River 130, 137
Regiments (American): *365th* 173–175 see also Combat Teams; *370th* see Combat Teams; *371st* 173–175 see also Combat Teams; *366th* 47–49, 53–56, 58, 60–81, 83–87, 97; *473rd* 147–148, 150–151, 157–166, 170–172, 174
Regiments (German): *281st Grenadier* 111, 116, 151, 154; *286th Grenadier* 87, 175
Regiments (Italian): *1st Bersaglieri* 87, 175; *San Marco* 174
Replacements 46, 146

Rhodes, Fred D., Staff Sgt. 50
Robinson, James, PFC 40
ROCKY RIDGE 94–97, 110–112, 118, 175
Rover Joe 83, 87, 95, 133–134
Rowny, Edward L., Lt. Col. 100–109, 114–116
Runyon, John F., Capt. 152–153, 158
Russell, Dudley, Major Gen. 74

Sarzana 164
Scarpello 42, 62–65, 75
Seay, Albert E., 1st Lt. 32–35
Seravezza 31, 34, 37, 39
Serchio Valley 19–26, 30–31, 35, 39–48, 53, 56–81, 128–129, 132, 147–149, 160–168
Sherman, Raymond G., Col. 12, 15, 18–19, 44, 71, 73–74, 78–79
Silver Stars 18, 22–23, 25, 28–29, 33, 39–40, 43–46, 49–52, 56–57, 63–66, 68, 81, 93, 96–97, 104, 106, 131, 141–144
Simpson, Oscar, Staff Sgt. 25, 29, 144
Skinner, Ralph, 1st Lt. 22, 25
Smallwood, Millard B., 2nd Lt. 38
Smith, Ezekiel C., Capt. 79
Sommocolonia 35, 40, 61–66, 74
South African Armored Division 23
Steinman, Murray L., Capt. 164, 170
Stevens, Warren B., 2nd Lt. 106
Strettoia 116, 154–155, 159–160
Strettoia Mountain 28–30, 154–160

Tank Battalions: *751st* 45; *758th* 116, 148, 151, 158, 162, 164, 169; *760th* 100, 105–106, 110, 114, 122, 148, 161–162
Tank Destroyer Battalions: *701st* 21, 100; *679th* 148, 168; *894th* 148, 158, 164
Task Forces: *#1* 98–107, 112–116, 129, 135; *#45* 19–20, 23–24, 169, 174; *#92* 23–24, 26–27; *Curtis* 164; *Sturtevant* 125
Tatum, Richard, Jr., PFC 142
Taylor, James, Tech. 4th Grade 52
Thayer, Philip, Capt. 108–109
Thomas, James, Private 153
Thompson, Sidney S., Jr., 2nd Lt. 47, 60–61
Tiglio 67, 74
Tindall, Richard G., Jr., Major 107–131

Toliver, Johnnie L., Sgt. 142
TOT 55
Trassilico 74
Trasimeno Line (German) 13
Truscott, L.K., Jr., Lt. Gen. 78–79, 127–129, 132, 137–139, 145–148
Tucker, Samuel, Capt. 61–62, 64, 72, 80

Vano Mountain 66–71
Vergemoli 44, 46, 56, 59, 70
Viareggio 56–59, 60, 147
Villa Franca 168

Walker, Arthur, Lt. Col. 33, 43–44, 116–117, 131
Walker, Melvin W., 1st Lt. 81, 103
Watkins, Kenneth, PFC 143
Weber, George O., Lt. Col. 33
Welliver, Warman, Capt. 129
Wetlaufer, Winston D., Capt. 34, 96–97
Whisonant, Frank, 1st Lt. 25
Williams, John A., Staff Sgt. 81
Wood, John E., Brig. Gen. 77, 83

www.ingramcontent.com/pod-product-compliance
Ingram Content Group UK Ltd.
Pitfield, Milton Keynes, MK11 3LW, UK
UKHW041956140426
5217IPUK00015B/825